The Japanese Tradition
in British
and American Literature

To *have gathered from the air a live tradition*
or from a fine old eye the unconquered flame
This is not vanity.
   Here vanity is all in the not done,
all in the diffidence that faltered.

—EZRA POUND

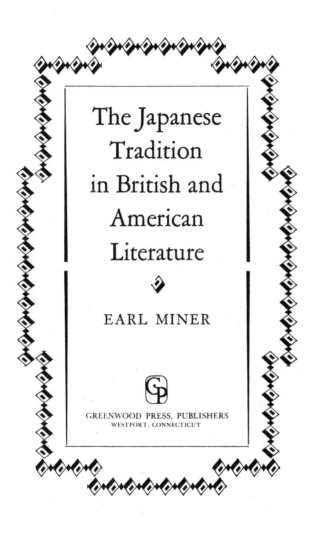

The Japanese Tradition in British and American Literature

EARL MINER

GREENWOOD PRESS, PUBLISHERS
WESTPORT, CONNECTICUT

Library of Congress Cataloging in Publication Data

Miner, Earl Roy.
   The Japanese tradition in British and American literature.

    Reprint of the ed. published by Princeton University
Press, Princeton.
    Bibliography: p.
    Includes index.
    1. Literature, Comparative--English and Japanese.
2. Literature, Comparative--Japanese and English.
3. Literature, Comparative--American and Janapese.
4. Literature, Comparative--Japanese and American.
5. Arts, Occidental--Japanese influences. I. Title.
[PR129.J3M5 1976]   820'.9'32   76-3698
ISBN 0-8371-8818-0

Originally published in 1958 by Princeton University Press,
Princeton, N.J.

Reprinted by arrangement with Princeton University Press

Reprinted in 1976 by Greenwood Press,
a division of Williamhouse-Regency Inc.

Library of Congress Catalog Card Number 76-3698

ISBN 0-8371-8818-0

Printed in the United States of America

中川宰平ぬ一夫妻丁捧ぐ

PREFACE

THIS STUDY is not the first one to deal with Japanese-Western cultural relations—an increasing number of excellent books and essays has appeared since the third quarter of the last century—but it is the first to give extended analysis of the role Japan has played in our literature and the ideas which have helped shape our literature over a period of four centuries. Other studies have dealt with single authors, topics, literary genres, or short historical periods and, by virtue of the singleness of their subjects, have been relatively simple and consistent in their approach. Such a consistent or simple approach has not been possible for the greater historical and topical scope of this study, because it would distort the complexities of the subject and reduce it either to mere generalities or to a sequence of facts with little meaning.

My reasons for seeking a new approach to the study of intercultural literary relations can be best understood by consideration of this greater scope. The period covered extends from 1549 to 1956, with the most detailed treatment given to the years since 1853 when Commodore Matthew Perry first visited Japan to reopen it to the West. Marco Polo is the first writer mentioned, Mr. I. A. Richards the last; a seventeenth-century Spanish nobleman is the first writer quoted, and W. B. Yeats the last. There are dozens in between. At one time or another, the subject

of discussion is a literary genre, literary criticism, or belles-
lettres; painting, opera, or the film; historiography, social
mores, cultural images, or religion. The subject is clearly
a protean one requiring a greater flexibility, more careful
interpretation, and more meaningful selection from the
well-nigh limitless materials than perhaps any author
could muster.

Such requirements are very exacting, and in fairness
to the reader I should like to be as explicit as possible
about the principles and methods I have followed. The
overall principle of method has been the eclectic one of
using that approach—whether historical, topical, biographical, critical, or otherwise—which has seemed to
me to be most useful in any given instance for elucidating
the nature of the effect of Japan. There are certain other
principles besides this one of flexibility. The first is that
I have felt that such a study as this, written by an American, could best deal with the effect of Japan on English
and American—or at most, Western—writers, artists, and
thinkers, and not the wholly separate subject of the effect of the West upon Japanese literature. Second, the
broad scope of the subject demands that the treatment be
limited to writers of real literary merit or of considerable
historical importance, although it has obviously been necessary to cut a wider swath in research, to base many generalizations on the works of writers not mentioned, and
to interpret according to one's critical sense the significance
of what has been chosen for its importance. The third
principle to which I have tried to adhere is that of proportion, because a proper proportion of emphasis and
treatment is essential if the important literary and intel-

lectual values are to be kept clear. Such great writers as Ezra Pound or W. B. Yeats who have been materially affected by Japan, or such a seminal literary and artistic movement as Impressionism, have seemed to me to deserve an extended and detailed analysis which would be out of place for lesser writers or for less influential movements.

In addition to these general principles, I have had two personal aims in writing—to tell an interesting story and to dispel certain illusions about Japan. I have made every effort myself and with the advice of friends to treat the story of four centuries of cultural relations as a continuous and integrated narrative which may best be read from the first page to the last. I hope that a reader who reads from beginning to end will find the book just such a narrative, that themes will become clear, that the dominant characters and their accomplishments will emerge in proper perspective, and that the story will come to a satisfying conclusion. The chapter titles and subtitles have been made as accurately descriptive as possible—both for such an ideal reader and for the more casual reader whose interest lies more in one subject, author, or period than another. For readers of either kind, I have tried to make the index as full as possible and to discuss my indebtedness to specific books by adding a section of Notes to the end of the book. Short descriptions of the Japanese literary forms are also to be found at the beginning of the Notes, along with a short bibliography for further reading and of earlier comparative studies.

I have also wished to dispel certain illusions about Japan, because I can remember with some embarrassment the misconceptions in my mind when I first set foot there.

I have since found that my misconceptions have been
shared, and even shaped, by the illusions of others, including many of the writers treated in this study. The
falsest and most unfair images of Japan have been the
unquestioningly sentimental image, the condescending
image of a toy-like nation, and the spiteful image of a
nation of barbarians. It has often surprised me that two
or even all three of these images may be held by people
who are otherwise sophisticated and mature. My own
conception of the Japanese is what I believe is the obvious
one, of a people who—whatever their cultural or national
differences from us—are human beings with virtues and
faults, aspirations and needs, more like to than different
from our own.

My urge to dispel such illusions may have made me
more intrusive than a well-mannered author ought to be;
but I hope that my other aim, to tell a coherent story,
has been carried off well enough to keep the intrusiveness
from becoming an annoyance. And the risk of intruding
my attitude is one which perhaps must be run, because
some overall concept of Japan and its effect upon our
literature seems indispensable for a study which deals
with many changing and often conflicting attitudes toward Japan over a long period of time. Good and even
great literary works may be based upon a false or only
partially true image of another nation, as Webster's "Italian" or Shakespeare's "Roman" plays show; but the historian must still say whether the image is true or false,
partial or whole. I have run the risk, then, because the
response to Japan of a Lafcadio Hearn or a W. B. Yeats
has a dual artistic and cultural aspect. To understand

the literary aspect of the response, one must question the literary quality of the resulting work in the light of one's literary standards; and to understand the cultural aspect of the response one must also question the fullness of the understanding of Japan upon which the literary work is based—and this requires an idea of what a proper response to Japan is.

The results of such an approach to intercultural literary relations have convinced me that Japan has had a recurring but widely varying significance for our writers. There have been what may be called three cycles of literary or artistic interest in Japan. The first began with the visit of St. Francis Xavier to convert the Japanese in 1549 and ended in the mid-nineteenth century. This long period of interest was important chiefly for its effect upon certain general intellectual concepts and for certain images and techniques which it gave to our literature. But the response was sporadic and light, and this period is quickly discussed in the first half of the first chapter. The second period of interest began with the reopening of Japan in 1853-1854 and ended about the turn of the century, a period which is treated in the first, second, and third chapters. The major portion of this study deals with the third cycle of interest which began in the first decade of the twentieth century and seems to have ended—or to be taking new directions—today. I have called these periods cycles, because in each one there seems to be a repeated pattern of developing interest. The pattern begins with excited and often over-enthusiastic interest, goes on to fuller understanding and borrowing from Japan, and ends with consolidation and slackening of interest. The pattern may be called one of exoticism, imitation, and absorption if the terms are given a somewhat different significance than usual. Each of the cycles has been shaped in part by the ones preceding, but each has also had a logic of its own derived from the concerns and experience of the age.

I believe that it is also possible to go one step further and to say that there has been an overall development of the interest in Japan from the day in which Europe had little knowledge of the Orient, to the excited fascination with Japan in the later nineteenth and the first decades of the twentieth century, and to the increased knowledge of Japan which vastly improved methods of communication and the cumulative work of dozens of eminent scholars have recently made possible. Over the long period of four centuries, Japan and its culture have become increasingly important to our writers and have assumed the role, to use the phrase of Ezra Pound, of "a live tradition" which has modified, refreshed, and helped shape much of the finest modern English and American literature.

In pursuing such a study as this over a period of years, one contracts debts to friends and books scarcely without knowing it. And although gratitude is not possible where memory fails, it is a real pleasure to acknowledge the assistance and encouragement given so generously by so many people. My wife, an American friend, several Japanese friends, and a German friend have given me that fundamental knowledge of Japan and its literature which alone makes such a study as this feasible. Many writers and critics have been gracious in answering letters full of questions, and their replies have often given an assurance to my work which had otherwise been lacking.

These writers and critics have frequently been quoted and their letters acknowledged in the Notes to the Chapters. Professor William Van O'Connor of the University of Minnesota has been suggestive with ideas and generous with his time over a period of six years as a teacher and a friend. Three of my colleagues at the University of California, Los Angeles, have given me invaluable advice. Professor John J. Espey has read and corrected the chapter on Ezra Pound. Professor Robert P. Falk has spent the large part of a summer in making the book more readable. And Professor Leon Howard has done more for the organization, method, and tone of the book than any but his large number of friends and students can understand. Mr. Frederick Morgan, Editor of the *Hudson Review,* has been drawn into this study so imperceptibly but generally that it is difficult to thank him properly for the benefits of his judgment, candor, and patience. My friend Professor Jin'ichi Konishi of Tokyo Educational University has kindly designed and drawn the characters for the jacket and dedication page. The President and Trustees of Williams College and the Research Committee of the University of California, Los Angeles, have been generous at different times in giving financial assistance. Finally, there is that debt of friendship and kindness which it has seemed possible to repay only by the dedication of this book.

Two other kinds of acknowledgment are in order. Parts of this book have appeared in different form in several periodicals: some of the remarks on Whitman in *American Literature,* parts of the chapter on Ezra Pound in *The Hudson Review* and the *Ezra Pound News letter;*

some of the discussion of Wallace Stevens in *The Explicator*, and a few of the remarks on W. B. Yeats's *Words Upon the Window-Pane* in *Modern Language Notes*. It is a pleasure to acknowledge the kindness of the editors of these periodicals in permitting me to redo and republish the materials they had published previously.

The large number of quotations from various authors has made it necessary to receive permissions from numerous writers, publishers, and agents. These permissions have been generously given, and I should like to express my acknowledgements and gratitude for them: To Mr. Richard Aldington and Miss Ann Elmo, agent: for permission to quote from Richard Aldington, *Collected Poems*, 1928. To Mr. Edmund Blunden: for permission to quote from his *Japanese Garland*, 1928. To Mr. Witter Bynner: for permission to quote from Witter Bynner and Arthur Davison Ficke, *Spectra*, 1916. To Jonathan Cape, Ltd.: for permission to quote from William Plomer, *Collected Poems*, 1936. To Chatto & Windus, Ltd.: for permission to quote from William Empson, *Collected Poems*, 1949. To Doubleday & Company, Inc.: for permission to quote from Rudyard Kipling, *Rudyard Kipling's Verse Inclusive Edition 1885-1932*; reprinted by permission of Mrs. George Bambridge and Doubleday & Company, Inc. To Faber & Faber, Ltd.: for permission to quote from Wallace Stevens, *The Collected Poems of Wallace Stevens*, copyright 1931, 1954 by Wallace Stevens. To Mrs. Arthur Davison Ficke: for permission to quote from Arthur Davison Ficke and Witter Bynner, *Spectra*, 1916; for permission to quote from Arthur Davison Ficke, *The Earth Passion . . . and Other Poems*, published by the Samurai Press, 1908; and for permission to quote from Arthur Davison Ficke, *Japanese Prints*, published by M. Kennerly, 1918. To Mrs. Charlie May Fletcher: for permission to quote from John Gould Fletcher, *Irradiations —Sand and Spray*, 1915; for permission to quote from John Gould Fletcher, *Goblins and Pagodas*, 1916; and for permission to quote from John Gould Fletcher, *Japanese Prints*, 1918. To *The Fortnightly*: for permission to quote from Ezra Pound, "Vorticism," *The Fortnightly Review*, CII, September 1, 1914. To Harcourt, Brace and Company, Inc.: for permission to quote from William Empson, *Collected Poems*, 1949; and for permission to quote from T. E. Hulme, *Speculations*, 2nd ed., 1936. To William Heinemann, Ltd.: for permission to quote from Algernon Charles Swinburne, *The Complete Works of Algernon Charles Swinburne*, 1925. To Henry Holt and Company, Inc.: for permission to quote from Robert Frost, *Complete Poems of Robert Frost*; copyright 1930, 1949 by Henry Holt and Company, Inc.; copyright 1936, 1948 by Robert Frost; by permission of the publishers. To Houghton Mifflin Company: for permission to quote from Amy Lowell, *Can Grande's Castle*, 1918; for permission to quote from Amy Lowell, *Pictures of the Floating World*, 1919; and for permission to quote from Amy Lowell, *What's O'Clock*, 1925. To Alfred A. Knopf, Inc.: for permission to quote from Witter Bynner, *The Beloved Stranger*, copyright 1919 by Alfred A. Knopf, Inc.; and for permission to quote from Wallace Stevens, *The Collected Poems of Wallace Stevens*, copyright 1931, 1954 by Wallace Stevens. To The Macmillan Company (London) and Mrs. W. B. Yeats: for permission to quote from *The*

Collected Poems of W. B. Yeats, 1952; and for permission
to quote from *The Collected Plays of W. B. Yeats*, 1953.
To The Macmillan Company (New York): for permission to quote from John Masefield, *The Poems and Plays
of John Masefield*, 1918; for permission to quote from
W. B. Yeats, *The Collected Poems of W. B. Yeats*, 1952;
and for permission to quote from *The Collected Plays of
W. B. Yeats,* 1953. To New Directions: for permission
to quote from Ezra Pound, *Personae*, copyright 1926 by
Ezra Pound, reprinted by permission of New Directions;
for permission to quote from Ezra Pound, *The Translations of Ezra Pound*, 1953, all rights reserved, reprinted
by permission of New Directions; and for permission to
quote from Ezra Pound, *The Cantos*, copyright 1934,
1937, 1940, 1948 by Ezra Pound, reprinted by permission
of New Directions. To Mr. Alfred Noyes: for permission
to quote from Alfred Noyes, *Collected Poems of Alfred
Noyes,* 1913; and for permission to quote from Alfred
Noyes, *The New Morning*, 1918. To the Oxford University
Press: for permission to quote from Conrad Aiken, *Collected Poems*, 1953. To Pearn, Pollinger & Higham Ltd:
for permission to quote from Robert Frost, *The Collected
Poems of Robert Frost*, 1930. To Mr. Ezra Pound and
Shakespear & Parkyn, agents: for permission to quote
from Ezra Pound, *Personae*, copyright 1926 by Ezra
Pound; for permission to quote from Ezra Pound, *The
Translations of Ezra Pound,* 1953; and for permission to
quote from *The Cantos*, copyright 1934, 1937, 1940, 1948
by Ezra Pound. To Routledge & Kegan Paul, Ltd.: for
permission to quote from T. E. Hulme, *Speculations,*
2nd ed., 1936; and for permission to quote from Edward

Storer, *I've Quite Forgotten Lucy*, n. d. To St. Martin's
Press, and The Macmillan Company (London), Mrs.
Cecily Binyon, and the Society of Authors' (agent):
for permission to quote from Laurence Binyon, *The
North Star and Other Poems*, 1941. To The Society
of Authors, agent: for permission to quote from *The
Poems and Plays of John Masefield*, 1918, by permission of
The Society of Authors and Dr. John Masefield, O. M. To
Mr. Walter Sherard Vines: for permission to quote from
Pyramid, published by R. Cobden-Sanderson, 1926; and
for permission to quote from *Triforium*, published by R.
Cobden-Sanderson, 1928. To A. P. Watt & Son, agents:
for permission to quote from Rudyard Kipling, *Rudyard
Kipling's Verse Inclusive Edition 1885-1932*, reprinted
by permission of Mrs. George Bambridge; for permission
to quote from W. B. Yeats, *The Collected Poems of
W. B. Yeats*, 1952; and for permission to quote from *The
Collected Plays of W. B. Yeats*, 1953. To Dr. William
Carlos Williams: for permission to quote William Carlos
Williams, "Marriage," *Poetry,* IX.

E.M.

CONTENTS

CONTENTS

CONTENTS

The Japanese Tradition
in British
and American Literature

I. THE MEETING OF
EAST AND WEST

"The glory of one country, Japan alone, has exceeded in beauty and magnificence all the pride of the Vatican at this time and the Pantheon heretofore."—JOHN STALKER, *Treatise of Japanning*, 1688.

THE ARMIES of Alexander and Napoleon, the caravans of the Polos, and the imagination of Christendom have turned to the East in an attraction not to be explained merely by the history of Western political and economic policies. As the westward journey has represented to many cultures the passage of the soul after death, the East has long symbolized the mysterious origin of life and the birth of history. No satisfactory explanation for this magic fascination of the Orient is likely ever to be given, and certainly not here where the aim is to describe the discovery and increasing understanding of only one Far Eastern country, Japan, and the effect of this discovery upon the imaginations of writers in English. But this pervasive if ineffable attraction exists and has existed in different forms throughout Western history as one of the strongest imaginative forces to grip the human spirit. It is easy to forget the fact that, considering his purpose, Columbus' voyages ended in failure, since his goal was India and trade with the rich and spicy East, not a land for empire in the West.

This appeal of the Orient has frequently merged with less imaginative interests. Marco Polo wrote enviously from China that the Japanese tile their roofs with gold while even the cathedrals of the West had to be content with lead. From such remarks it is easy to see that no small part of the interest in the Orient has been in its barbaric pearl and gold, and there is little doubt that the East India ventures aimed at a profitable holding of the East in fee. It remains true, however, that the mere thought of gold-shingled houses was thrilling to the imagination and that many of those who went to trade with or to convert the Chinese and Japanese were all but converted themselves to the civilizations which they sought to enlighten with the religion, science, and commerce of the West. As one noble Spanish traveler is said to have written of Japan in the seventeenth century, "if he could have prevailed upon himself to renounce his God and his king, he should have preferred that country to his own." Many an imagination had been kindled by the Orient before Lafcadio Hearn decided to change his name to Koizumi Yakumo and become a Japanese subject; many men since have delighted more in the title of Old China or Japan Hand (or Expert on Japan, in present-day parlance) than in the circle of acceptance on Beacon Street or the closed ranks of Bloomsbury. The more conventional of us find it difficult to understand or wish to approve of this enthralling appeal of the Far East or of those who succumb to it; but it remains true that although European progress has gazed steadily west, when the rigors of an age of strife have ended and men have settled in ease and safety for a time, they have turned their eyes back to the East again with the questioning of memories and impulses which can more easily be felt than explained. The greatest of the mythical exploits of Dionysus, and the one which fired the heart of the young Alexander, was the conquest of India, a rich land to the east of the dividing deserts and the Valley of Cush.

i. Renaissance and Augustan Images of Japan (1550-1850)

The imaginative appeal of the East has led men to search out or discover the Orient and then to attempt to bring the fruits of such discovery into accord with the beliefs, desires, and knowledge of their age. The first period of modern European discovery of the East began some four centuries ago, when, in 1549, Francis Xavier, the sainted Jesuit, arrived in Japan to commence missionary work in the western part of the country hoping, with the blessing of God upon his endeavors, to convert that country and to go on to China and India. He discovered a surprisingly astute and civilized people in the two years of his visit, and only his tact, insight, and force of conviction enabled him to prosper in his efforts. By 1600 there were about 300,000 converts, among them many of the most important members of the feudal nobility. The conversion of these leaders even lent something of the quality of a holy war to a few of the campaigns of Japan's great if capricious military leader,

Hideyoshi, when his battles in the 1580's were directed in part by Christian generals and fought by troops marching behind Christian banners. But the tolerance of Christianity had been motivated partly by a desire to suppress bellicose Buddhist sects, and in 1587 Hideyoshi —for no reason historians can satisfactorily explain—proscribed Christianity. The laws were, however, lightly enforced until the salvationist Franciscans came to Japan, bent upon immediate conversion of Japanese souls to the Kingdom of God, and Japanese territory and treasure to the Kingdom of Spain. The Franciscans openly flouted the laws and in 1598, with the accession to power of Tokugawa Ieyasu, a Domitian-like era of persecution began. The careful work of St. Francis Xavier had been undone; Japan gave up its own hopes of empire in the Philippines, turned towards Korea, and closed itself to the West. For two and a half centuries only a limited number of Dutch ships, and Dutch alone, were allowed to harbor in the one port of Nagasaki. The open door had been closed and sealed from visitors. Death was the penalty for foreigners who landed on Japan by accident or design, and death for Japanese who returned after leaving the country. When Melville wrote of "impenetrable Japans," he was speaking from the experience and fears of American and European whalers in Japanese waters.

There were several important results from this first contact with Japan and a growing excitement over the small but steady flow of goods which the Japanese allowed to trickle out with the Dutch. The Jesuits had appreciated the alien culture they discovered to a degree which was sure to have an effect upon Western thought. In 1577, when Edmund Spenser was beginning to complain of the lawless savagery of Ireland, one Jesuit wrote from Japan: "It must be understood that these people are in no sense barbarous. Excluding the advantage of religion, we ourselves in comparison with them are most barbarous (*siamo barbarissimi*). I learn something every day from the Japanese and I am sure that in the whole universe there is no people so well gifted by nature." The Jesuits knew, and soon their correspondents knew, what they admired in Japan: government by law (instead of by personalities) and the peaceableness of the citizenry, the stable Japanese family and social system, their courage, their adaptability to foreign ideas, and their skill in the arts and crafts. Europe was by comparison nervous and unsettled, provincial, and uncivilized. When these opinions were confirmed by secular travelers, and as European appreciation for the Orient grew, a revolution began to take place in Western thought. The fact that the Japanese, and later the Chinese, were found to be peaceable, intelligent, cultured, and endowed with every merit "excluding the advantage of religion" forced reconsideration of traditional European ideas of culture. For centuries men had assumed that with the possible exception of Greece and Rome, the pagan world was lawless and primitive, but now the widely circulated writings of the Jesuits led many thinkers to a relativistic attitude toward cultures and toward history. Although many, no doubt most, writers chose to ignore Japan and China, the Far East was one of the forces which began to insist that

Europe re-examine itself in less flattering and absolutist terms.

The Western image of Japan for the next two hundred and fifty years (1600-1850) was that of a faraway, intelligent, civilized nation which had chosen to isolate itself. The cruelty of the Japanese persecutions of converts to Christianity was gradually forgotten because most of the martyrs were Japanese—the English, at least, could look upon the execution of converts to "papistry" with a certain amount of detachment and parochial equanimity. And while Japan was content to do without the rest of the world, the Jesuits were endeavoring to plant the Christian faith in China. The soil was less hospitable there, but careful Jesuit nursing and accommodation to Chinese peculiarities helped the faith to grow until, as in Japan, Franciscans and Dominicans destroyed their efforts. Chinese Christians had never totalled more than those converted in Japan, and by 1800 Christian influence was waning rapidly. In the Middle Kingdom as well as in the Eastern Isles, a period of Western relationship with the Orient had come to an end.

Japan and China had been closed to all but a few Dutch merchants hardy enough to venture so far for a profit, but there were many important consequences of this first modern contact with Japan. For the first time since Pythagoras set out upon his fabled travels to India, the extreme Orient had touched Western imaginations and thought in a way not to be denied. This discovery was of immense importance, but it must not be exaggerated. Voyages to the Far East were scarcely more fabulous and were considerably less numerous than those to American shores, and it was a rare European who could distinguish between Japan, China, and India in any meaningful geographical or cultural way. The Far East was a more or less homogeneous whole to the imagination of Christendom. It was rich and wise Cathay, or the ancient mother East of which Sir William Temple writes in his *Essay upon the Ancient and Modern Learning* (1690). "Science and Arts have run their circles, and had their periods in the several Parts of the World," he observes. "They are generally agreed to have held their course from *East* to *West*."

Three images of "Cathay" stirred the Renaissance imagination—the idea of the Oriental languages, the ideal of Oriental government and, for literature, the image of a sage Oriental spectator beholding the follies and vices of Europe. Sir Francis Bacon, Sir Thomas Browne, and others contemplated what little was known of the Sino-Japanese written characters from philosophical and religious viewpoints. The possibility of a written language whose characters represented ideas as well as sounds was wonderful to contemplate, while Sir Thomas and others debated whether the Oriental tongues, somewhat confusedly apprehended as a unit, might not be the primitive language which existed before sinful mankind erected the Tower of Babel and God set

> Upon their tongues a various spirit to rase
> Quite out their native language, and instead
> To sow a jangling noise of words unknown.

Conservative philosophers and the Jesuits' enemies at the court of St. Peter's were skeptical of the Jesuits' panegyrics on the stable, just governments of the Orient and sought some Aristotle or Augustine to justify them. The Orientophiles had in Confucius a ready answer to this demand for a political and social philosopher in the East. The enthusiasm for Far Eastern polity grew, but it developed as much from the Renaissance enthusiasm for perfect states—More's Utopia, Bacon's New Atlantis, and behind these Plato's ideal republic and Cicero's *De Republica*—as from an absolute admiration of the Orient. Something of the Renaissance attitude remains even today when people use Confucius—or Lin Yutang—as a byword for homely wisdom or maxims of folk truth, and when such a social critic as Ezra Pound advocates the Confucian writings as a solution for the ills of Western culture. The Oriental sage developed into a Utopian philosopher.

Once the sage became a literary type, he was employed as a mirror or "spy" of Western society, useful to satirize European governments and society from a point of view which was at once fresh and nominally non-partisan. This type of satire emerges in the eighteenth century, usually with a Chinese observer like Goldsmith's Lien Chi Altangi, but in a few instances employing a mythical Japan to expose Western social and political evils. The most important English example is probably Tobias Smollett's *Adventures of an Atom*, which appeared in 1769. While there is no Oriental sage here, English politics are allegorized in the guise of a description of the Japanese political scene, a trenchant satire which is, however, even less knowing about Japan than its nineteenth-century counterpart, Gilbert and Sullivan's *Mikado*.

The Chinese and Japanese goods of art which fascinated the tastes of Europe had another literary effect in England. Images of "china" (ceramics) or "japan" (lacquerware) begin to occur increasingly in poetry, where before these countries had been only examples of the most distant reaches of the earth. The highly colorful, fragile, and splendid porcelains, lacquerware, and brocades easily became apt metaphors for the equally stylized, rich, and brittle emotional and moral life of the Augustan *haut monde*. Chinaware is a bitter and unforgettable metaphor for all but open adultery in Wycherly's *Country Wife* and a delightful ambiguity for passion and glazes in John Gay's "To a Lady on her Passion for Old China." But it remained for Pope to develop this imagery to its finest point in *The Rape of the Lock*, for him to ask of the multi-motivated Belinda,

> Whether the nymph shall break Diana's law,
> Or some frail China jar receive a flaw,
> Or stain her honour, or her new brocade.

After our initial shock from the anti-climaxes, we are startled again by the acute resemblance between chinaware and chastity in the society which Pope describes. This poem represents the typical use of Oriental art in the eighteenth century—absorption of Oriental images or references into the general literary stream without surrender of the standards of the age. Some writers, however, were willing to overthrow the accepted values of their time and write in the extraordinary fashion of John Stalker in his *Treatise of Japanning* (1688): "Let not the Europeans any longer flatter themselves with the empty notions of having surpassed all the world. . . . The glory of one country, Japan alone, has exceeded in beauty and magnificence all the pride of the Vatican and Pantheon heretofore."

These philosophical, literary, and social responses to the Orient represent an important part, but only a part, of the impact of the East upon Western thought in this period. In the long view these literary conventions and images were to fade as new ones arose, and the effect of the Orient upon historiography and cultural philosophy was to have more lasting significance. Ernst Cassirer remarks in *An Essay on Man* that the "historical consciousness" does not appear until the eighteenth century; nothing contributed so much to this consciousness as the growth of historical relativism. It is true in a sense that medieval and Renaissance history grew out of Saint Augustine's *City of God* and its source, the historical writings of the two Testaments. Traditional histories began, like Sir Walter Raleigh's *History of the World*, with the Creation and the Fall and time was to end with the New Jerusalem. This teleological view presumed a single, coherent culture—the Hebraic, classical, Christian civilization of the West, and could stand only as long as pagan civilizations could be absorbed into the view or ignored. Africa was one matter, but the Jesuits' enthusiastic account of Japan and China was another, very different question. Even while the traditional Christian world-view was being subjected to cool scrutiny by the natural scientists, the historians were faced with the necessity of finding an explanation for cultural differences more sophisticated than the dispersal of the sons of

Noah to the four corners of the earth. It would be foolish to argue that the Orient alone brought about acceptance of historical and cultural relativism, but it played a large part in dramatizing the issue and demanding settlement. It is curious that the effort, which seems so eccentric today, to call the Oriental tongue the pre-Babelian language of man was a last, desperate attempt to bring the Far East within the Biblical outlines of history. And in the realm of art, the more absolutely critics rejected porcelain or lacquer on the grounds that it was unartistic by accepted standards, the clearer it became that other standards existed. Goldsmith's Lien Chi Altangi, the sage Chinese, could write in his eighth letter of *The Citizen of the World* that, "In spite of taste, in spite of prejudice, I now begin to think [English] women tolerable; I can now look on a languishing blue eye without disgust, and pardon a set of teeth, even though whiter than ivory. I now begin to fancy there is no universal standard for beauty"; but the "fancy" was the discovery of the Western mind, not of the Chinese, that standards of beauty and truth are relative to time and place. Japan had closed itself to Europe, but Europe could no longer shut its eyes to the Orient.

The growth of relativistic thought has a dual relevance to this study. This growing eighteenth-century belief in relativistic standards prepared the way for the next age to attempt an understanding of Japanese literature and art by what could be discerned as Japanese standards. This was a necessary step if the Japanese cultural contribution was ever to be fully understood and adapted to Western modes. Secondly, with the rising interest in esthetic "taste," in the "sublime," in the "sensible," and in other psychological approaches to art, the same relativism which we find in historiography is gradually transferred to the observing individual. Art and nature become relative not only to time and place, but also to the mind perceiving them. Berkeley's idealism and Kant's unknowable *Ding an sich* are different expressions of this revolution in Western philosophy. In the wake of this development, the poet studies the Grecian urn or daffodils for what they mean to his "inward eye," not to universal man; and still later the artist insists that his impression at any given moment of the shape of the urn or the color of the daffodils is as real as anyone's—only impression is real. This is not to say that Oriental art suddenly produced the Romantic age and then Impressionism, since these developments were slow processes with many other complex causes of lesser or greater importance. Still, as Beverly Sprague Allen's study of *Tides in English Taste (1619-1850)* shows, Orientalism was one of the important currents flowing under the stately bridge of neoclassicism. And as another chapter will show, when Impressionism formulates and justifies its theories, it turns to Japanese art.

This first period of discovery and adaptation of the Orient, roughly 1550-1850, is also important because it establishes the typical pattern of interest in the Far East. Each successive wave of interest has begun with a fresh or renewed moment of contact. This confronting of cultures produces excited interest in what is distant, unknown, and different—the exotic—an interest which may kindle serious as well as frivolous imaginations.

The Renaissance sought the wonders of exploration and the prodigies of nature and treasure; the Augustans sought to absorb as much of the variety of the novel and dissenting as it could into its flexible but unified world view; and the early nineteenth century found pleasure in the far-off worlds of romance and the fruits of imperialism. The pattern is complete when writers have absorbed the new experience into such images and conventions as the sage Oriental, and when scholars have tried to achieve as sufficient an understanding as they can from the facts which are available. By 1850, books on Japan have lost the speculative, fascinated, excited tone which characterizes early books like Stalker's. One book tends to be like another in mood, organization, and even phraseology. There really was little more to be done until Japan would once more open herself to the West. A representative English book, fittingly anonymous, was published in 1841—*The Manners and Customs of the Japanese*, compiled from many acknowledged sources. The author begins in typical fashion: "Whilst English travellers are almost overwhelming the British public with information concerning the most remote, the most savage, and the least interesting regions of the globe, there is an extensive, populous, and highly though singularly civilized empire, which remains as much a *terra incognita* now, as it was an hundred years ago." The typicality of this work lies in its mingling of the old enthusiasm for the highly civilized Japanese and the curiosity for the remote in the sober cadences of the scholar's language. It was time for the East and West to meet once more.

ii. The American Rediscovery of Japan

One of the "Several Remote Nations of the World" into which Swift sent Gulliver on his third voyage was Japan, a country as remote to most Englishmen as Laputa and Balnibarbi. But in addition to the fictional *Amboyna* which carried Lemuel Gulliver out of Nangasac (Nagasaki) on his voyage home, real ships from another nation were sailing regularly in the profitable whaling waters off Japan. Among them in the 1840's was the *Acushnet,* with Herman Melville aboard. Melville learned from his experiences that Japan was a dangerous shoals to be avoided at the peril of death at the hands of the militantly self-isolated inhabitants, however convenient the country would have been for laying in supplies and making repairs. When, in 1851, Melville launched his *Pequod* and Captain Ahab in search of the white whale in Japanese waters, there was still a mysterious beauty and danger which he expresses in the sober close of one of his finer passages in Chapter CXI of *Moby-Dick*:

"To any meditative Magian rover, this serene Pacific, once beheld, must ever after be the sea of his adoption. It rolls the midmost waters of the world, the Indian ocean and the Atlantic being but its arms. The same waves wash the moles of the new-built Californian towns, but yesterday planted by the recentest race of men, and lave the faded but still gorgeous skirts of Asiatic lands, older than Abraham; while all between float milky-ways of coral isles, and low-lying, endless, unknown Archipelagoes and impenetrable Japans."

The Pacific is serene only to the Magian rover, to the

Narcissus who peers lovingly at the water which drowns him. Japan and Moby Dick alike rise with great beauty from the blue depths of the Japanese seas, both with outward beauty but fundamentally unknown, unexplored, and inimical. Both challenge the heart of man only to destroy it.

Not all American vessels of this period were sailing ships, however. Many of those with which the United States hoped to engage in the imperialistic game were coal-burning sidewheelers, but without an Asiatic coaling-station they could not compete effectively with the English, Dutch, and French ships. American imperialistic necessity and a period of almost revolutionary change inside Japan combined to make it possible for Commodore Matthew Perry to gain an attentive if somewhat hostile audience when, on July 8, 1853, he steamed into Tōkyō Bay to bargain politely in the shadows of the guns of what the Japanese called his "black ships."

Although the success of Perry and the first great American imperialist gambit had a noisy and ebullient response from the press, writers were slow to make Japan a part of their literature. The career of Bayard Taylor may illustrate why. He had inveigled his way into Perry's expedition as a kind of secretary for the venture and sent off accounts of the little fleet's travels to the *New York Tribune*. The same experiences made up a volume of travel sketches, *A Visit to India, China and Japan* (1855), but in spite of these writings, and in spite of his use of nearly every other subject for his poetry, he wrote nothing in poetry or fiction which utilizes Japanese materials. And what is true for Taylor is also true for Emerson, Whittier, and Lowell. Japan was not yet a proper literary subject because, for poetry at least, the Orient either meant an India imaged in the vague transcendentalism of many a poem like Emerson's "Brahma," or it meant the Near East, whose exotic and mildly amorous subjects were moralized to varying degrees in poem after poem which appeared in the wake of Goethe's *West-Östlicher Divan* and Edward Fitzgerald's translation of the *Rubáiyát of Omar Khayyám*.

A few signs of a growing interest in Japan can be discovered. When Commodore Perry stopped to see Nathaniel Hawthorne, then the American consul in Liverpool, to ask him to write up the narrative of the expedition, Hawthorne declined, saying that he was committed to his present post. But he wrote in his journal for December 28, 1854, words which show that he pondered Japan as a literary subject, for "the world can scarcely have in reserve a less hackneied theme than Japan." A little later, Sidney Lanier wrote a few epigrams on his contemporaries in the pose of a Japanese—a vague reflection of the lively vogue of the sage Oriental in eighteenth-century literature. Longfellow's versatility helped him find one way of including Japanese materials, by writing on ceramics in a poem for *Harper's* in 1877. *Kéramos* tours the ceramic centers of the world, and comes to its climax with a lofty, aerial view of Japan in some twenty or thirty verses. His conclusion is not a moral, but a decision that the natural and colorful designs on Japanese ceramics represent

The counterfeit and counterpart
Of Nature reproduced in Art.

This is remarkably close to what the Impressionists would say about Japanese art in the heyday of their enthusiasm, but this one poem can scarcely be said to be representative of Longfellow or to indicate a change in the basic interests of the age. If there were not yet enough swallows to make a Japanese summer, however, American taste was beginning to change and the Orient was about to become a subject again.

Perhaps no one provided the change in manner, form, and subject matter of nineteenth-century American poetry more radically than Walt Whitman, who often seems to write of any slight shift in the cultural breeze as if it were a major change in the prevailing winds. While only one of his poems is completely Japanese in subject, many treat it and its people along with other subjects. His constant theme that he is brother and transcendentally part of all men leads him to beckon all of Asia as well as Europe and America into his generous arms. Sometimes he seems merely to exclaim in appreciation, as in his *Salut au Monde!* where he raises "high the perpendicular hand" as a signal to "You Japanese man or woman! you liver in Madagascar, Ceylon, Sumatra, Borneo," and elsewhere. The welcome changes to musing in "Facing West from California's Shores" (1860), where he ponders age-old thoughts which were to be expressed repeatedly by him and later poets. Asia is "the house of maternity, the land of migrations," the source of life and death alike, the *Ur-Mutter*.

The event which suddenly made Japan a part of American experience and the subject of one of Whitman's poems was the visit to America in the early summer of

1860 by the Japanese mission to ratify the treaty brought
about by Perry's visits. The Japanese visited several American cities and took part in parades and similar festivities
which the *New York Times* for June 26th called "de-
cidedly the most magnificent display our city has ever
seen." Among the rapt crowds which thronged Broadway
for a view of the Japanese was Walt Whitman, who gave
eloquent expression to the more serious thoughts of New
Yorkers in a poem published by the *Times* for June 27th.
Originally titled "The Errand-Bearers" and published a
scant ten days after the event, "A Broadway Pageant"
begins by describing the unparalleled spectacle:

> Over the Western sea hither from Niphon come,
> Courteous, the swart-cheek'd two-sworded envoys,
> Leaning back in their open barouches, bare-headed,
>   impassive,
> Ride to-day through Manhattan.

As if his own prophecies in earlier poems are now fulfilled, Whitman exclaims, "to us, then at last the Orient
comes,"

> The Originatress comes,
> The nest of languages, the bequeather of poems,
>   the race of eld,
> Florid with blood, pensive, rapt with musings . . .
> The race of Brahma comes.

But when he also chants "America the mistress . . . a
greater supremacy . . . My stars and stripes fluttering in
the wind," we see that idealism can easily give way;
Manifest Destiny has thrust its mailed hand into Mel-

ville's "unknown Archipelagoes, and impenetrable Japans" and wrenched them open. "Passage to India" was published eight years later, after Whitman's imperialistic enthusiasms had been quelled by the rigors and sufferings he witnessed during the Civil War. Now India is the symbol of the Orient, and passage to it is once again

> to primal thought,
> Not lands and seas alone, thy own clear fresh-
> ness . . .
> To reason's early paradise,
> Back, back to wisdom's birth, to innocent in-
> tuitions,
> Again with fair creations.

Most of the American public was content with less sober thoughts. The eighteenth-century device of the sage Oriental observer was refurbished by the *New York Times* with the pretense that some letters of a member of the Japanese embassy had been found, letters which satirized the habits of Americans by the standards of Japanese cleanliness and decency, just government, and lack of factious religious sects. "Japanese" plays were hurried to the stage with such enticing titles as "Our Japanese Embassy" and "Tycoon: Or, Young America in Japan." P. T. Barnum, who knew a good thing or fresh dollars when he saw them, advertised Japanese coins, lanterns, autographs, and other curiosities in addition to his usual prodigies of art and nature.

Japan was now in the American consciousness; the question was how long it would take the country and its

writers to gain anything like Whitman's appreciation of
the significance of the Orient. His dream of full Western
knowledge of the East and its culture was to remain
unrealized for many decades, if indeed it can be said that
it is fully realized today. In the meantime, such early
scholars as B. H. Chamberlain, W. G. Aston, and F.
Brinkley were at work studying, translating, and explaining—laying the groundwork for genuine understanding of Japan.

In the year Whitman died, 1892, Ernest Fenollosa—
the man who has perhaps done as much as anyone else
to fulfill the hopes of "Passage to India"—was back from
Japan in time to write a long poem for the Phi Beta
Kappa society of Harvard University. *East and West* is
an attempt, as he says in the Preface, "to condense my
experiences of two hemispheres, and my study of their
history." The refined East becomes feminine and the
action-minded West masculine in the symbolism of the
poem, although he also finds feminine renunciation and
softening in Western codes of love and masculinity in the
Oriental "martial faith of spiritual knighthood": "This
stupendous double antithesis seems to me the most significant fact in all history. The future union of the two
types may thus be symbolized as a two-fold marriage,"
as it is in this poem. The poem is brilliantly conceived
and ordered in its opposition of the double types of East
and West, but its heavy intellectuality and fumbling
verse fail to arouse poetic interest. Nonetheless, even if
Fenollosa fell short of writing moving poetry, he did
create a poetic genre out of the relatively formless mus-

ings of Whitman, a genre whose finest expression is the attempt of Ezra Pound to unify Eastern and Western experience and history in the *Cantos*.

Fenollosa wrote other "Japanese" poems of less importance. A sonnet, "Fuji at Sunrise," develops the metaphor of *East and West* by describing the arrival of the "prince of day" to the half-clad, feminine Mt. Fuji in terms of sexual union. He experimented with musical effects in "The Wood Dove," just as the Imagists and T. S. Eliot were later to do, and in "Karma" and "Maya" attempted to bring Eastern thought into English poetry in a much livelier way than the paradoxes of Emerson's "Brahma" and the poems which it inspired.

Although Fenollosa's attempts to marry East and West were far from successful, he left behind him a poetic domain for other writers to explore and develop. Ezra Pound, who has owed most in his poetic career to Fenollosa and who has been most successful in developing his legacy, has summed up Fenollosa's career best: "In America and Europe he cannot be looked upon as a mere searcher after exotics. His mind was constantly filled with parallels and comparisons between eastern and western art. To him the exotic was a means of fructification." For their part, the Japanese did what they have never done before or since, and what perhaps no other nation has done, when they sent a cruiser to bring Fenollosa's ashes to Japan for burial. Whitman and Fenollosa had performed what they could to bring Japan to the attention of America and England. Their contemporaries and the succeeding generation were left with the task of assessing what had been known and what could be newly discovered. The measure of their success and failure in this attempt to interpret Japan and adapt it to literature represents the second chapter in our intercultural history and brings very different images of Japan to our literature.

II. NEW IMAGES AND STEREOTYPES

OF JAPAN

Wer den Dichter will verstehen
Muss in Dichters Lande gehen;
Er im Orient sich freue
Dass das Alte sei das Neue.
—Goethe, *West-Östlicher Divan*

IT CANNOT be said that Japan or the greater Orient
changed the Victorian sensibility to any calculable degree, or that it forced a new world-view upon the nineteenth century comparable to the impetus the Orient
gave to relativistic thought in the century before. The
changes which took place came about gradually, and
had already been under way in the eighteenth century.
For all of the doubt and indecision commonly associated
with mid- and late-Victorian poetry, it would appear that
the Victorian temper was, if not strong, then extremely
flexible before the variety and contradictions of the realities of the age. It was a curiously mixed temper which
could absorb both progress and conservatism, exploita-
tion and humanitarianism, economy and display, or hard-
headedness and sentimentality. Japan was only one of the
many forces which touched upon, and was absorbed by,
the Victorian sensibility; but if Japan failed to produce
any great change in nineteenth-century thought or feel-

ing, it did nonetheless bring many uniquely Victorian problems to a significant and illuminating focus.

i. Japan and the Victorian Muse

Just as Dryden's and Addison's generations were sturdily confident that they had reformed and refined the civilizations bequeathed to them, so the Victorians were sure that they had brought Civilization and Morality to their highest development. They were sure they could carry the progress still further, if only the ideas of right-thinking men were allowed to prevail; and since the world acknowledged that England was the Glory of Europe, one way to improve the world was to send emissaries of light from Britannia into the heart of darkness, to the heathen peoples. Such a project requires considerable faith in the rectitude of one's own ideas, and it appears that the Victorians possessed whatever confidence was necessary. This robust attitude is clearly visible in their attitude toward Japan. The anonymous author of *Manners and Customs of the Japanese* (1841), who was quoted in the first chapter, expressed considerable hesitation in describing or passing judgment on Japan. Little more than a decade later, a more typical contemporary of Macaulay, Charles MacFarlane, who has no new information of any importance, can write a book with a long and pretentious title—beginning, *Japan: An Account. . . .*—with the assurance of his age: "It appears to me erroneous to say—though it very commonly *is* said—that we know next to nothing of Japan and the Japanese." But in the next breath he says that this knowledge

comes from books which are "mostly old and voluminous," and which he has perhaps found too ponderous
to read.

MacFarlane's confidence hesitates briefly over an issue
of international law. Is Japan really a civilized nation?
This is not clear—for all the weighty evidence at hand.
He wonders whether "a nation which, like Japan, refuses all intercourse with the rest of the world, may claim
all those privileges of neutrality for its harbors which
other civilized nations have created and sanctioned for
their mutual convenience." How Japan could keep its
harbors closed by opening them is somewhat difficult to
understand. Sensing that his logical ground is uncertain,
he shifts his approach to an argument *ad hominem.*
"Even if the rights of nations justified a government
playing the part of the dog in the manger, it would be
found that men are not quite so patient as oxen. The
instincts of nature, the natural law, stronger than all
others, will impel mankind to invade and break up such
excluding systems as those which obtain in Japan, China,
and Annam."

The fruits of Progress (and English industry) shall
be willy-nilly forced upon the Orient by "the instincts of
nature." This is a grim business, but we cannot understand the age unless we also see the qualifications and
contradictions in its attitudes. Speaking of Perry's expedition, then out to force a little natural law upon the
Japanese, MacFarlane sighs hopefully that it will be done
"with prudence and gentleness," lest the Japanese, "an
interesting people, will be plunged back into complete
barbarity." The terrifying amount of condescension here

is unlike anything in preceding centuries, but the ideal-ism and hopes are real, just as the iron-spined Perry was polite and considerate, and full of idealistic talk of car-rying civilization to the East.

Another topic, Japanese women, shows a wholly new side of MacFarlane and his age. As we all know, he says in effect, the character of a nation's women is the ulti-mate and readiest test of the height of its civilization. He quotes an old and revered friend who had known the most cultured women of all parts of the world and who had declared that the Japanese "are the most fas-cinating, elegant ladies that I ever saw in any country of the world." They would be admitted immediately "at St. James's, or in any other court in Europe." To this MacFarlane adds a sentence which is astounding in the sincerity of its feeling: "As these words were spoken many years ago, I need not now be ashamed of con-fessing it was they that first excited me to a deep and lively interest . . . in Japan." As this reflection of the Vic-torian temper in the faraway mirror of Japan shows, the imperialistic impulses are no more the dominant part of the spirit of the age than those last refinements of the Ro-mantic sensibility which make up Victorian idealism.

It was not books such as MacFarlane's, however, which excited national interest in the Japanese, but the Eng-lish counterpart of the Japanese embassy to America— the Japanese Court at the International Exhibition of 1862. Of the various excited notices in the press, the most informative is the article by a certain W. Burges in *The Gentleman's Magazine* for July. His special interest is in medieval arts and crafts, and although he is dutifully impressed by the European exhibits, it is the Japanese Court which takes his heart: "Truly the Japanese Court is the real medieval court of the Exhibition." This curious coupling of Japan and the European middle ages is not something we dare pass off simply as evidence of undiscriminating Victorian taste. Horace Walpole, a "neoclassical" connoisseur of the best taste, had had Chinese chairs and Japanese screens purchased for his "Gothic" estate, Strawberry Hill. And the Esthetic movement at the end of the nineteenth century paired Japanese with medieval European art in spite of W. S. Gilbert's attempt in *Patience* to laugh the country back into its senses. Burges' article is but one expression of what is a general problem of European taste.

The problem is one of exoticism, a taste which appears to run, like primitivism, in two courses, the chronological and the cultural. Chronological primitivism seeks its ideal "state of nature" in a utopian past, cultural primitivism in a contemporaneous but distant civilization. Similarly, Walpole, Mr. Burges, and Oscar Wilde saw common ideal and exotic elements in the distant European past and in the newly discovered art of Japan. The cultural relativism of the eighteenth century had prepared the way for a second step, an idealizing of a culture different from one's own. If the idealized culture is simple, then the urge to idealize it is primitivistic; if it is less primitive than unfamiliarly refined, then the idealizing is exoticism. The International Exhibition laid the basis of an exoticizing of Japan which lives on to this day.

The failure of the greatest Victorian poets—Tennyson, Arnold, Browning, and Hardy—to respond in any important way to Japan seems at first to suggest that, as in the United States, so in England Japan had not yet become a useful poetic subject for expressing the concerns of the age. This is not the case, however, for as with Whitman in America, the poets of a more popular nature in England found that Japan was significant in their lives and work. Three such typical and popular poets are Sir Edwin Arnold, Rudyard Kipling, and Alfred Noyes. Sir Edwin is now "glad to be hid and proud to be forgot," but in his own day he had a wide following. He was a poet, a writer of travel sketches, a translator of sorts, a convert to a mild Buddhism, and later in life one of the first prominent Englishmen to marry a Japanese. He published his *Light of Asia* in 1881, a prolix poem on the life of Prince Gautama, full of quasi-Indian materials and a belief, which seems to anticipate Lafcadio Hearn, that Buddhism and evolutionary science reveal the same truths. The poem was denounced as heretical from many a pulpit, but it was also read in many a parlor for its exotic, lilting lines. It is characteristic of the age that after this effusion of unorthodoxy Sir Edwin should bow to his Queen's request and write an equally prolix and equally devout, or perhaps heretical, poem on the life of Christ.

Sir Edwin's visit to Japan shows how precarious the Victorian ideal of feminine refinement and respectability was. There is no evidence to show that Japanese women were sexually any less moral than English women, but there were undoubtedly more women entertainers of various sorts, and the early visitors to Japan were at once shocked and pleased to discover that a woman of pleas-

ure might also be a "lady" of culture. In his *Japonica*
(1891), a collection of travel essays, Sir Edwin has a
great deal of praise for the "musmee"—i.e., *musume,*
"girl" or "daughter," but with connotations of "mistress"
or "pleasure-girl" in the literature of this period. And
the unforewarned reader is open to something of a
shock when he discovers that the book's photographs
show some of Arnold's lady friends, now in refined
activities with musical instruments or flower-arranging,
and now disrobed, posing by a bath-tub. Part of what
pleased the English in these Japanese women can be
seen in the six restless stanzas of Sir Edwin's poem,
"The Musmee," of which two lines will do—"The
Musmee's heart is slow to grief / And quick to pleasure,
love, and song." And the poem on the "Summit of Fuji-
yama, August 26, 1890" insists that in spite of the
wonderful view, "I like the Mountains of Japan / Best,
at your side, O Yoshi San!" His idealizing and his
affection for his friends are genuine, however, as "Tan-
gled and torn," a poem written on his return voyage,
shows.

Too free! too fast! With memories laden,
   I gaze Northward, where lies Japan.
You are there—so far! friend, teacher, and maiden!
   Haru and Mina and Yoshi San!

These poems on Japanese women do not suggest his
true range, however. He translated Japanese poems of a
folklorish and ethical stripe; he wrote others based on
Japanese legends; and even made up a hodge-podge section called "Poems of Japan" in a later volume, *The*

Tenth Muse and Other Poems (1895). The first of these, "A Japanese Lover," tells, in a riot of Japanese and English words, how the man hastens by jinrikisha to a tryst with his beloved. One group of poems is called "Some Japanese Uta," that is, tanka (also called waka) or thirty-one-syllabled lyrics. The series begins inauspiciously with a haiku, or seventeen-syllabled nature-poem, passed off as a tanka and ascribed to the poetess Ono no Komachi instead of to its proper authoress, Kaga no Chiyo. About a millennium and two poetic genres separate these two writers, so Sir Edwin is somewhat shaky as a scholar. The last poem, "The Japanese Soldier," is a curious affair which stretches on for some ten pages. The verses tell with unhappy glee the response of a country militiaman to his Emperor's call to leave his sweetheart and go off to fight the Chinese. It is shocking to see that the Chinese are invariably referred to contemptuously as "Pig-tails." The Japanese can be sword-rattlers in their own right, but there is something unnatural in the European imperialistic swaggering of the man who had translated the Indian scriptures hallooing the Japanese militia off to fight the Chinese for the sovereignty of Korea.

The gentle and charming sides of Sir Edwin's personality must be remembered along with those others which make him such a representative European in Japan, but he is a writer whom we have not found it difficult to ignore. Rudyard Kipling is another matter, for although he possesses a similarly mixed sensibility, his limitations and his undoubted powers have brought admirers and detractors to the same uneasy stance. Whatever his literary abilities, no one has disputed the fact that he represents the popular tastes and ideals of late Victorian England better than any other prominent literary figure. He also shows, better than any author of his time, the richness and humane integrity of the Victorian sensibility absorbing the experience of Japan.

Like Sir Edwin Arnold, he was a traveler in Japan who sent travel essays back from his points of call. He arrived at Nagasaki in the spring of 1889, wending his way slowly up towards Tōkyō. His first article contains a lengthy title concerning "Japan at Ten Hours' Sight . . ." which satirizes the fatuously ponderous titles of books like MacFarlane's. His first impression is that everything Japanese is wonderful and everything copied from foreigners execrable. He is struck by the beauty and number of the children, by the refinement of Japanese architecture, and especially by the cleanliness of the people. Of course, he had just come from India and China, but Japan was even cleaner and neater than Europe, a fact which invariably impressed Europeans and Americans all out of proportion to the significance of such matters, and usually led visitors to belittle the great civilizations of India and China. Chinese godliness was only barely next to Japanese cleanliness.

The comparisons he chooses to describe what he sees imply the extent of the Japanese vogue in England. Japanese womankind first reminds him of Pitti-Sing in *The Mikado,* but later, when he claims to have fallen in love with an O-Toyo in a teahouse, he says that she is "ebon-haired, rosy-cheeked, and made throughout of delicate porcelain." And to convey what the actors looked like on the kabuki stage, he advises his readers to "Look at the nearest Japanese fan." The wonder of what he sees is due in no small part to the fact that the people really appear like the representation of them in Japanese art. But the assurance with which he can refer his readers to "the nearest Japanese fan," *The Mikado,* or porcelain, testifies to something else, to the familiarity with Japanese art which the vogue for *japoneries* had brought. The country remains strange, but the very strangeness is familiar. Later, while in Ōsaka, he was treated to the thrill which has been perennially enjoyed if not always actually sought out by visiting Westerners. He is intruded upon in the bath by a woman willing to scrub his back. Of course she is young, "a pretty maiden," and clad in Eve's naked honour. The thrills of her good manners and beauty as well as her nakedness—the mixed idealism and light eroticism—are concomitant and inseparable.

His most significant essays are those which deal with what was named Civilization by the Victorians. He visited Ōsaka castle and certain "manufactories" and returns to generalize in a queer way for a man committed to Empire and Progress: "Thus we talked of the natures and dispositions of men we knew nothing about till we decided . . . that the cultured Japanese of the English pattern will corrupt and defile the tastes of his neighbours till . . . Japan altogether ceases to exist as a separate nation and becomes a button-hook manufacturing appanage of America . . . and . . . that it was foolish to form theories about the country until we had seen a little of it."

For Kipling, humility and perception have overcome any desire to be an emissary of European civilization, and exoticism runs counter to the ideals of industrial progress. The white man has no burden to bear to Japan as he does to China and India. An essay from Kyōto continues in this serious vein. The beauty of nature and of the children there attract him, especially in contrast to the corruption of the imperialistic tea-merchants from China lounging on vacation at the hotel bar. After visiting one of the city's beautiful temples and seeing its dazzling artwork, he writes: "Japan is a great people. Her masons play with stone, her carpenters with wood, her smiths with iron, and her artists with life, death, and all the eye can take in. Mercifully she has been denied the last touch of firmness in her character which would enable her to play with the whole round world. We possess that—We, the nation of the glass flower-shade, the pink worsted mat, the red and green china puppy-dog, and the poisonous Brussels carpet. It is our compensation." This statement of artistic sensibility and cultural humility from the man often reviled as the poet-laureate of imperialism is a rich tribute both to his own integrity and insight and to the richness and flexibility of the Victorian temper.

After eleven articles, he bade Japan goodbye with a last look of admiration for almost everything Japanese but of dismay at the confusion of Western modes and the influx of industrialism. His second trip to Japan in 1892 led him to write four more sketches, but he is wearied by the tourists and even his prose style seems tired. Only one piece, "Half-a-Dozen Pictures," is fresh and interested, but in spite of the Impressionistic skill with which he draws it, the article ends tentatively and he left Japan not to return again.

Some of Kipling's prose and verse attest to his visits in Japan. "Griffiths the Safe Man" is a farcical story of a traveler in Japan who keeps his passport so closely locked up that children, militia, and hotel servants cannot find it until he discovers it in his coat pocket. The Japanese setting is used for its incongruity, because what the narrator cannot understand about Griffiths in one set of terms baffles the Japanese on other grounds. In addition to this story, three of Kipling's poems are touched by Japan, but two only superficially. "The Undertaker's Horse" has a so-called Japanese proverb for an epigraph built upon a Chinese name, and "The Rhyme of the Three Sealers" employs Japan merely as an exotic setting for a sea-ballad, "Away by the lands of the Japanee / Where the paper lanterns glow . . . ." These trivial poems were probably written before he visited Japan, but "Buddha at Kamakura" gives meaningful expression to what he had learned from his careful observation. The experience it implies is very much like the proverbial visit to scoff which ends in prayer, as four stanzas from it show.

> A tourist-show, a legend told,
> A rusting bulk of bronze and gold,
> So much, and scarce so much, ye hold
>   The meaning of Kamakura?
>
> But when the morning prayer is prayed,
> Think, ere ye pass to strife and trade,

Is God in human image made
No nearer than Kamakura?

Yet spare us still the Western joke
When joss-sticks turn to scented smoke
The little sins of little folk
   That worship at Kamakura . . .

And whoso will, from Pride released,
Contemning neither creed nor priest,
May feel the soul of all the East
   About him at Kamakura.

The poem is perhaps the best example in his poetry of humility and condescending imperialism in a delicate balance which shifts to humanity and humility. Curiously enough, in the *Collected Works,* "Buddha at Kamakura" is followed by "The White Man's Burden" in which the same elements are in the same uneasy balance ending there in as decisive a shift to Empire, Militant Christianity, and Civilization. Seen together, these poems show that like the greatest Victorian poets, Tennyson and Arnold, Kipling finds himself in a world of rigid principles and ideas, ideals which are necessary to maintain human culture from the anarchy which would follow their discard, but that like them, he found it equally necessary to doubt the validity of these ideals in order to maintain his humanity and account for the nature of things as they are. The dual necessity to believe and to doubt, to keep firm hold on the belief and also to accept the emotion or experience which would destroy it, is one of the distinguishing characteristics of the age and is all the more discernible when its representative men come into contact with Japan. As with Kipling, this contact is apt to bring about a momentary confusion before a new, and typically paradoxical, harmony of attitude is achieved.

There were, of course, a number of Victorian poets who were undisturbed by the contradictory opinions of the age, and who contented themselves with as superficial a treatment of Japan as of the other subjects which the age offered them. These writers were apt to be affected by the advance-guard, but not deeply. W. E. Henley was one of these. He writes of the currently popular Japanese prints and of Buddhist transmigration of souls in a "Ballade of a Toyokuni Colour Print," but all is superficial as he wonders if he were "a Samurai renowned" or of what social station when he was a Japanese in a previous existence. He cannot decide, but, "Child," he ends, "What time the cherry-orchards blow/ I loved you once in old Japan." Such poems were ubiquitously popular in the 'Eighties and 'Nineties, and later even among the Imagists, if one allows for differences in technique. Perhaps the first example of an English poem on these *japoneries* is a dramatic monologue by Margaret Veley in *Cornhill Magazine* for September, 1876. The speaker is a man who asks the woman he is courting of the figure drawn on a fan,

> Will you say she is not lovely?
> Do you dare?
> *I* will not! I honour beauty
> Where I can,

Here's a woman one might die for!
—In Japan.

European interest in Japan was greatly stimulated by
the Japanese victory in the Russo-Japanese War of 1904.
There was a lot of talk and some articles on Japan as
the "Britain of Asia." George Meredith wrote an introduction to Yoshisaburō Okakura's widely read book, *The
Japanese Spirit* (1905), which told the English about the
spiritual basis for the courage of the Japanese soldiers at
Port Arthur. Herbert Spencer corresponded with a Japanese statesman and somewhat gratuitously offered his advice to Japan. It is clear that by the turn of the century
British interest in Japan was becoming more serious than
it had been—in recognition of the fact that Japan was
becoming a world power. But there were still those poets
who wrote of Japan as a pretty-pretty land over distant
seas, continuing, as Alfred Noyes did, exotic Victorianism
into the twentieth century. In no less than "A Triple
Ballad of Old Japan," he makes it a shore of heart's desire,
a lost, golden land: "That land is very far away,/We
lost it long ago." "Haunted in Old Japan" talks of serious
matters in a trifling fashion—

We the sons of reason, we that chose to bride
Knowledge, and rejected the Dream that we denied,
We that mocked the Holy Ghost and chose the Son of Man,
Now must wander haunted in the heart of Old Japan.

Whatever thought was in the poem vanished when Noyes
later revised the heresy of the third line. "A Japanese Love
Song" is interesting for its almost desperate use of color,

perhaps under the influence of Whistler's advocacy of block prints and their coloristic technique.

> Though the great skies are dark,
> And your small feet are white,
> Though your wide eyes are blue
> And the closed poppies red . . .

It is somewhat difficult to decide which part of Japan he had in mind when he talks about women with wide, blue eyes. A long narrative poem, "The Two Painters," amply illustrates the familiarly uneven course of true love, and talks boldly about art conquering "Time and Fate," but its only excuse for its demands upon the reader's credulity seems to be that the events occur in far distant Japan where anything may happen. There are other similar poems and a short story, "The Log of the Evening Star," which vend the same exotic wares, but the total result of Noyes's contact with Japan can be summarized in four lines from "Nippon."

> I saw that fairy mountain. . . .
> I watched it form and fade.
> No doubt the gods were singing
> When Nippon isle was made.

ii. Tales of Japan

Noyes is by no means the last writer to watch Japan "form and fade" into the exotic mist before him, for the cherry-petal exoticism of the Victorian period has continued and has even cast, at times, a warm, pink glow over the unlikely domain of cold prose. There are several hundreds of travel books, libraries of pseudo-Japanese fiction, and novels and short stories using Japanese materials of various kinds, but almost all are of dismayingly low literary quality. It is inadvisable for anyone with normal demands on his time to enter this realm of literature when a poet like Alfred Noyes can quickly give all that most of them have to offer in a few lines of exotic atmosphere. Most of these writers may be ignored in good conscience, but it will pay us to look at a few of historical importance or at those who have made important contributions to the popular image of Japan. Otherwise, we shall do well to hasten by to writers of undoubted literary importance who used Japan to add a new color to their style.

Perhaps the proper background for an understanding of the kind of fiction which was written on Japan in the late nineteenth century is the extensive travel literature. The names of the authors are more important than the works in most cases; they certainly make an impressive list. Bayard Taylor, Sir Edwin Arnold, and Rudyard Kipling were fellow travel-writers with such notables as General U. S. Grant. Henry Adams and John La Farge, the artist, went to Japan in 1886 and sent back some of the most interesting reports. Percivall Lowell represented the United States government in several countries of the Far East, and shipped back rooms full of Japanese art objects which Amy Lowell said filled her imagination as a child; and he wrote of Japan so persuasively that Lafcadio Hearn was induced to go there. William Sturgis Bigelow and Ernest Fenollosa not only went to Japan, but also were converted to Buddhism. Of the French and German visitors to Japan, only one is important for our literature, "Pierre Loti," of whom there will be more to say in another connection. Mr. John Ashmead, Jr., has analyzed the image which these travelers created in an excellent unpublished study, "The Idea of Japan 1853-1895": "In general Japan was described as on the one hand, fairy-like, quaint, childish, toy-like, polite, and honest, while on the other hand it was called proud, militaristic, cruel, revengeful, and treacherous." This, in a few words, is the dual popular image of Japan at the time, and an image which persists in some minds to this day. Such distorted conceptions are behind the shuffling, giggling "Japanese maidens" of *The Mikado* or the Metropolitan Opera Company's productions of *Madama Butterfly* and underlie the horror of the "Yellow Peril" which has determined our immigration legislation and which became an inhumane stereotype in movies, comic strips, and "patriotic" fiction during the Second World War. So fixed has the dual image become that even a capable anthropologist, Mrs. Ruth Benedict, succumbed to it in the double metaphor she chose for her book, *Chrysanthemum and the Sword* (1946). The small element of truth which may lie in this double image does not alter the fact that neither aspect of it pictures the Japanese as human beings with human faults and virtues. But happily, as Ashmead shows, there was another image of Japan, one no doubt exaggeratedly enthusiastic, but for more sensible reasons: "Some observers felt that East and West would find a common meeting ground in Japan. . . . As the art of Japan became known, there was a new growth of the

[Augustan] idea of Japan as a Utopia, now as an artistic Utopia. To Fenollosa, La Farge, Hearn, and others, Japanese art was a refreshing change from the commercialized art of the West."

As the second cycle of Japanese interest progressed— the cycle of exoticism, imitation, and absorption—these enthusiasts for Japanese art helped make the print and even the more serious art of Japan seem worthy of respect and a fruitful source of technique. But the various stages of the cycle of interest overlap, and all three modes of appreciation are often evident in the same period. For even while Fenollosa and Pound were studying Japan and its literature seriously, the stock image of the humorous Japanese bumbles through the pages of a Wallace Irwin's *Mr. Togo, Maid of All Work* (1913), and the eighteenth century's Oriental sage dwindles to a private detective in the stories of Charlie Chan and John P. Marquand's Mr. Moto.

The new understanding of Japan was growing, however, in France and England, among painters and poets, and it was becoming reasonably easy for a poet like Oscar Wilde to adapt the Impressionistic pictorial art, taken in part from the Japanese block print, to poetry by the use of coloristic images which created "studies" and "impressions" in verse. But novelists face their most difficult problems in conceiving the disposition of their plots, in devising narrative techniques, and in developing characters—problems not to be solved by pictorial methods—so that it is not surprising to discover that few novelists could find techniques which would absorb Japan into their art. The readiest way was the use of exotic detail, usually in what may be called Japanese similes. The fact that these similes appear in the works of writers of all sorts shows what many critics have pointed out—that one of the curious sides of avowedly tough-minded Naturalists is their tendency to lapse either into exoticism or sentimentalism, or both at once. Such exotic detail is frequently Japanese. Stephen Crane writes in *Maggie* of a character whose face "looked like a devil on a Japanese kite." Jack London frequently employs similar Japanese comparisons when he turns lyrical over such women as Ruth Morse, the finest woman in the life of Martin Eden. Her voice was like "silver, he thought to himself . . . and on the instant . . . he was transported to a far land, where under pink cherry blossoms, he smoked a cigarette and listened to the bells of the peaked pagoda calling straw-sandalled devotees to worship." It would have been altogether too incredible for Frank Norris to transport to Japan, even in thought, that unlikely pair in *The Octopus*, the rugged Annixter and the willowy Hilma, when the time came for a declaration of love; but he does the next most unbelievable thing when he has them weep over each other in San Francisco's Japanese gardens, where "They wiped each other's eyes like two children and for a long time sat in the deserted little Japanese pleasure house, their arms about each other, talking." Another early realist, Henry B. Fuller, employs the same technique in his two principal novels, and even Theodore Dreiser finds it helpful to explain in *The Titan* that "Sohlberg was interesting as an artistic type or figure—quite like a character in a Japanese print might be."

When naturalists allow themselves such licenses of style,

surely writers less committed to describe the stark and degrading spectacle of humanity may permit themselves an occasional Japanese detail. William Dean Howells seems to have thought so, and also to have believed that his heroine, Penelope, in *The Rise of Silas Lapham* would be enhanced when her mother declares, "She can't step out of the house without coming back with more things to talk about than most folks would bring back from Japan," or when he describes her appearance before the fire in terms of the "Japanese effect" of "her little visage," "dusky hair," and the fan held before her face. It is easy to infer from such remarks that Bostonians provided their fair share of the tourist business in Japan and that the Japanese prints from which the description of Penelope was drawn were expected to be familiar to Howells' large audience. However refined Henry James's admirers (and detractors) find him, there are few exotic details in his novels; instead, such a metaphor as the famous one of a pagoda at the beginning of the second volume of *The Golden Bowl* is used as a conceit extended over a page and a half, more to show the perplexities which confront Maggie Verver than as Orientalia. Edith Wharton uses Japan similarly in *The Age of Innocence* as a symbol of Newland Archer's tumbled state of mind. He wishes to flee with the Countess Olenska from the rigid society of New York to Japan, where he seeks to lead a life as free from American social restrictions as that of Lieutenant Pinkerton and Madame Butterfly.

These and the many other comparisons and references to things Japanese which might be exampled add up to little more than a stylistic device which shows the increasingly widespread and accepted presence of Japan in American and English life. The country and its art were now sufficiently well known and popular enough for these allusions to make immediate sense to the many varieties of popular audiences which read the novelists from whom these examples have been selected. This is of importance, but it is also plain from the allusions themselves that the novelists had little or no knowledge of Japanese fiction. The reasons for this are simple enough. There had been few translations of Japanese stories, and none of them had had any literary quality; but more importantly, the Japanese novel has had, on the whole, a good deal more to learn from the West about the craft of fiction than it has had to teach.

Japan does enter English and European fiction in other ways than this one of style, however. The country itself provided subject matter for interested writers, most of whom had traveled in Japan. The bulk of this fiction is, unfortunately, made up of the exotic staple of halcyon "Old Japan"—as if that were the world's golden age— and belongs to the limbo where time has left it. But Japan could also engage the mind of such a writer as Robert Louis Stevenson, who retold the story of "Yoshida Tora-Jiro" in *Cornhill Magazine* for March, 1880. In the overtones of his beautiful prose, one can sense the admiration which Stevenson felt for the courage which helped Yoshida make victories out of the successive defeats to which impetuosity and reforming zeal led him as he attempted to modernize and shape the destiny of Japan.

The most important novelist in this period to use Japan as a subject was not, however, the author of *Treasure*

Island or even an Englishman. This dubious honor goes to Louis Marie Julien Viaud—"Pierre Loti"—whose importance in exotic literature can scarcely be exaggerated. His most popular book, *Madame Chrysanthème* (1888), grew out of his experience as a naval officer on call in Japan, and it went through many editions and into many translations in a few years, as Europe seized upon Viaud's picture of Japan, a picture which was to hold all but complete sway over the popular mind until Lafcadio Hearn enlarged it and softened its harshness. To understand the peculiar quality of this novel, one must see it in the context of Viaud's other writings. He wrote other pieces on Japan, and in addition to this, his best known subject, he wrote on the larger Orient—Egypt, Turkey, India, and China. Add to these Iceland, children, and cats as his subjects, and it is plain to see that he exhausted every possible source of the exotic and sensational. Compared to him, Hearn was a realist with a limited subject matter.

Few things would justify Kipling's mature if ambiguous treatment of the experience of English imperialism more than a comparison with Viaud. The attitudes of both men toward the Orient are ambiguous, but Viaud's writing shows a mingling of the most trivial exoticism with a conscienceless imperialism. The slow-paced morality of the Victorian English is absent from the pages of *Madame Chrysanthème*, where the pleasures of exoticism and imperialism permit moral indifference and forms of spiritual brutality. The "marriages" between the French naval officers and Japanese women are only a joke; the women are, in the words of one of the officers, bibelots—

ugly, but droll and amusing; and when the officers set sail from Japan, they are more concerned for their cartloads of curios than for the women they leave behind. It is an ugly novel, but basic reading to understand what imperialism means to the Orient today: if America and its women were to be judged by "quaint" prostitutes at the docksides of New Orleans the effect would be much the same.

Ugly as it is, the novel has literary as well as historical importance, for in it the Japanese subject crosses the line into literary form. From his own experience, and out of the realities of imperialism, Viaud created the novel of desertion. This theme usually revolves around Europeans, especially naval officers, who visit Japan, acquire "wives," and desert them. Moral issues are often obscured, as in *Madame Chrysanthème*, behind the exotic mist, although later novels in this form usually soften the theme by making the woman something other than a prostitute and by attributing reluctance to the man who leaves her. A further step came when the narrative point of view was shifted from the titillated officer to the suffering woman, changing exotic sensation to pathos or even tragedy, although the exotic element remains in the setting. The most famous story of desertion is the tale which ultimately found its greatest setting in the haunting music of Giacomo Puccini's *Madama Butterfly*, but the genre was widely popular. It reached the "little magazines" when *The Chapbook* for January 7, 1897, carried "In the Shadow of the Daibutsu" (Kipling's "Buddha at Kamakura"), where the Japanese girl is a graduate of Vassar visited in Japan by a classmate who innocently steals away the

American naval officer. Our heroine Sakura has, indeed, not stooped to folly, but the only thing left for her to do is pine away and die. The heartlessness of foreign sailors is set to rights in *A Japanese Nightingale* (1901), a sentimental and melodramatic novel by Winnifred Eaton Babcock who wrote under the pseudo-Japanese name, Onoto Watanna. The heroine of the novel is Yuki, a Eurasian and a geisha, whose mother was deserted by a Dutch Pinkerton at Nagasaki. Yuki succeeds where her sisters had failed, in marrying the American, but the author has had to make her a Eurasian in order to get her past the immigration officials and racial prejudice. Mrs. Babcock published several other novels which deal with Japanese girls in similar social problems, but they have even less to recommend them than this well-intentioned book.

It would be agreeable to say that these ephemerae disappeared completely in December, 1941. Unfortunately, they were replaced by the still less acceptable image of the brutal Japanese during the war, and the exotic genre revived itself with amazing vigor after the war. The best-known of the postwar novels is probably James Michener's *Sayonara* (1954), where the tendency to deal with social problems which is evident in Mrs. Babcock's work and other prewar novels produces a new incredibility. The lightly exotic and erotic treatment of the Japanese woman has now made her incredibly superior to the American women on the scene. The unfortunate result is, as usual in do-gooding novels, that the story has more good will than credibility.

If there are exceptions to this generalization about the low quality of "Japanese" novels, William Plomer's work is one of them. His is perhaps the only fiction which reads like a splendid translation from a modern Japanese novelist. It is even possible—and useful—to compare him with famous Japanese authors. "A Brutal Sentimentalist" (1929) analyzes Japanese personality in the manner of the stories of Mori Ōgai; his "Yōka Nikki" is written in the peculiarly Japanese genre, the fictionalized diary; and his "Nakamura" is frequently reminiscent of the prewar Japanese Naturalists and the psychological studies of Akutagawa Ryūnosuke. But the most extraordinary literary echo—extraordinary both because a skillful English writer has chosen to imitate a Japanese novel and for the degree of the imitation—is "Mother Kamchatka," a bitter satire on the worst sides of Japanese life, whose source is the greatest of modern Japanese satires, Akutagawa's *Kappa*. The mordant analysis of Plomer's long story follows Akutagawa's technique of using short chapters in which Kappas (here, Kamchatkans) introduce the horrified narrator to the country which is transparently Japan.

Plomer has also written a "Japanese" novel, *Sado* (1931, 1951), which deals with the conflicts of personality among four complex characters—an English artist visiting Japan, a young Japanese intellectual, an Englishwoman married to a Japanese, and her husband. In this example of Bloomsbury in Japan, the author is not very sympathetic to his Japanese characters, but the same thing may be said of his attitude toward the English; and one is moved to sigh in relief, at last, over a realistic novel with a Japanese setting. The limitations of Plomer's accomplishment are inherent in a certain autobiographical and journalistic flavor to his writing. His desire, throughout all his Japanese fiction, to deal with the Japanese National Character in terms of his own experiences makes the stories fall somewhere between recorded observation—the journalistic quality—and *Bildungsroman*. For while a Japanese novelist could deal with Plomer's subjects unconsciously, so to speak, Plomer is forced to deal too closely with his own experience; how closely one can discover by comparing the characters in his fiction with the people in "Not by Eastern Windows Only," the Japanese portion of his autobiography, *Double Lives* (1943). Unfortunately, the reader who lacks Plomer's experiences is apt to find that the author's compulsion to give them expression does not wholly correspond with his own literary interests.

These varied fictional treatments of Japan show that the reasons for re-creating Japan in novels and short stories vary with the writer, but there are some constant historical motives which can be discussed. For many writers—and readers—Japan takes them to another, happier world where they may, for a time, forget their own troubles and moral conventions in an Oriental Garden of Bliss. Other writers like Viaud treat Japan for the variety of sensations it affords, and still others because it enables them to treat subjects which would otherwise be considered immoral or distasteful. What, one wonders, would be the American reaction if the dying Madame Butterfly were Bostonian and Pinkerton and Kate were Italian? And finally, there are those writers like Plomer who seem to have written of Japan from a desire to interpret their own experience in the Orient. While these novels show that Japan is no longer what it was for Hawthorne, the least hackneyed subject in the world, and while no great novel has been written on Japan, the example of Plomer proves that it is now possible to treat Japan as a fictional subject apart from the intolerable exoticism or condescension which for so many decades has prevented any mature use of Japan in our literature.

iii. Japan on the Stage

It is a curious fact that while the Japanese subject on the English and American stage has been even more primitive and intolerable than in the novel, the actual literary results have been generally happier. The explanation of this literary curiosity is no doubt the fact that the stage has had a longer and more successful tradition of adapting the strange, the exotic, and the spectacular to its medium. The novel is, perhaps, basically a more realistic genre; certainly, *A Midsummer Night's Dream*, Dryden's *All For Love*, or the libretti of the most famous operas would either be dismissed as second-rate, incredible novels or have to be cast in the form of children's fiction. The stage has had an initial advantage over the novel in dealing with Japanese subjects.

This advantage was, however, slow to appear. The theatrical magazines of the 'Seventies often mention a stage-type called "the heathen Chinee" who is by turns comic in his efforts to speak English, exotic in his outlandishness, and evil in his opium—this last strangely inconsistent with the thriving opium monopoly of the British China trade. A few years later, the stage Japanese appears, at first indistinguishable from the stage Chinese, but increasingly associated with exotic refinement or fumbling jollity. "The jolly Jap" is a frequent type in variety shows, musicals, and as a fillip to otherwise tame productions. The exotic type is usually an unutterably refined woman or an equally intrepid samurai—types which seem to be the idealized noble savage filtered down through Oriental exoticism. "The jolly Jap" may well have grown in part out of English contact with the Japanese who came to London for the International Exhibition of 1862, or with those who came to establish shops and even small factories to cater to the craze for Japanese bric-à-brac in the last decades of the century. The jollity itself may owe something to the remarkable affability of the Japanese or to their disconcerting habit of laughing when embarrassed by foreigners whose demands or customs seem strange. But no small part of the "jollity" probably originated in the delight which coarse audiences have always felt when foreigners of whatever description appear different from themselves and still not seem to realize or to mind it. The extent to which the craze for things Japanese affected England can be understood in two ways. One of the amusements of Londoners from the 'Sixties on was to visit the Japanese colony at Knightsbridge for an exotic adventure, a craze whose results can be seen in magazine illustrations of the interiors of Victorian houses or of stage sets. The ubiquitous Victorian surfaces of parlor or stage—the shelves, mantles, chests, tables, and even floors—are laden with vases, fans, and other bric-à-brac.

It was not just the bourgeoisie or stage managers who

seemed to the more sober-minded to have taken leave of their senses, however. This was also the age of "Whistler and the Japanese," the time when the advance-guard called itself by such names as Aestheticism and Impressionism. Aestheticism seems to have been composed of two parts of medievalism and one of Orientalism, a combination particularly vulnerable to the charge of preciosity which was brought against it. No one made the charge more amusingly than Gilbert and Sullivan in 1881 when they and the Savoy Company offered *Patience* to a delighted public. Oscar Wilde becomes Reginald Bunthorne, a "Fleshly Poet," and Algernon Charles Swinburne becomes Archibald Grosvener, an "Idyllic Poet"—two aesthetes well calculated to enchant the "young ladies dressed in aesthetic draperies" and all "in the last stages of despair." When the haughty Dragoon Guards march in to claim these moribund creatures as their own, they are horrified to hear Lady Jane deplore the primary colors of their uniforms, even when she encourages them that there is some room for hope if only they would add "a cobwebby grey velvet," various medieval garnishes, and surmount the whole "with something Japanese—it matters not what" as a *pièce de résistance*. Bunthorne-Wilde does manage a moment alone to complain wearily that "I do *not* long for all one sees/That's Japanese," but when he offers himself at auction, he must proffer his usual wares.

Put in half a guinea and a husband you may gain—
Such a judge of blue-and-white and other kinds of pottery—
From early Oriental down to modern terra-cotta-ry.

And when Bunthorne and Grosvener are impelled to confess, in unison, to the virtues which they share, each acknowledges himself to be

> A Japanese young man,
> A blue-and-white young man,
> Francesca da Rimini, miminy, piminy,
> *Je-ne-sais-quoi* young man.

While Gilbert was contemplating what seemed to him the aberrant taste of his time, the Japanese stage-types were appearing with greater frequency. The reviewer of "The Japs" in *Theatre* magazine for October 1, 1885, despaired: "In the first place, I do not understand the mania for Japanese pieces." These "Japanese pieces" might well have passed from view had not the "Japanese" fantastics been given something of an immortality by Gilbert and Sullivan's most popular opera, *The Mikado*, which appeared in the same year. The story of how this opera came into being, a story Gilbert often told, attests more eloquently to the power of the Japanese vogue than anything else which might be said. In 1884, during one of the fits of mutual dislike which the collaborators were given to, Sullivan insisted upon a plot more realistic than the airy nothingness of *Princess Ida*. Gilbert was mulling over the request in his study one day when a souvenir fell from the wall. It was not one of the usual stage-souvenirs but a *japonerie*, a samurai sword, which clattered to the floor and gave Gilbert his inspiration. Here then, is Sullivan's new, realistic play, made to order by the man who shortly before had satirized the craze for "all one sees/That's Japanese." When "realism" begins with bric-à-brac and ends with Nanki-Poo, it is easy to see that the popularity of Japan at the time was great enough to dazzle even those who bemoaned it.

To people his play, Gilbert exploited the stock theatrical Japanese types which had been infesting the stage for a decade or more. In the Mikado and Poo-Bah we have the cruel Oriental; Ko-Ko is the "jolly Jap"; and Yum-Yum and her classmates parody the refined Japanese woman— all of course with the saving comic gusto which makes them so entertaining. The types also had relevance to scandals at the English court and in the government of the time, and in this respect the play is curiously like the satire of the eighteenth century, where Japan was used as an allegorical disguise for the England of the day. To playgoers of the time, Gilbert's satire was interesting both for itself and for its pleasing distortions of the popular image of Japan. The names of the characters are, of course, names never heard of in Japan, and the only knowledge of Japan really necessary to understand the opera could have been gained from any of the pseudo-Japanese plays of the time. Except for the Japanese façade, the opera is as English as anything Gilbert ever wrote for Sullivan. There are a couple of exceptions to this statement, perhaps. When Katisha threatens to reveal that Nanki-Poo is not a second trombone but the son and heir of the Mikado, the other characters clamorously "sing Japanese words"—"O ni! bikkuri shakkuri to! oya oya!" —an un-Japanese conjunction of words which may be freely rendered, "You devil! with fright, with hiccups! hey! hey!" And there is also the legend that the "March of the Mikado's Troops" ("Miya sama, miya sama . . .")

is an obscene song. Actually the text is more corrupt than the words, which probably signify:

> Honored Prince, Honored Prince,
> What does this mean—
> This business of fluttering
> About before the ladies?
> Hey, nonny, nonny, nonny, hey!

The Japanese have never had much enthusiasm for *The Mikado*, any more than the English would for a French comic opera which depicted their young queen as Mae West. But there is a tale of a postwar adaptation of *The Mikado* which delighted Japanese and Americans alike with its topical overtones and its suggestions that the "Mikado" personified the Supreme Commander for the Allied Powers, a title as weighty as most of Poo-Bah's.

The enormous success of *The Mikado* guaranteed a large progeny and a continuance of the Japanese vogue. Not a month passes after 1885, until the international tensions of the 'Thirties, without some journal carrying mention of a Japanese play or an article either on pseudo-Japanese plays or on the real Japanese drama. The titles need no comment—*The Geisha, The Mayor of Tokio, Cherry Blossom River, A Flower of Yeddo, The Lady of the Weeping Willow Tree*—and so on. But the fact that an interest was developing in the native Japanese drama led to more serious efforts to put Japan on the stage. Sir Edwin Arnold, whom we have met before, published *Adzuma: or the Japanese Wife* in 1893. In this melodrama, the slandered Adzuma saves her reputation by arranging to be decapitated in place of her sleeping husband at the hands of the slandering suitor who has been inflamed by the devices of a black-hearted villain and the cross-currents of karma—the same story which the Japanese movie *Gate of Hell* made current to thousands of Americans in the early 1950's. The play is more sentimental and melodramatic than anything else, but Sir Edwin added talk about fate and karma which attempts to give a serious meaning to the action.

As the years passed, various devices were employed to give greater accuracy to the Japanese setting. Well-documented stage sets, Japanese words in the text, and supposedly typical Japanese modes of behavior were employed to give an air of realism. But the "realism" is only the fictive, holiday realism of Hollywood spectaculars, a factitious realism which has nothing to do with fundamentally human and Japanese truth. But this is also the period of the novel of desertion, of Ibsen's problem plays dealing with such social issues as "the woman question," and of a tendency to theatrical display. These elements—an attempted realism, dramatic "problems," and display—began to alter the character of the stage representation of Japan. Such an English play as *The Geisha* was so lavish and the sets so carefully made along Japanese lines that the reviewer for *Theatre* could not "recall a more sumptuous or tasteful spectacle" and regarded its success as a foregone conclusion. The play is really more melodramatic than problematic, but it does skirt interracial issues, and has the usual naval officer and disappointed Japanese woman of the desertion-plot.

It was the American rather than the English stage which produced the best known of the Japanese plays, however. In a tight spot for a new play, David Belasco seized upon a novel which had been recommended to him by a friend. The novel had been written by John Luther Long and published in 1897. After a tremendous, hurried effort and great financial investment, and having secured the services of one of the most prominent American tragediennes, Belasco finally brought *Madame Butterfly* to the stage of the Herald Square Theatre on March 5, 1900. It was an immediate success—perhaps second only to *Uncle Tom's Cabin* among American tragedies—and Belasco always said that his "most successful achievement in stirring imagination" was the illusion of a whole night's passing in fourteen minutes of complete stage silence and changing lights in this play. His great success in the New York production led him to open the play concurrently in London, where, at the first night's performance, Giacomo Puccini—who understood no English—watched the play intently, and rushed backstage afterwards in tears —as Belasco told the story—begging him for permission rights to make the play into grand opera. As novel, play, and opera the fate of Cho-Cho-San remains the finest version of the theme of desertion. Although the moral problems of Pinkerton are not so much solved as flooded away by the surge of emotion from Butterfly's suicide according to another moral code, there is a truly tragic quality latent in Butterfly's dilemma. The play is of course only a melodrama, but one which has some truth and, as an opera, the haunting magic of Puccini's tender music. Belasco was encouraged to try another Japanese play by the second night of the American run of *Madame Butter-*

fly, and in 1902 produced *The Darling of the Gods*, a latter-day *Venice Preserved* set in Japan, but preserved only indifferently in the costly, accurately Japanese settings. Where *Butterfly* was truly melodramatic, this play was only fatuously pathetic, but Belasco's enemies, the Theatrical Trust, busied themselves in hurrying to the boards a rival play based upon the novel by Mrs. Babcock mentioned earlier—*A Japanese Nightingale*. Butterfly held the boards against all her sisters, however, and even John Luther Long, her author, could not repeat his and Belasco's success when he tried to produce *The Dragon Fly* independently in Philadelphia in 1905.

Such plays went on and off the stage in persistent succession for about thirty years. The last play with a Japanese subject before the war seems to be the Civic Repertory Theatre's production of Paul Green's *Hymn to the Rising Sun*, which opened in Chicago on January 12, 1936. The type left the stage at this time, presumably because of the friction between Japan and the United States, and during the war the old image of the "heathen Chinee" made Japanese carried the movies and the comic strips alike. Since the war, an uncertain period of peace and political realignments has impelled the popular mind to shift this inhuman image back to the mainland Chinese. There was a degree of softening toward the Japanese even in Rodgers and Hammerstein's *South Pacific*, first performed in New York in April, 1949. And with John Patrick's adaptation of Vern Snider's novel, *The Teahouse of the August Moon* (October, 1953), the old stage conception of Japan returned in full force. The play condescends to the "jolly Okinawans," and is also something of a gentle satire on American Military Government in Okinawa. The play differs from prewar Japanistic plays in the greater realism, if not necessarily greater truth, of the action and in the casting of a Japanese, Mariko Niki, as the geisha in the teahouse.

It is interesting that this stock image has proved as hardy as it is in this play produced exactly a century after Perry's squadron first sailed off the coast of Japan. One would have expected that a more mature interpretation of Japan would have been achieved after so long a period, but literary images and forms are as slow to die as international misconceptions, and dramatic conventions probably change even more slowly than the conventions of other forms. Moreover, Japan has had to struggle to emerge in its true form from the false images with more effort than most countries. The reasons for the formation and persistency of these images have been discussed in part already, but no account of the images and stereotypes of Japan would be complete without some reference to Lafcadio Hearn.

iv. The Popular Image of Lafcadio Hearn

There are probably three Lafcadio Hearns, enough alike so that they merge confusingly, but fundamentally different enough to require different approaches for understanding them. The first is Hearn the person, a shy, complexly motivated personality who must be left to the disputes of his biographers. The second is Hearn the literary artist and thinker who is more properly the subject of the next chapter. And the third is the popular conception of Hearn—the only man really to have understood Old Japan, that lovely land of mists, gentle and sensitive if rather bloodless people, cherry blossoms, and amiable legends. It is this view of Japan replacing Loti's harsher one, which probably helped give currency to the stage and fictional types of the refined and intrepid Japanese, which makes dowagers gush and gruff men sigh, and which the mature reader can only feel is an impairment of the spirit called Lafcadio Hearnia.

There is reason enough for this conception of Hearn and Japan in the titles of the books he published between 1894 and 1905: *Glimpses of Unfamiliar Japan, Out of the East, Kokoro, Gleanings in Buddha Fields, Exotics and Retrospects, In Ghostly Japan, Shadowings, A Japanese Miscellany, Kotto, Kwaidan,* and *The Romance of the Milky Way and Other Stories.* Only *Japan, An Attempt at Interpretation* (1904) is apt to strike the ordinary reader as a title which does not suggest the exotic. And *Japan* is the only book in which he does not collect a number of largely unrelated pieces which swell by many times the actual number of subjects dealt with in the eleven titles first listed. These many separate chapters with their novel and exotic titles—"Karma," "Insect Poems," "Nirvana" and the like—and countless fugitive pieces published posthumously in book form often seem to be merely stories of pathos, of a strange ethical code, of the mysterious and the supernatural. Small wonder, then, that Hearn brought Japan, or at least a romantic conception of it, into the homes and the hearts of the West.

The question of where exactly Hearn's enormous popular appeal lay is one for which hindsight has few advantages. Perhaps one explanation is that his peculiar talent came at a propitious time. The movement of art for art's sake and the growing protest in many circles against the ideas of Progress and Respectability and what they connoted in social and economic terms came to a climax in the years between 1885 and 1905. The public as a whole was scarcely ready to endure what Whistler, Wilde, Symons, Beardsley and their fellow radicals were demanding be done in England and America, but the popular imagination was sufficiently attuned to the Aesthetic Revolt to welcome enthusiastically what Hearn had to say about Japan. He may have made a great deal of bother about Oriental refinement which treated of realms above the popular mind, but it was all very quaint and pretty. He may have proclaimed the superiority of Buddhism to Christianity and science, but all of this protest against the ideals of the age was safely off in faraway Japan, and not in London or Boston. He offered aestheticism and unorthodoxy to his large audience at an easy remove, and flights into the strange or the exotic which were a welcome escape from the strenuous life of the late nineteenth century in England and America. The age seems to have found in Hearn a compromise with Whistler, the French, and unorthodoxy.

There was in addition the sop of exoticism, a taste whose appeal seems to be proportional to its ineffability. People who turn with warm expectations to a book called *Exotics and Retrospects* have tastes which the soberminded find difficult to explain. But exoticism runs closely parallel to cultural relativism, and the popular imagination seems to have discovered both at this time, without of course ever really losing hold of the absolutes of Protestant orthodoxy.

For his part, Hearn contributed an element which was essential to capture the taste of his time. Although he was orthodox in no common acceptance of the term, he was idealistic, and intensely so. This idealism echoes in the tone of every paragraph he wrote. Impelled by Percivall Lowell's *Soul of the Far East* (1888), he seems to have gone to Japan as if he expected to find a Utopia, and in any case wrote as if he had. The characters who float through his stories are either very good or very bad, and although the criteria by which we are to judge them are often not Western standards, this is only part of the secret between the author and us—we are never in doubt about the nature of heroism or villainy. It is also significant that he idealized the people of Japan and their culture, not simply or blindly, but in the terms in which the Japanese themselves like to think they excel. The Japanese ideals were close to his own—or he never would have become a Japanese subject under the conditions he did —and he communicates them to the Western reader with a fine fervor. This fact accounts for a situation with which the West is not too well acquainted, Hearn's continuous popularity in Japan. A nation which found somewhat to its embarrassment that it was far behind in what the West liked to think was civilization was naturally happy to find itself praised for what it was, rather than blamed for what it failed to succeed in becoming; and later, in this century, when the Japanese found they had become rather too drably the Westernized nation which they had once sought to be, it was pleasant for them to be able to return to his praise in the hope that what he saw was still basically true, after all. In a sense, the Japanese have fallen prey to a foreign exoticizing of themselves.

Lafcadio Hearn is in part a symbol, then—to the West of the exotic, of the ideal, and of that which is safely heterodox because it is in a far-off land. And to Japan he is a symbol of true appreciation of the Japanese spirit. The West and Japan have shared the idea that he has understood Japan as no Westerner ever had before or is likely to again and, in certain rather limited senses, this is true. With the help of a sensitive personality which was akin to Japanese aestheticism and with the aid of the sentimental image of Japan which the travelers had established before him, he more than any other man gave Japan an appeal that it had never before exercised over the imagination, especially the popular imagination, of the West. When people thought of the ideally strange, they thought of Japan; and when they thought of Japan, they were sure to glow with a warm feeling for Lafcadio Hearn. There is scarcely another man in history who has become to such an extraordinary degree a sympathetic symbol to two different cultures, who could appeal so much to the nation he visited, or create as warm an image of that nation in his own culture—at the very time that his writings were only half understood. To appreciate the other, unfamiliar half of his writings, however, it is necessary to take cognizance of a very different stream of events from those examined so far. It is necessary to look at the French response to Japan, and at Impressionism.

III. FROM *JAPONISME* TO IMPRESSIONISM: THE CHANGE FROM NINETEENTH TO TWENTIETH-CENTURY ARTISTIC AND POETIC MODES

"The search after *reality* in literature, the resurrection of eighteenth-century art, the triumph of *Japonisme*—are not these the three great literary and artistic movements of the second one-half of the nineteenth century?"—ARTHUR SYMONS quoting Jules de Goncourt in *Dramatis Personae*.

THE EARLY DECADES of nineteenth-century literary and artistic interest in Japan seem to have had most importance in supplying exotic subject matter to poets and prose writers and in contributing a wider realm of experience to be absorbed by the already existing attitudes of English and American writers and, to an increasing extent, by the popular imagination. The Victorian image of Japan—an Eastern country which was curiously civilized but hardly European, a nation of beautiful and refined but also enticing and "improper" women, a land which needed the benefits of civilization through trade and yet one which had a splendid culture to confer upon the West—this ambiguous image of Japan had not yet faded from Western minds when a new wave of interest flooded France and soon spilled over into England and the United States.

The proper philosophical and historical conditions had been formed for a more appreciative interest in Japan. The gradual acceptance of historical, cultural, and critical relativism from the eighteenth century onward was about to culminate in Taine's theories of art arising from a cultural "milieu." The increasing interest in sensibility and emotions and in the psychological processes of artistic composition and appreciation might have led at any moment to the Impressionistic assumption that beauty and even reality lie in the eye of the beholder. These and other elements in the thought of the second half of the nineteenth century needed only some fresh impetus to bring them together into a new theory of art and literature. Although it might well have happened under a wholly different stimulus, the new movement in French art and literature seemed to the artists and writers of the time to have been touched off by Japanese color wood-block prints. What began as a vogue ended by shaping or affecting several literary and artistic movements.

i. French Interest in Japanese Art

It is a melodramatic oversimplification of the complexities of art and reality to say that any artistic movement began on a certain sunny morning in such-and-such a place, and yet once the vogue which was soon called *Japonisme* became established, there were many claims and counterclaims for the credit of beginning the movement.

The bemused historian can only stroke his chin, take his choice, and begin somewhere. There is no more credible evidence to rely upon than the somewhat sensational story of the day in 1856 when Félix Bracquemond discovered a volume of Hokusai's *manga* ("drawings," but often, as here, drawings made prints) in the possession of the printer Delâtre. The details of the discovery vary with the teller, but all versions attest to Bracquemond's excitement. For some reason, Delâtre refused to part with the sheets then but later sold them to an engineer, Lavielle, from whom Bracquemond triumphantly captured them, after all. It is said that the volume of drawings "became Bracquemond's breviary," and as shipments of Japanese art increased after Perry's visit to Japan, other artists and citizens were soon acquiring the prints, ceramics, and paintings for themselves. Their demands for things Japanese echoed Bracquemond's, and the discovery became a fad.

Japonisme, as the fad was called, grew in part out of an earlier vogue for Chinese art and poetry. The period of Chinese exoticism was largely fostered by Théophile and Judith Gautier and lasted from about 1800 to 1870. Their understanding of China was as partial and exotic as Alfred Noyes's later understanding of Japan, but Judith enjoyed composing stories supposedly about China and Théophile delighted in the pose of the mandarin-poet. He submitted some of his "Chinese" poems to the first issue of *Parnasse contemporain*, where there were allusions to China in the work of Mallarmé, Popelin, Verlaine, Maupassant, and Renard. Superficial, faddish, and drenched with exoticism as the Chinese vogue was, it was nonetheless symptomatic of the wide search for literary and artistic materials which characterizes this era of excited experimentation.

Growing out of the Chinese vogue as it did, the period of *Japonisme*, 1865 to 1895, might well have remained as superficial as the craze for *chinoiseries* had it not attracted the interest of some of the most important artists and critics of the day. The Gautiers and the brothers Goncourt soon took up Bracquemond's interest, and stores selling Japanese art were enthusiastically patronized by Heredia, Regnier, Voisins, and Clemenceau. Montesquiou employed a Japanese gardener, Huysmans was defending Japanese art, and A. Renan was writing poetry on Japan.

More important than this popularity of Japanese art in Paris, however, was the fact that from the early 'Seventies Japanese prints were taken as models of technique and were the justification and frequently the origin of the theory of the Impressionists and the painters associated with them. Manet, Monet, Duret, Degas, Gaugin, Toulouse-Lautrec, Van Gogh, the Americans James A. M. Whistler and Mary Cassatt—to name only the most important—extolled the Japanese print, borrowed both subject matter and technique from it, and used it to justify their own creations. Duret's declaration that "the Japanese are the first and finest Impressionists" and Van Gogh's belief that Japanese art was the "true religion" are typical responses. In the strange perspectives and frequently unbalanced compositions of the prints they found a liberation from academic formalism. In the brilliant, unusual colors and combinations of colors in the prints they found an excuse for their own many-hued palettes. And from the peculiar, stylized features of the figures drawn in the prints and from the Japanese indifference to Western ideas of representational art, these painters found a way of expressing their personal impressions of reality and beauty in new techniques and ideas of form.

The Impressionists had, after all, worked themselves into something of a dilemma. Denying the rules of the academicians, and depending upon the validity of the individual artist's perceptions as they did, they were on the verge of saying that art is solely a matter of impression, of individual taste. Hostile critics could have condemned them by their own theory, for if the impression or whim of any individual were valid—of Impressionist, academe, or laundry-woman—then anyone could call the Impressionists' own work bad, and artistic anarchy would prevail. It is not clear that this vulnerability in their theory was ever acknowledged by the Impressionists or fully exploited by their enemies, but it is clear from their pronouncements at the time that they repeatedly turned for proof to the Japanese prints which, they declared, ignored the old, traditional rules and achieved a beauty of the artist's own devising. The surprising thing—and that which attests to the power of Japanese art in the minds of this generation—is that they assumed that if they could convince their detractors that their new theories were deduced from the print, they would be justified. Or perhaps it is still more astounding that their critics should, for the most part, agree to the logic while denying the proof. To add irony to perplexity, the Japanese themselves in these years regarded the block

print with the same contempt that painters today feel
for photographs, because they felt that the prints lacked
universality and truth in their depiction of human activities taken out of nature and depicting transitory moments.
Paradoxically, this realism of the moment was one of the
elements of the prints that the French painters appreciated most, but they failed to see that the techniques
employed by the genre were as stylized as the paintings of
the academicians.

ii. The Effect of Japan on
French Literature

The relevance of the Japanese interests of the painters
to literature and literary theory was great, although perhaps it is not immediately apparent today. From the
outset, the writers had been as enthusiastic Japanophiles
as the artists, as Manet's painting of Zola at his desk
(1868) illustrates. The picture shows a panel of a Japanese
screen to the left and prints of an actor (by Toyokuni
or Kunisada) over the desk which itself bears some
Oriental bric-à-brac. Zola's rooms were filled with *japoneries*, and his staircase is said to have been lined with
that kind of print which he chose to call "my furious
fornications." Moreover, he had been anticipated as a
collector by the Gautiers, Huysmans, the Goncourts, and
others.

Most writers experienced some understandable difficulty in transferring their interest in Japanese art to
literature. The simplest solution was to make verbal comparisons between some person, object, or situation in

their writing with something they remembered from prints or Japanese art. These Japanese similes appeared soon after 1877—and probably inspired the American novelists examined in the last chapter—on the pages of the Goncourts' in *La Fille Éliza, Frères Zemganno, La Faustin;* in Huysmans' *À Rebours;* in Maupassant's *Mouche;* and in Proust's *Le Côté de Guermantes, A l'ombre des jeunes filles en fleurs,* and *Sodome et Gomorrhe.*

Japan also contributed to the literary theory of the French novel. Two general approaches to literary Naturalism were propounded, the "scientific" by Zola, and the more Impressionistic by the Goncourt brothers. Zola's philosophy of Naturalism owed little to Japan, but he felt a strong kinship with the technique of the Impressionists which is expressed both in statements like the one about Pissarro—"He is simply a naturalist . . . he straightforwardly shows you what he sees"—and in his interest in the slice-of-life or the focus on the moment in the Japanese prints. Precision and exactitude were necessary, but he held with the Goncourts that the disorder and shapelessness of life requires an expressive form like the casual disarrangement of composition which they saw in the Japanese print. The Goncourts practiced this theory more earnestly even than Zola, so earnestly that Professor William Schwartz—the first person really to study the role of Japan in modern French art and literature—has been led to say that "The influence of Japanese art . . . seems to have affected the arrangement or construction of all the later Goncourt novels," as *Manette Solomon,* for example, "and also affected to some extent their choice of subjects," as in the courtesan-Life of *La Fille Élisa* and the acrobats of *Les Frères Zemganno.*

It does indeed appear strange that the vogue for Japanese art which was at first exotic should insist upon the absolute value of the prints outside of their cultural context and help establish the realism of the Naturalists. But this development seems less strange when it is placed against the background of increasingly relativistic thought which opened the way for both the appreciation of Oriental art and the formation of the determinism— that is, the relativism of place, social position, and the like —which underlies Naturalism. And in the realm of technique, it is plain to see that what Professor Schwartz characterized as "the accidental or trivial but veracious groupings of things and events that is found in nature and produced in Japanese art" is as relevant to the methods of Naturalistic realism as to Impressionistic painting. For literature at least, "realism" is as much a matter of technique and convention as it is of subject matter.

Impressionism was various and fertile enough to lead to another literary movement, "Decadence," which opposed itself to the Naturalistic effort to make art as much like life as possible. The Decadents deplored Naturalistic reality, which they found ugly and misshapen, and instead advocated *l'art pour l'art,* beauty instead of reality. The two movements were theoretically so opposed that it seems impossible that they could have stemmed from Impressionism or have shared an interest in Japan—and yet they did. Because while a Huysmans and a Zola or a George Moore and an Oscar Wilde are most notable for their differences, they shared with the Impressionists an urgent desire to separate art from morality. Whether they chose to describe the real or the beautiful, life as it is or art for its own sake, neither school shared with Pope any desire to moralize their song. Moreover, the distinction between the real and the beautiful—between Zola's lyrical romanticizing of sex and meadows in *Germinal* and various Decadent treatments of prostitutes— is as difficult to separate as the real and the beautiful sides of the Japanese print which both schools admired.

The transition from Impressionism in painting to Decadence—or to Symbolism as the movement was more often called in England—in poetry was, then, very complex and can be treated in many ways. Two further lines of transition are important, however, and must be mentioned. Many poets tried to adopt the techniques of the Impressionists directly and even called their poems "impressions." Many of these "impressions" employ Japanese detail, as we might expect. And there is the second bond, the common interest of Impressionist and Symbolist alike in Japan. When writers as different as Viaud ("Pierre Loti") and Paul Claudel go to Japan and find it important to their experience and art, Japan and its culture may fairly be called one of the important determinants of modern literature. The Goncourt brothers realized this, and so did Arthur Symons when he asked with Jules Goncourt, quoting him in *Dramatis Personae*, "The search after *reality* in literature, the resurrection of eighteenth century art, the triumph of *Japonisme*— are not these the three great literary and artistic movements of the second one-half of the nineteenth century?"

iii. The French Discovery of
Japanese Literature

While travelers and the admirers of Japanese prints
were responding to Japan with varying degrees of emotionalism and sobriety, writers were composing poems
which they thought might be in the Japanese manner.
The exoticism of these poems makes them unreadable
today, but they soon passed from the literary scene and
were replaced by the translations and then the imitations
of Japanese poetry which were beginning to appear.
The distinction between using Japanese materials or
posing in pseudo-Japanese manners on the one hand,
and employing forms, images, and techniques modelled
upon Japanese poetry on the other, is an important one
and one which may be made in French imitations after
the turn of the century. While there seems to have been
some confusion between what was really Japanese and
what was only called so, true Japanese modes made head-
way and the death knell of the pseudo-Japanese verse of
the preceding decades was surely rung by Marcel Revon's
authoritative *Anthologie de la Littérature Japonaise*
(1910). Almost immediately, and for the next fifteen years,
French poets imitated the techniques of Japanese poetry
and even adapted the five-seven-five syllabic arrangements
of haiku (lyrics of nature) to French poetry. While Couchoud may be credited with originating haiku in French,
and while his practice was followed in one way or another
by Baldensperger, Paul Fort, Vocance, Jean Breton, Éluard, and literally hundreds of others who sent French
haiku to competitions held by the *Nouvelle Revue Franç-*

aise, it is probably most significant that when, in 1916, Couchoud republished his essay, "Epigrammes lyriques au Japon," he could put Japanese poetry "under the aegis of Mallarmé."

While the French discovery of the haiku had the appearance of the excitement and significance of the Renaissance English discovery of the sonnet, Professor Schwartz's claim that haiku "started the present tendency toward condensation in French poetry" is no doubt at once too great and too narrow in its generality. It is too great because too general, but haiku did offer such new techniques as precision or objectivity of imagery and justified methods which had already been devised. Japanese poetry also had the effect of confirming the earlier literary interest in Japanese art and, after the Japanese victory in the Russo-Japanese war, of establishing the European reputation of the country and its culture on a sounder and more mature base than exoticism of whatever degree of enthusiasm could have created.

iv. Whistler's Role in Popularizing Japan

Such a long, if nonetheless hasty and superficial, excursion as this into the importance of Japan for modern French painting, criticism, and writing may well seem to have taken us far afield from the subject of this study unless it is recalled that in this period all artistic roads led to and from Paris, and that from Paris the most excited praise of Japanese art spread over Europe and to the

United States. France, America, and England discovered Japan, it may be said, in three events which happened within a few years of each other: Bracquemond's discovery of block-print art in 1856, the visit of the Japanese mission to the United States in 1860, and the English International Exhibition of 1862. Whitman and Fenollosa showed that the American discovery led to philosophical and political speculation, and the English writers showed that Japan entered into Victorian social attitudes. But the French interest in Japan was artistic and literary from the outset, and it was therefore extremely important to the developing English and American literary interests. What was most urgently needed if Japan was ever to become truly important to our writers was a man who could combine the interests of all three countries, and such a man was soon to be found in the midst of a dozen and one controversies—James Abbott McNeill Whistler, an American who had studied in France and who lived most of his adult life in England.

It seems highly likely that the period of the Etching Revival in France, the early 1850's, laid the technical basis for intelligent interest in the Japanese prints. If this is the case, Whistler's inclusion in the group of this period —with Delacroix, Delâtre, Bracquemond, and Meryon— entitles him not only to the claim that he was the popularizer of Japan in England, but also to being one of the men who made possible the discovery of Japanese prints as a step forward in the graphic arts. He was soon as enthusiastic a collector as the other Impressionists and furnished his studio with Japanese and Chinese silks, porcelains, prints, and curios which readily became accessories or exotic details in his pictures, much as these same *objets d'art* were being used as exotic detail or for Japanese similes by the writers of the time.

In 1863 Whistler took his enthusiasms to England, where in the next few years the surprised British public was treated to the sight of his most patently Japanese pictures. "Arrangement in Rose and Silver: La Princesse du Pays de la Porcelaine" (1864) was the first to show —in the "princess's" stance and the flowing lines of her clothes—how the block-print figures might be made into European art. "Caprice in Purple and Gold: the Golden Screen" (1864) is another such imitation, and "Variations in Flesh Colour and Green: The Balcony" (1867) is almost a translation. The clothes, the sake cups, and the three-stringed lute in this painting are Japanese enough, but the whole composition of horizontal balcony lines crossed variously by the lithe bodies of the women make this picture an almost slavish imitation of Kiyonaga's famous balcony scenes. Also, what is probably the first example of Whistler's famous butterfly signature appears in the conventional Japanese manner—stylized and in a rectangle at the lower left-hand corner.

The gain from these careful imitations of Japanese prints was, in part, the exacerbation of such critics as Ruskin, who claimed that one of Whistler's Battersea Bridge studies—modelled on a print by Hiroshige—flung "a pot of paint in the public's face"; but also a gradual absorption of the best aspects of the technique of the prints and their transformation into a style wholly his own in such paintings as his three "Symphonies in White" and the many "Nocturnes" and "Harmonies" of his mature

style. Sadakichi Hartmann, who moved in the circles of
the advance guard from Whistler's to Pound's day, commented significantly on Whistler's mature work: "Never
have the elements of Eastern and Western art been so
originally united as in these poems of night and space."
Hartmann's mingled European and Japanese ancestry and
his acquaintance with Impressionist and post-Impressionist
artists enable us to put considerable stress on his phrase,
"these *poems* of night and space," for in it he points to
the significance of Whistler for the poets who followed
him. One of the outstanding characteristics of the Impressionist movement in its most inclusive sense is the
way in which the arts are mingled and the aims, techniques, and critical vocabularies of art, music, and literature are freely exchanged. One need only compare the
titles or subtitles of the works of Debussy, Whistler, and
the early Pound to see how far this is the case. This synesthetic aspect of what may be called pan-Impressionism
enabled composers to influence painters, painters poets,
and so on in a way which is probably unique in cultural
history. And this same intermingling of the arts made
it possible for Japanese art at first, and Japanese literature
later, to interpenetrate art and poetry to a degree which
probably would not otherwise have been possible. Whistler recognized the significance of this pan-Impressionism
and even fancied himself something of a prose stylist. It
was inevitable that writers should gather about him and
that he and his ideas should leave their impress upon the
poets with whom he was acquainted.

v. Whistler's Influence on
English Poetry

Whistler's role in popularizing Japan in the artistic world can best be compared to the way in which "Pierre Loti" and Lafcadio Hearn captured the imagination of the public at large. From the 1870's to the pronouncements of Pound in the 1910's, literary and graphic artists repeated the phrase or slogan, "Whistler and the Japanese." Many of the writers most significantly influenced by Whistler's interests are more properly the subjects of later chapters, because his influence lived beyond his own lifetime and acquaintance. But he also had an importance in the development of new modes of poetry which can be understood best by comparing the effect which his infectious ideas had upon two very different poets who had in common a friendship and later enmity with Whistler—Algernon Charles Swinburne and Oscar Wilde. The important thing is that both men had a first-hand introduction to Japanese art and to Impressionism through him, and that they responded differently. In that difference lies the change from late Victorian to modern poetic style, although it would take two or three more decades for the change to be realized.

Swinburne's talents and tastes led him to reject in his poetry the most important techniques of Impressionism, although he toyed with the language of the Impressionists and may be said to be—with a convenient typographical distinction—a Victorian impressionist. The distinction between Impressionism and impressionism is just the difference to be found between those poems of Swinburne and of Wilde which were influenced by Whistler. Swinburne achieved breadth and a connotative richness through emotive details, skillful rhythms, and connotative diction. Wilde's Impressionist poems achieved their richness through color and precise imagery. Swinburne did indeed sometimes use the popular language of the Impressionists which he had learned of from Whistler, but for all that his rosy muse did not lose her sweetness by another name. It is somewhat unfair to quote from Swinburne's later, unhappy period, but during these years he wrote the only poems comparable to Wilde's. One title, "Étude Réaliste" for example, leads us to expect an Impressionistic study of adults, of an interior, or of a brightly lit landscape, but the poem begins:

> A baby's feet, like sea-shells pink,
>   Might tempt, should heaven see meet,
> An angel's lips to kiss we think,
>   A baby's feet—

and continues in this manner which is its own best criticism. But the title is Impressionistic, and he was inspired on other occasions to imitate the Impressionist painters. Whistler's closest friend among the French painters was probably Fantin-Latour, and "A Flower-Piece by Fantin" ought to give Swinburne a fair chance to achieve an Impressionistic quality:

> Heart's ease or pansy, pleasure or thought,
> Which would the picture give us of these?
> Surely the heart that conceived it sought
>   Heart's ease.

He writes as if he has no eye for seeing, intruding thought and moralizing upon what is representational. When Whistler exhibited his "Symphony in White Number Two: The Little White Girl in the Mirror" at the Royal Academy in 1865, a poem by Swinburne was attached to its frame. "Before the Mirror" began:

White rose in red-rose garden
  Is not so white;
Snowdrops that plead for pardon
  And pine for fright
Because the hard East blows
Over their maiden rows
  Grow not as this face grows from pale to bright.

Behind the veil, forbidden,
  Shut up from sight,
Love, is there sorrow hidden,
  Is there delight?
Is joy thy dower or grief,
White rose of weary leaf,
  Late rose whose life is brief, whose loves are light?

The fluent versification which nonetheless follows the intricacies of syntax and logic is a typical Swinburnian triumph, but it would require a vivid imagination to obtain any sense of Whistler's painting from this poem. The poem is less a beginning of a new tradition than the end of Romantic exclamation over works of art and an exercise in Victorian amorous poetry.

The not overly close cooperation of painter and poet ended, and a much warmer enmity grew between them.

When they began to attack each other in public gatherings and print, the issue between them naturally became Whistler's advocacy of Japanese art. When Whistler first made his famous "Ten O'Clock" speech on February 20, 1885, he opposed the beautiful in true art to the moralizing in false art, and ended his speech with a Japanese climax, saying that even if the artist of the gods were not to appear on earth, "the story of the beautiful is already complete—hewn in the marbles of the Parthenon—and embroidered, with the birds, upon the fan of Hokusai—at the foot of Fusiyama." Swinburne was enraged, and in *The Fortnightly Review* for June, 1888, trusted that the audience "remembered that they were not in a serious world; that they were in the fairy-land of fans, in the paradise of pipkins . . . and all the fortuitous frippery of Fusi-yama."

"Fly away, butterfly, back to Japan," Swinburne later wrote "To James McNeill Whistler," but the butterfly remained to hover over English art and poetry. Even such a poet as Alfred Noyes was impressed and attempted coloristic poems in the confused mode of "A Japanese Love Song" with its blue-eyed Japanese girls and red poppies. The degree to which he reflected the ideas of his poetic betters can be seen in the first fifty-odd pages of his *Collected Poems* which alternate the Swinburnian mode with the Japanese and the Impressionistic. Change was in the air, but while Noyes scented it and Swinburne resented it, neither was able or willing to actualize it in his poetry.

Wilde was enough a figure of the 'Nineties to seek out change. As Holbrook Jackson points out in *The Eighteen*

Nineties (1913), the most commonly heard slogans proclaimed what was new—the new woman, the new art, and so on. Whistler, Japan, and Impressionism were still new enough, still fresh enough in people's minds from the squabbles with Swinburne and others, to become useful poetic material for Wilde. He wrote a number of poems whose titles either begin, "Impression . . ." or which reflect other critical terms of the Impressionists. The techniques by which he attempted to translate Whistler's and his own interests into poetry are largely pictorial and coloristic, and avoid the intrusion of personal feeling, thought, or moralizing. While Swinburne might compose a poem which tells how he *feels* about one of Whistler's pictures, Wilde in effect reproduces the picture in language—sharply focused, visible, and full of color. "Impression du Matin," for example, employs the critical terms for which Whistler was being berated and, in its resemblance to the technique of the Imagists, represents a considerable step in the direction of the New Poetry movement.

> The Thames nocturne of blue and gold
>   Changed to a Harmony in gray:
>   A barge with ochre-colored hay
> Dropt from the wharf: and chill and cold
>
> The yellow fog came creeping down
>   The bridges, till the houses' walls
>   Seemed changed to shadows, and St. Paul's
> Loomed like a bubble o'er the town.

These first two stanzas lead us out of the Victorian era and into the modern world of Whistler's colors and T. S.

Eliot's fogs. The sense of the first two lines is that "Dawn is breaking," but it breaks in the terms of Whistler's paintings—from a picture of night to a pale "harmony" of dawn. The Whistlerian or Impressionistic vocabulary appears in many such poems. "In the Gold Room: A Harmony," for example, might have been a picture by Whistler; and "Impression—Le Reveillon" uses the technical, painter's term for the strong employment of light in a poem expressing the changing brightness of dawn. A stanza from "Les Silhouettes"—

> The sea is flecked with bars of gray,
> The dull dead wind is out of tune,
> And like a withered leaf the moon
> Is blown across the stormy bay—

or another from "Le Jardin"—

> The gaudy leonine sunflower
> Hangs black and barren on its stalk,
> And down the windy garden walk
> The dead leaves scatter,—hour by hour—

gives some sense of the way in which Wilde had learned his Impressionist lessons, especially when they are compared with the mist and moralizing of Swinburne's "A Flower-Piece by Fantin."

The extent to which these "Impressions" have a Japanese origin other than the indirect ancestry through Whistler is made clear in "Le Panneau," which employs exotic Oriental details and originally bore the title, "Impression Japonaise." Also, in his essay on the "Decay of Lying" ("lying": the Impressionist dictum that art does not faithfully describe life, but reshapes it in the personal vision of the artist), he uses "Japanese things" as "an example from our own day" to make his point that art is not a mere representation of reality. And another essay, "The English Renaissance," makes it clear that he felt there was a kinship between his own poetry and Japanese art: "And this indeed is the reason of the influence which Eastern art is having on us in Europe, and the fascination of all Japanese work. While the Western world has been laying on art an intolerable burden of its own intellectual doubts and the spiritual tragedy of its own sorrows, the East has always kept true to art's primary and pictorial conditions."

It is one of the ironies of literary history that Wilde's life was so sensational that those poems of his which are familiar today are those which stagger under "the intolerable burden" of his "own intellectual doubts and spiritual tragedy." Those of his poèms which satisfy his own requirements—the "primary and pictorial conditions" of art—have been unfortunately ignored, although they represent the real continuity, the vital and developing tradition of English verse from the Victorian to the modern period. To say this is to make a somewhat exaggerated claim for the importance of Wilde, since he had little influence over his successors; but the point remains very much the same, because in order to produce the New Poetry of the next two decades, poets had to turn to the same sources from which Wilde had borrowed and learn the same lessons which he recites so well in his Impressionistic verse. In fifteen years or so, Ezra Pound would be proclaiming the importance of "Whistler and the Jap-

anese." Wilde had made a start which soon ended, but
had his personal life been other than what it was, he
would in all probability be regarded with T. E. Hulme
as one of the founders of modern poetry. In the meantime, the Impressionistic style, Impressionistic thought,
and the popularity of Japan were being kept warmly
alive by Lafcadio Hearn, whose thought and style represent a transition or, more properly, a continuum of Impressionism and Japan in the period when there were few
poets worthy of note to keep the tradition alive.

vi. Hearn's Synthesis of Science and Impressionism in Japanese Buddhism

The popular image of Hearn the exoticist discussed in
the last chapter was not so much wrong as superficial, as
a closer examination of his development will show. His
career as a wandering journalist, which ended in Japan,
stopped momentarily at an earlier date in New Orleans
where he discovered two elements which he sought
throughout his lifetime—the unusual and a rich historic
past. His taste for the unusual was really a taste for the
exotic in both the cultural and chronological senses, but
it also directed him to his métier as an Impressionist.
What Impressionism meant for him at this time is clear
from the epigraph he chose from Eugène Delacroix for
his *Leaves from the Diary of an Impressionist.*

> Jeune artiste, tu attends un sujet? Tout est sujet;
> le sujet c'est toi-même: ce sont tes impressions,
> tes émotions devant la nature. C'est toi qu'il faut
> regarder, et non autour de toi.

He had learned to trust to his own responses for inspiration, and this meant that the fine shades of perception of which his sensitive personality was capable were more important than the perceived object itself. This theory might well have been a pernicious stylistic influence had he not taken Flaubert as his literary model and had he not always sought to convey the quality of his own impressions to his reader. As he said of his more macabre writing, he wished to make his reader feel "a ghostly shudder."

Hearn's mature style was formed by the time he had written *Chita* (1889). It is a periodic style which is typically formed of units with complex sentence structure, slight inversions, or series; these units are loosely co-ordinated by semicolons or co-ordinating conjunctions. He achieved a style of seeming simplicity and freedom and of real ease in these rhythms of loosely joined complex units. The reader proceeds on wave after wave of the small, qualified, and controlled vibrations of Hearn's fine sensibility. Stylistically, he is reminiscent of Hawthorne, but he lacks Hawthorne's tough-mindedness and the necessity, which goes beyond technique, of holding evil and pessimism at bay with his style.

One of the themes of this study is that Impressionism owes a great deal to Japan, not only generally in its inception as many people have recognized before, but also particularly in theory, in subject matter, and even in the style of the Impressionist writers. While it is fortuitous as proof, it is nonetheless illustrative of the theme, that Hearn should find in Japan his proper spiritual and artistic home. There he found a refinement he could not discover in the West, the exoticism he had discovered in New Orleans, and an even deeper sense of the past. There, more than anywhere else, he could find a world to stimulate the fine reactions of his sensibility. And he also found there a technique to enrich his Impressionistic style, the characteristically Japanese device of interspersing short poems in the flow of his prose.

The differences between his first book on Japan, *Glimpses of Unfamiliar Japan* (1894), and the usual traveler's account lie in the Impressionistic description and the beautiful prose style. The earlier of the twenty-seven "pictures" of this book deal with his impressions of the busy life about him, but soon alter their concern to the inner depths which he believed lay under the businesslike manner of the people. This search for more subjective material soon led him to discover the literature, the art, and the religion of the country, and although he never did learn enough of the language to become even moderately fluent, he had an intuitive grasp or affinity for Japanese ideals which overcame his handicap. For example, his own spiritualistic tendencies gave him a keen appreciation of the animism which Japanese culture has inherited through Shintoism. In "Beside the Sea" he writes in his characteristic reflective style of people who have died in shipwreck as if they had become the *kami,* the tutelary spirits, of the locality: "Still, I cannot convince myself that even that grosser substance of vanished being ever completely dies, however dissolved or scattered,—fleeting in the gale,—floating in the mists,— shuddering in the leaf,—flickering in the light of waters, —or tossed on some desolate coast in a thunder of surf, to whiten or writhe in the clatter of shingle." The essentially Japanese and un-Occidental quality of passages like this can be best understood by comparison with the tone and assumptions of such passages in English poetry as that where Milton insists that Lycidas "is not dead / Sunk though he be beneath the wat'ry floor" or Wordsworth's grief for "Lucy" "Rolled round in earth's diurnal course / With rocks, and stones, and trees." Such intuitively Oriental perceptions as this, stories which were told to him, poems which were explained, and events and sights which required no translation made up the stuff of his writing. Only a mind with an extraordinary sensitivity and responsiveness and only an Impressionistic style could have made what he did out of such difficult materials. What Japanese he learned was never sufficient for him to open his mind to his wife, and there were no neighbors who understood enough of the fine shades of English to understand him. The result was that he was forced to be an Impressionist, forced to rely on his perceptions and intuitions, and that he wrote for an audience he could only dimly imagine across thousands of miles of seas.

His literary accomplishment is difficult to judge. Most of his readers wrongly assumed that he was the creator or at least the translator of the stories with which he charmed them. Actually, he only adapted and rewrote stories he heard from others—lacking any real knowledge of the language and with only an indifferent inventive gift, he had to have them translated into English before he could begin to work. And, as he recognized himself, he had no poetic genius. He did have a talent approach-

ing genius for that rhythmical prose which is frequently
and mistakenly called poetic, but it is easy to see that
concentrated and brief poems like the Japanese forms
cannot be adequately translated by a writer of periodic
prose. The popular image of Hearn the translator remains, however, and if one asks the writers who were
forming their styles just after the turn of the century
which translations of Japanese poetry they read, they are
apt to reply vaguely as the late John Gould Fletcher did:
"I recall reading *haiku* in Lafcadio Hearn's translation
(not very exact), also in Basil Hall Chamberlain's book
on Japanese poetry," and in French and German translations. Hearn did adapt the translations of his acquaintances, but only to flavor his prose or for short chapters
on special subjects such as poems about insects or folk
songs, and with no aim to set himself up as a translator. All
of his translations of Japanese poetry, culled from here
and there, have made up only one small, posthumous
volume. Another limitation of his literary accomplishments has already been suggested. His Impressionistic
method was ill suited to sustained writing. His usual piece
is picture, an Impression, or a reflection; and his only
treatment of a single subject throughout a book is his last,
most laborious work, *Japan, An Attempt at Interpretation*, which is political and philosophical rather than
literary.

Hearn's chief claim to literary fame lies in his style
and his finely adjusted tone. The style varies as his purpose changes from reflection to description and from
narration to analysis; the tone is more consistent—such
typical words as "fleeting," "death," and "shadows" sug-

gest the note of anguish which the falling cadence of a period often conveys. He undoubtedly belongs to the foremost group of nineteenth-century American prose stylists and, while he is no Thoreau or Henry Adams, it is true of him as of all superior stylists that his style reflects his ideas. Paul Elmer More was perhaps the first to observe that Hearn's thought involved Buddhism and evolutionary science and that this combination determined his whole mode of expression and thought. But there is a third element as well, the Impressionism which taught him that truth is made up of varying perceptions and is relative to the perceiver. Evolutionary science told him that there is little scope for mere sentience in the struggle for survival which goes to the fittest, and Buddhism declared that all of what science calls the objective world is illusory, a vanity and striving after wind. These three different, one might say dissident, elements in his thought produce a certain tension which makes Hearn something other than a mere stylist.

But three such various interpretations of reality needed some unifying solution. Hearn felt that he had begun to deal with the problem when he discovered Huxley's and Spencer's interpretations of evolutionary science. Spencer emphasized the process of change or flux in evolution and once said in a sentence which Hearn was fond of quoting, "The one thing permanent is the Unknowable reality hidden under all these changing shapes," a statement which Hearn believed echoed the Buddhist distinction between the reality of Nirvana and the illusion of Maya. Paul Elmer More observed that this identification is too simple, that however phenomenal Western science may conceive objective reality to be, it is still the only world open to scientific cognition and endeavor. Thus this innocent mistake contributes to the intensity of his style: "In the fusion of Mr. Hearn's thought the world of impermanent phenomena is at once knowable and unknowable: it is the reality of Western cognition, and therefore is invested with an intensity of influence and fulness of meaning impossible to an Oriental writer; and at the same time it is the unreality of Eastern philosophy, and hence is involved in illusion and subtle shadows into which it threatens momentarily to melt away . . . . It is a new symbolism that troubles while it illumines."

The artistically profitable if philosophically mistaken identification which More points out was one matter, but it cost Hearn greater pains to unify Impressionism and Buddhism, because here the question of whether the impressions gained from the objective world express truth or false illusion could not be ignored. "Nirvana, A Study in Synthetic Buddhism"—a title which echoes Spencer—shows Hearn attempting to solve his dilemma. Since the vibrations of impressions from the perceived object to the perceiving subject constitute the truth and delight of Impressionism, he tries first to redefine the perceiving subject: "It is not the sentient and conscious Self that enters Nirvana. The Ego is only a temporary aggregate of countless illusions, a phantom-shell, a bubble sure to break." The only subjective self remaining after this definition is an intuitive, nonsentient, unconscious being—a very different self from the one he accepted from Delacroix for the epigraph to *Leaves from the Diary of an Impressionist.* But this could not really satisfy him, and at other times he seems to wish to redefine the objective world in subjective terms, as when he says that the world is *"the integration of acts and thoughts."*

Neither of these answers is really satisfactory, however, and he turns to postulating the nature of the ultimate good:

In Buddhism the only entity is the absolute; and to that entity the false self [of Western science] stands in the relation of a medium through which right perception is deflected and distorted . . . and everything relative is possible. But the absolute transcends the subject and the object and time and space . . . . The Buddhist admits the absolute as something more than an intellectual conception. It is the perception of the feelings that are eternal and the abnegation of the false self, that is the aim and end of Buddhist teaching."

He neglects to say how there can be "feelings that are eternal" without a subject to perceive them and goes on to define his ideal as perfect selflessness, "Infinite Space, or Emptiness." The self must be eliminated through successive transmigrations and purgings to the final perception of "the dreaming Buddha, freed from the last ghostly bond of self." This selflessness hardly strikes a Westerner with very happy conviction, and indeed at this point one feels that Hearn can only verbalize his way free: "Nirvana is no cessation, but an emancipation. It means only the passing of conditioned being into unconditioned being." In this statement, the Christian selflessness which presumes oneness with God who is infinitely good in positive qualities is exchanged for unity

with what is good for the infinite lack of negative qualities. This is the contradiction or evasion, but he found
in it a way of unifying Buddhism and Impressionism,
since his favorite impressions, experiences, and thrills of
emotion arise from the inexpressible, but ideal unknown.
But "arise" is the wrong word for a relationship in which
subject and object have become at once nothing and
everything: all is impression, but nothing is perceived.
Raise the Unknown to a Kantian noumenon, call it
good and make it selfless, and it becomes not sensation
but the highest ethical and artistic desiderative. Perhaps
any layman courageous enough to attempt a theory of art
and reality based upon a metaphysic and eschatology
outside his own culture may be allowed a few contradictions.

It is more than likely that few readers understood
this synthetic philosophy and that they turned pages
somewhat more rapidly when Mr. Hearn began to treat
of Buddhism. However, this theory or philosophy is
pervasive in most of his writing from Japan, all the more
pervasive, probably, for the inchoate and contradictory
form it assumes in such an essay as "First Impressions"
(of faces) where we see that, for him at least, Impressionism and Buddhism are the same:

"But no face at all moments remains exactly the same;
and in cases of exceptional variability the expression does
not suffice for recognition . . . . All expression has but a
relative permanency: even in faces the most strongly
marked, its variations may defy estimate. . . . And what
are these ["fugitive subtleties" of expression and person-
ality] but the ebb and flow of life ancestral—under-rip-

plings in that well-spring unfathomable of personality whose flood is Soul. Perpetually beneath the fluid tissues of flesh the dead are moulding and moving—not singly (for in no phenomenon is there any singleness), but in currents and by surgings."

In accepting Buddhism, and by uniting it with Western knowledge, Hearn brought Impressionism full circle to one of its origins, Japan. The movement which had begun with Japanese art as its shibboleth found its finest expression in English prose when Lafcadio Hearn went to Japan. Although Impressionism was antithetical to Buddhism both in its psychological theory and in its veneration of the block prints which Buddhists held in contempt for their celebration of the fleeting, "unreal" world, Hearn reconciled the two at least for his own satisfaction. That he did this in a prose style of very real beauty is his personal accomplishment as a writer, an accomplishment which cannot be dismissed by exposing the half-errors of the image of him which have arisen in the popular imagination. But the popular mind was not wholly wrong in its view that Hearn was, by Western standards at least, something of an exotic; and this exoticism and the distortions of the popular view of him at least played the valuable role of keeping Japan alive in the minds of writers till the day when a new generation of poets might turn to Japan for one of its sources of ideas and verifications of artistic principle—when it announced to the world that it had created a "New Poetry" to replace the Victorian forms and styles which no longer seemed expressive of the realities of changed experience and a new view of the world.

IV. TRANSITION TO THE
"NEW POETRY"

"We proposed at various times to replace [conventional poetry] by pure *vers libre*; by the Japanese *tanka* and the *haikai*; we all wrote dozens of the latter as an amusement." —F. S. FLINT on the Poets' Club.

THE SECOND GREAT CYCLE of interest in Japan had begun in the mid-nineteenth century with Perry's visits to Japan and had quickly developed and defined itself with the discovery of Japanese block prints in France, the visit of the Japanese embassy to the United States, and the Japanese Court at the International Exhibition in England. The response to Japan had been variously simple-minded and sensitive and at its best had furnished the age with a new experience which had to be fitted into the assumptions of the age, with ideas which altered the assumptions to a degree; and as Impressionism grew and exfoliated into other movements, the meaning of Japan was gradually diffused into much of the art of the age. This second cycle continued to have its effect upon the practice and theory of art, and to a lesser degree, upon prose and drama. But the effect of Japan upon English poetry, both directly and indirectly through Impressionism, waned as Wilde's generation of innovators came to its heady climax in the 'Nineties and was discredited on moral rather than literary grounds. If Japan still seemed important, the credit was due to a popularizer like Hearn who was only half understood, or to the artists who now wrote of Japanese art as something wholly familiar and even commonplace. The few poets like Alfred Noyes who continued to write poetry colored by Japan obviously belonged either to the dying Victorian age or to the quiescent Georgians. The lull of interest in Japan coincided with an ebb-tide in English poetry.

Meanwhile, certain forces were quietly in motion to produce a fresh poetic start. The work of the first great scholars of Japan and its culture was becoming known, partly through the publicizing of Hearn, and partly through a genuine desire to understand this newest of the world's major powers. And in France, the discovery of Japanese poetry had added real meaning to the interest in Japan on the part of poets and writers. If the lessons which Whistler had taught about the importance of France and Japan had been ignored or forgotten by the majority of English poets, a new generation of experimenters was beginning to learn them over again and to declare its intentions of creating a fresh start in a poetic revival which soon came to be called "The New Verse," "The Poetic Renaissance," or more commonly, "The New Poetry."

The date of renewed interest in French poetry and of the discovery of Japanese poetry by English poets may be fixed with some confidence at about 1907 or 1908. In 1908 a group of young poets and artists gathered about T. E. Hulme to discuss poetry, art, and philosophy. Calling themselves the Poets' Club, the group met weekly to discuss poetry and literary theory, to compare discoveries, and to read their poems to each other. Hulme was the leader of this group and of the second which he formed after a falling-out with some of the members of the Poets' Club. He propounded a break with "Romanticism" —by which he meant not only the English Romantics, but also the Victorians and the Georgians—and a return to "Classicism." The poetry he advocated was to have what he regarded as classical qualities: "dryness" or lack of sentimentality, compactness and economy, accuracy of specification, and imagistic technique. The following aphorisms, culled from here and there in his haphazard writings, represent the poetic principles which he and his group considered to be the most important.

"Always use the hard, definite, personal word."

"Each word must be an image *seen*, not a counter. . . . it is this image which precedes the writing and makes it firm."

"Style is short, being forced by the coming together of many different thoughts, and generated by their contact. Fire struck between stones."

"Thought is prior to language and consists in the simultaneous presentation to the mind of two different images."

"The great aim is accurate, precise, and definite description."

"Visual images can only be transferred by the new bowl of metaphor. Images in verse are not mere decoration, but the very essences of an intuitive language."

Professor Glenn Hughes, whose *Imagism and the Imagists* (1931) is probably the most important study of the poetry of this period, has observed that in Hulme's scattered notes there are "dozens of the most astonishing poetic statements, as concentrated as the finest *hokku* [i.e., haiku] from Japan, as penetrating as the epigrams of Wilde, as fresh and startling in their imagery as the best efforts of his associates and followers, the professional imagists." This evaluation no doubt places too high a literary value upon Hulme's critical *dicta*, but the comparisons chosen by Professor Hughes are very suggestive for the light they shed on the sources and effects of Hulme's theories: the accounts of Hulme's associates and the poetry they wrote show that the two most influential literatures were the Japanese and Wilde—if by "Wilde" one may symbolize the Whistlerian and French interests of the 'Nineties.

The French and Japanese interests of this group are clear from explicit statements by F. S. Flint, who was with Hulme from the beginning, was later associated with the Imagists, and who has left a very careful account of the enthusiasms and experimentation of these years in his "History of Imagism" in the *Egoist* for May 1, 1915. The importance of Japanese poetry had even been stated in print: "I had been advocating in the course of a series of articles on recent books of verse a poetry in *vers libre*, akin in spirit to the Japanese." The group was made up, he continues, of F. W. Tancred, Edward Storer, Joseph Campbell, Florence Farr (the friend of Shaw and Yeats), Hulme, and himself. They were agreed in their contempt for contemporary verse and experimented with many techniques and forms, hoping to transform the poetry of the time, of which Flint writes: "We proposed at various times to replace it by pure *vers libre;* by the Japanese *tanka* and the *haikai* [i.e., haiku]; we all wrote dozens of the latter as an amusement; by poems in a sacred Hebrew form . . . by rimeless poems like Hulme's 'Autumn,' and so on . . . . We were very much influenced by modern French symbolist poetry."

Biblical, Symbolist, Japanese poetry, and *vers libre* were what they set up as examples or goals; and all are represented, usually in interminglings, in their poetry and in the poetry of the Imagists who succeeded them. The "sacred Hebrew form" turns out to be chiefly the poetry of the Canticles, which the Imagists imitated in most of their love poems, borrowing (from the King James Version) diction, images, and to a lesser degree, balanced syntax. Japanese poetry, especially haiku, seems to have meant primarily three things—concision or economy of style, precise imagery, usually taken from nature, and the avoidance of moralizing or didacticism. The influence of Symbolist techniques is somewhat more complex. In part it brought a new subject matter, especially descriptions of subjects which would have seemed unpoetic to earlier poets. But chiefly it meant firmer intellectual control and the tone of "dryness" advocated by Hulme—irony, paradox, and even morbidity. It is impossible in practice, however, to distinguish neatly between the effects of French and Japanese poetry. On the one hand, Symbolist poetry had itself been affected by Japan; and on the other, Flint's calling haiku by the alternative name, haikai, which was used almost exclusively by the French, shows that the group had probably discovered Japanese poetry from the French and in French translations which tended to blur the lines of difference between what was essentially Japanese and what was typical of French taste at the time. It is only a few years later, when the Imagists made use of English translations, that the distinctions can be made with any great certainty.

Flint mentions that Hulme's "Autumn" was a poem which seemed to represent the qualities they sought in their writing. A careful examination of it ought to reveal the extent to which it reflects their avowed interests.

> A touch of cold in the Autumn night—
> I walked abroad,
> And saw the ruddy moon lean over a hedge
> Like a red-faced farmer.
> I did not stop to speak, but nodded,
> And round about were the wistful stars
> With white faces like town children.

The quality which seems most Symbolistic and least Japanese in the poem is what might be called the tone of the images—the moon a sunburned farmer, the stars like pale children—an ironic use of metaphor which reflects a tighter intellectual control than was common in the poetry of the time. The qualities which seem most Japanese are the brevity and concision of the poem; the concern with objects of nature as the subject of the poem; the speaker's venturing out at night to look at the moon and stars—the subject of countless Japanese poems; and above all, the reliance on images to bear the meaning of the poem without any explanation or additional comment. It would be too much to say that the poem is modeled upon Japanese poetry and so an example of the imitations the group made of haiku, but it seems safe enough to assume that the poem shows an awareness of Japanese poetry which is new to English writers.

The other four poems which Hulme wrote as blackboard exercises—"Above the Dock," "The Embankment," "Mana Aboda," and "Conversion"—are even less successful as poems, but they combine to show the difficulty which even this revolutionary group faced in emancipating itself from current poetic modes. Sometimes the faintly precious tone suggests that Wilde and the 'Nineties had not been altogether forgotten, and there is a tendency toward pictorial technique which suggests the attempt to reproduce Impressionistic painting which Whistler inspired—"The Embankment" has a Whistlerian subtitle calling it a "fantasia." But these suggestions are only reminders of what might have been had Wilde and others really succeeded in developing an Impressionist poetry; and if Hulme's poetry shows anything apart from its probable sources, it shows that the Poets' Club had learned in a short time all that Wilde might have had to teach, and that they had taken one step further in the direction of modern poetry.

What they had learned was the imagistic method which enabled the poet to present, rather than to describe and then moralize—the *ut pictura poesis* of Impressionism. In part this discovery, or rediscovery, was made possible by the imagistic techniques discovered in Japanese poetry, in part by the Symbolist method of suggesting ideas through a tone which was usually complex or ironic. The step taken toward modern poetry was their advocacy of *vers libre*. Since Flint uses the French term consistently, it is clear enough that Symbolist poetry was the chief source and justification for this technique. But Flint's repeated conjunctions of *vers libre* and Japanese poetry in such phrases as "a poetry in *vers libre*, akin in spirit to the Japanese" or "by pure *vers libre*; by the Japanese *tanka* and the *haikai*" seem to indicate that these poets assumed that Japanese poetry was written in a free form. This is true to a degree, since Japanese poems have no meter or rhyme; but the fixed syllabic basis of Japanese prosody prevents one's calling tanka or haiku "free" in any real sense. It is impossible to say whether Flint and the others knew of the syllabic lines of Japanese poetry, because the dozens of haiku which he said all of them wrote do not seem to have survived. But the tendency of translators to render Japanese poems into free form without rhyme in order to avoid the effect of jingles may have led Flint to assume that the "spirit" of Japanese poetry which he speaks of was akin to the efforts of the Poets' Club to establish *vers libre* in English.

The issue of free verse is important because of the great controversy which developed about it. Poets differed about the nature as well as the desirability of free forms—whether, for example, Whitman or the French poets should be imitated—and so many extraneous issues were raised by the debate that Japanese poetry was soon lost sight of in this respect; but it is significant that such alien forms of poetry as tanka and haiku could be influential in the early stages of the development of an English *vers libre* and that they could help obtain serious consideration by the younger poets. *Vers libre* is also important because it distinguishes the poetry of the new movement from the poetry of Wilde and others who attempted to adopt Impressionistic technique. Wilde was still enough a part of the metrical nineteenth century to compose in the conventional forms which had to be broken before they could be remade into structures which seemed meaningful for modern poetry.

The poetry of the other members of the Poets' Club shares the qualities discoverable in Hulme's, qualities of the preciosity and decadence of the 'Nineties, of Symbolist poetry, and of Japanese poetry. The first poem in Edward Storer's *Mirrors of Illusion* was called simply, "Image."

> Forsaken lovers,
> Burning to a white chaste moon
> Upon strange fires of loneliness and drought.

Although the poem lacks the precise outlines of Japanese poetry or the intellectual tone of Symbolist verse, the three-line, asyntactical form does suggest the Japanese. This impression is given credit by Flint in his "History of Imagism," where he writes of Storer that he "was in favour of a poetry which I described in reference to his book, as 'a form of expression like the Japanese, in which an image is the resonant heart of an exquisite moment.'" Such a comment and other remarks quoted earlier illustrate the degree to which Japanese poetry was extolled and imitated by this group of proto-Imagists. Storer's later book, *I've Quite Forgotten Lucy*, continues to show the same qualities. The faintly decadent tone of the 'Nineties weakens most of the poems, but the long poems have the irony and morbidity which frequently characterize the Symbolists. The short poems are most like the Japanese, as one might expect, and their imagery is usually drawn from the natural sphere of haiku, as a poem like "Illusion" shows.

> Where the moon's image lay
> palely printed on the water,
> a summer moth
> lay happily dying . . . . . .
> She thought she had died upon the moon.

Before Japanese poetry became known to the West, few poets would have felt they dared to write such a short poem about a moth and the moon unless they could discover a suitable moral to draw from the description.

The poems of the other members of the Poets' Club are much the same. Walter Solomon's *Images Japonaise* expresses in its very title the mingled Japanese and French discoveries made by these poets, but the quality of most of their writing is not high enough to call for very careful consideration, and the period is more remarkable for its experimentation and formulation of a new poetic than it is for its actual literary accomplishment. When we look elsewhere in these years for other evidence of change, we see poets like Harold Monro who are enough interested in Japan to show their concerns in one way or another—Monro established the Samurai Press and struggled in his own poetry to combine Georgian traditionalism with the experimentalism of Hulme, Flint, and others —but these are only swirls and eddies in a back bay of English poetry. This beginning of the third period of literary interest in Japan is chiefly significant for its discovery of Japanese poetry and the experimentation which proved that this Oriental literature was useful in establishing modern poetic theory and practice. And if all was quiet temporarily, the discovery had been made, and in a few years there would be no end of literary storms at the appearance of Ezra Pound, who could both dramatize the discoveries which had been made and shape them into some of the most important poetry of the first half of the new century.

V. EZRA POUND

"Pound's nearest American analogue in the past is not Whitman, however, or Mark Twain, but a painter, James McNeill Whistler. . . . Like Pound in the literary art, it was in the extreme-orient that Whistler discovered the fundamental adjustments of his preference."—WYNDHAM LEWIS, "Ezra Pound"

IT IS SAID that when Ezra Pound visited a session of the Poets' Club for the first time the cafe in Soho shook under the vehemence of his reading "Sestina: Altaforte." He was "very full of his troubadors," sighed F. S. Flint in his "History of Imagism." He was full of many interests, but willing to undertake more, and gradually assumed leadership of the club from Hulme, who was really more interested in philosophy and esthetics than in poetry. Hilda Doolittle ("H. D.") joined the group in 1910, and Richard Aldington in 1911; some time during this period Pound learned about the poetic usefulness of Japanese poetry from Flint. By the time Amy Lowell, John Gould Fletcher, and such other diverse figures as Ford Madox Ford and D. H. Lawrence became associated with Imagism, Pound was leader of the group in every way, including the study of Japanese poetry.

i. "Whistler and the Japanese"

The steps leading to these interests and his leadership are, like many aspects of Pound's career, shadowy and legendary, but T. S. Eliot's Introduction to the *Selected Poems* gives the most plausible explanation. He wrote: "The earliest of the poems in the present volume show that the influences upon Pound, at the moment his verse was taking direction, were those of Browning and Yeats. In the background are the 'Nineties in general, and behind the 'Nineties, of course, Swinburne and Morris." The importance of Browning and Yeats to Pound's writing is well known, but the phrase, "the 'Nineties in general," is somewhat vague. Perhaps Eliot's fine critical instinct led him to feel that this decade was important but, unable to think of any poet who might have excited Pound, he left his statement vague. It is very unlikely that Pound should have responded to the *fin de siècle*—or to any period—as to a vague pressure, but in the light of his poetry, it is not necessary to assume that the influence of the 'Nineties had to come through poets alone. He shared Yeats's qualified admiration of Ernest Dowson and Lionel Johnson, and had discussed both of these poets and Japanese poetry with Victor Plarr. But what seems to have interested him most about the 'Nineties were the ideals of form and technique of the Impressionists—a movement best represented in England by Whistler, Symons and, to a lesser degree, Wilde.

That Pound was interested in Whistler and Symons is shown by his essay on Symons' poetry and by the frequent allusions he makes to Whistler. Wyndham Lewis has recognized the affinity between the two expatriate Americans and their common interest in Japan, as the epigraph to this chapter shows. There is a good deal of evidence besides. For instance, it is significant that Pound's first poem in the first issue of *Poetry* (October, 1912) was "To Whistler, American." What he gained from Whistler can be discovered indirectly by another look at Eliot's essay: "Technically, these influences were all good; for they combined to insist upon the importance of *verse as speech* (I am not excepting Swinburne); while from more antiquarian studies Pound was learning the importance of *verse as song*." A moment's consideration will show that this perceptive statement is suggestive as far as it goes, but it does not go far enough toward defining the nature of his early work: it is in fact a better description of Yeats's early poetry. What Pound also took from the 'Nineties, or from Whistler at least, was a belief in the importance of *poetry as picture*, to use Eliot's style of expression. Color, composition or form, and above all else visual perception are the elements which were increasingly important to him. The extent to which Whistler retained his influence can be seen from the poetry—for many years an image was to Pound either a pictorial or an abstract perception, and he loitered behind the Imagists in also using sense perceptions of sound or smell as images.

The question of the relation of all of this to the Japanese is another matter. It would not do to make too easy an identification of Impressionism and its influences with Japanese art and its influences, if only because Impressionism grew from many other causes as well. We know this in retrospect, but in the popular conception of Impressionism and Whistler just before the First World War, Japan was the dominant cause. There can be no doubt at all that Pound shared this idea. He wrote in the *Egoist* for

June 1, 1914, about Whistler and Japan in terms not calculated to be misunderstood.

"I trust that the gentle reader is accustomed to take pleasure in 'Whistler and the Japanese.' Otherwise he had better stop reading my article until he has treated himself to some further draughts of education.

"From Whistler and the Japanese, or Chinese, the 'world,' that is to say, the fragment of the English-speaking world which spreads itself into print, learned to enjoy 'arrangements' of colours and masses."

The dogmatic tone allows no moment to doubt—one either responds favorably to "Whistler and the Japanese" or is convicted of barbarism.

Pound's dogmatism has a personal logic, since the Impressionistic quality in his earlier poems is an element which distinguishes them from the work of Swinburne, Browning, and Morris. "Impressionistic" here does not mean vague and uncertain expression, but formalistic, perfectionalistic and, for poetry, pictorial technique. In such a poem as "Au Jardin," for example, it is not just the title, but also such lines as "she danced like a pink moth in the shrubbery," or "From amber lattices upon the cobalt night," with their Impressionistic palette, which allow us to associate the early Pound with Impressionism. There are many such poems equally clear in their descent. Although the poem is mostly a translation, the title of "Impressions of François-Marie Arouet (de Voltaire)" is significant, and the poem itself shows an awareness of the French fad for *japoneries* in its enumeration of "chests from Martin (almost lacquer), / And your white vases from Japan." Other similar poems are

the somewhat precious "Heather," the energetic "Game
of Chess" which is significantly subtitled a "Theme for
a Series of Pictures," the first section of "Phanopoeia"
with its Whistlerian subtitle—"Rose, White, Yellow,
Silver"—and "Albâtre" which is something of a "symphony in white" after the manner of Whistler's portraits.
Even the early Cantos frequently employ these " 'arrangements' of colours and masses" in the spirit of "Whistler
and the Japanese," as we see for example in this lovely
passage from the close of the second *Canto*:

> Grey peak of the wave,
>   wave, colour of grape's pulp,
> Olive grey in the near,
>   far, smoke grey of the rock-slide,
> Salmon-pink wings of the fish-hawk
>   cast grey shadows in water,
> The tower like a one-eyed great goose
>   cranes up out of the olive-grove.

The Impressionistic technique tends to disappear in the
middle, more expository cantos, and when it returns
in the Pisan Cantos, it appears in briefer passage. In all
of Pound's poetry, however, this technique lies at hand,
ready to be called upon for vividness, for beauty, and—
for reasons which now take us to another aspect of his
development—for contrast with more discursive passages.

ii. Haiku and the "Form of Super-Position"

The crucial period of Pound's development into a
mature poet and of the formulation of his poetic theory

are the years from 1912 to 1914 when he was strengthen-
ing and sharpening his borrowings from the Provençal,
from later nineteenth-century poets, and from Yeats,
with techniques borrowed from Whistler and Impressionism. "Whistler and the Japanese," he had proclaimed,
magisterially echoing the popular voice in 1914, but his
accent had a significance of its own, the significance of
a study of Japanese poetry which enabled him to respond
to Japan directly without Whistler as an intermediary.
When he set down his ideas on poetry and explained
his purposes in the well-known article on "Vorticism" in
the *Fortnightly* for September 1, 1914, he showed how
haiku (or hokku)—seventeen-syllabled Japanese nature
poems—entered into his poetic theory and enabled him to
compose one of his best-known poems:

"Three years ago [1911] in Paris I got out of a 'metro'
train at La Concorde, and saw suddenly a beautiful face
and another and another . . . and I tried all day for words
for what that had meant for me. . . . And that evening
. . . I found suddenly the expression . . . not in speech
but in sudden splotches of colour. It was just that—a
'pattern' or hardly a pattern if by pattern you mean something with a repeat in it. But it was a word, the beginning
for me of a new language in colour."

The pictorial terms suggest his admiration for Whistler,
but what he goes on to say links his technique with Japanese poetry (my italics).

"I wrote a thirty-line poem and destroyed it because
it was what we call work of the second intensity. Six
months later I made a poem half that length; a year
later [1912] I made *the following hokku-like sentence.*

> The apparition of these faces in a crowd;
> Petals on a wet, black bough."

He did not declare that this is a "hokku-like sentence" merely because the poem is short, or because the image is somehow Japanese. The significance of the phrase is explained by another passage.

"The Japanese have the same sense of exploration. They have understood the beauty of this kind of knowing [i.e., 'imagistic' as opposed to 'lyric' writing]. . . . The Japanese have evolved the form of the hokku.

> The fallen blossom flies back to its branch:
> A butterfly.

That is the substance of a very well-known hokku. . . .

"The one image poem is a form of super-position; that is to say it is one idea set on top of another. I found it useful for getting out of the impasse left by my metro emotion." The haiku, or hokku, he quotes here is one attributed to Moritake (1472-1549); its modernity, its importance for Pound, lies in the fact that it and similar haiku seemed to him to employ an important structural technique, "a form of super-position."

Since his concept of super-pository structure is important in understanding a technique used in much of his poetry, it is necessary to consider what he meant by it. The poem he wrote—"In a Station of the Metro"—is, again,

> The apparition of these faces in a crowd;
> Petals on a wet, black bough.

The poem is clearly divided into two parts. One part, the first here, consists of a relatively straightforward, unmetaphorical statement. The second part is a sharply defined, metaphorical image of light-colored petals on a moistened, dark bough. In its simplest form, as here, the connection between the "statement" and the striking image is one of seemingly simple contrast. There is a *discordia concors*, a metaphor which is all the more pleasurable because of the gap which must be imaginatively leaped between the statement and the vivid metaphor. After devising the technique for "In a Station of the Metro," Pound used the super-pository method, as it may be called, as a very flexible technique which provides the basic structure for many passages and many poems.

The discovery of this technique in a poetic form written in a language he did not know is one of the insights of Pound's genius. Haiku are written in three "lines" (usually not separated as such, however, when written by the Japanese) of five, seven, and five syllables, and frequently are divided by a "cutting word" (*kireji*), or caesura, into seemingly discordant halves. That Pound perceived this can only be appreciated properly when one realizes that this structural division was not perceived, or at least not discussed in print in English, until 1953, when Mr. Donald Keene discussed the matter in nearly the same terms, without reference to Pound, in his excellent little handbook, *Japanese Literature*. If this discovery has its historical importance, it is even more significant, however, that Pound had discovered in haiku a supple technique for his poetry.

Once discovered, the "form of super-position" soon became a technique for poems of more than two verses, as in "April."

> Three spirits came to me
> And drew me apart
> To where the olive boughs
> Lay stripped upon the ground:
> Pale carnage beneath bright mist.

The statement in the first four lines here is not, strictly speaking, abstract, since "the olive boughs" can be visualized to about the same degree as "the faces in a crowd." The statement is, however, more descriptive or situational than the vivid lyrical image which is set off by the colon and which draws the poem together in a metaphorical unity. This startling juxtaposition of an image of great intensity alongside a descriptive passage can be seen even more clearly in "Gentildonna."

> She passed and left no quiver in the veins, who now
> Moving among the trees, and clinging in the air she
> severed,
> Fanning the grasses she walked on then, endures:
>
> Grey olive leaves beneath a rain-cold sky.

Even his widely admired "Chinese" poems are apt to be given this structure borrowed from haiku. For this reason, and by virtue of the tone of restrained emotion, "Liu Ch'e" is as Oriental a poem as Pound has written.

> The rustling of the silk is discontinued,
> Dust drifts over the court-yard,

There is no sound of foot-fall, and the leaves
Scurry into heaps and lie still,
And she the rejoycer of the heart is beneath them:

A wet leaf that clings to the threshold.

Of the many things which might be said of this lovely
poem, three are relevant here. First, this is one of his
few early poems which employs aural images, and the
result is a vivid creation of the scene. More important,
the super-pository method has become almost a *tour de
force* here; there are four images in the first four lines,
and it is almost incredible that Pound should be able to
find, as he does, a fifth image which surpasses the rest in
intensity as a rich, sudden focus for the whole poem.
And third, the Chinese poem he "translates" (from
Giles's *History of Chinese Literature*, 1926) is completely
reconstructed in a form borrowed from the Japanese.

He soon found it convenient, perhaps for variety as
much as for anything else, to change the order of statement and image, as in "Alba," where the image comes first
in an explicit simile.

As cool as the pale wet leaves
of lily-of-the-valley
She lay beside me in the dawn.

In addition to experimenting with the order of statement and image, he quickly attempted to adapt the super-
pository method, to such different subjects as "Women
Before a Shop" and "L'Art, 1910," and he soon discovered that the technique was flexible enough for such
a comic piece as "The Bath-Tub."

As a bath tub lined with white porcelain,
When the hot water gives out or goes tepid,
So is the slow cooling of our chivalrous passion,
O my much praised but-not-altogether-satisfactory lady.

The humor here comes from the protraction of the initial, faintly ridiculous image—the parody of his own suppository technique—from the context into which the orotund Biblical cadence which the Imagists were fond of using for their love poetry is thrust, and from the ludicrous use of the diction of his Provençal love lyrics. "Fan-Piece, for Her Imperial Lord" is interesting for other reasons.

> O fan of white silk,
>   Clear as the frost on the grass-blade,
> You also are laid aside.

Like the better-known "Jewel Stairs' Grievance," this is a complaint; the subtle statement of desertion is expressed in the first and third lines, the conveying image in the second. The pathos of her complaint is told to the fan and expressed to her betrayer and the reader by the unobtrusive adverb, "also," in the third line. What gives the poem its real intensity is, however, the image of "frost on the grass-blade," whose only ostensible connection with the rest of the poem is the whiteness it shares with the fan. The real meaning of the image is an ever-widening circle of comparisons: as the clear frost melts quickly in the morning sun, so beautiful fans are the toys of the nobility for but an hour, and so a woman's beauty attracts a man for only a season. It also seems more than mere coincidence that the form of the poem is almost perfectly that of a haiku, especially since his source, Giles's translation, consists of ten lines of iambic pentameter! The alternation of syllabic fives and sevens in haiku is varied only in the last line, which has six, and the poem fulfills haiku's other requirement, that it specify or imply a season, in this case, autumn. The subject matter alone, love, is alien to haiku, but for subtlety of technique and by virtue of its form, this poem comes closer than perhaps any other attempt to meriting the title, "a haiku in English."

Many other poems employ the super-pository method. The most notable are "A Song of the Degrees," "Ts'ai Chih," "Coitus," "The Encounter," "Shop Girl," "Fish and Shadow," and "Cantus Planus." These are all short poems in which the technique is used variously and with great ease, but it is more interesting, in the light of his later poetic development, to discover that Pound was able to adapt the method to longer poems as well. There is something more than "an echo of Browning" in the close of "Near Perigord"; the something more is a superposed image.

> There shut up in his castle, Tairiran's,
> She who had nor ears nor tongue save in her hands,
> Gone—ah, gone—untouched, unreachable!
> She who could never live save through one person,
> She who could never speak save to one person,
> And all the rest of her a shifting change,
> A broken bundle of mirrors . . . !

"Mauberley" ends similarly, with the imagistic last four

lines set off from the rest of the poem to act as coherent summary for Mauberley's fate.

> Mouths biting empty air,
> The still stone dogs,
> Caught in metamorphosis, were
> Left him as epilogues.

It is remarkable that Pound was able to adapt this technique which he developed from the short, lyric haiku even to the lengthy, narrative *Cantos*. Generally speaking, he uses the technique in the *Cantos* in two ways, either as a striking ending for a canto or, more frequently, within a canto to express intensely in an image what has gone before or what directly follows. He uses the technique most freely in the first thirty and in the *Pisan Cantos*, which are less expository than the middle cantos with their concern with the evils of usury and certain forms of government. The "form of super-position" appears both within Canto XVII and, more strikingly, at its end:

> Thither Borso, when they shot the barbed arrow at him,
> And Carmagnola, between the two columns,
> Sigismundo, after the wreck in Dalmatia.
> Sunset like a grasshopper flying.

The third and twenty-first Cantos close with similar uses of the form, and one of the *Pisan Cantos* also, the eightieth.

> . . . and God knows what else is left of our London
>   my London, your London
> and if her green elegance
>   remains on this side of my rain ditch

puss lizard will lunch on some other T-bone.

sunset grand couturier.

The anthropomorphizing of the sunset brings an additional life to the preceding passage, casting a beauty over the "rain ditch" and perhaps making London a fine lady whose most becoming gown is primped by the sunset hovering about like a courtly lady-in-waiting.

The more common use of the technique is to be found within the cantos, however, usually to focus the meaning of a number of lines in one vivid and sudden image. While there are many such instances, a few quoted in a series will show the range of the technique from images of vivid contrast to images which seem to grow in part from the context. The super-posed images are italicized.

And the Castelan of Montefiori wrote down,
"You'd better keep him out of the district.
"When he got back here from Sparta, the people
"Lit fires, and turned out yelling: 'PANDOLFO'!"
In the gloom, the gold gathers the light against it.
—Canto XI

"Free by land, free by sea
    in their galleys,
ships, boats, and with merchandise
2% on what's actually sold. No tax above that.
    Year 6962 of the world
    18th April, in Constantinople."
Wind on the lagoon, the south wind breaking roses.
—Canto XXVI

Drift of weed in the bay:
She seeking a guide, a mentor,

He aspires to a career with honour
To step in the tracks of his elders;
a greater incomprehension?
—Canto xxix

and as for the solidity of the white oxen in all this
perhaps only Dr. Williams (Bill Carlos)
will understand its importance,
its benediction. He wd / have put in the cart.
*The shadow of the tent's peak treads on its corner peg
marking the hour.*
—Canto lxxviii

did we ever get to the end of Doughty:
The Dawn in Britain?
perhaps not
Summons withdrawn, sir.
(bein' aliens in prohibited area)
*clouds lift their small mountains
before the elder hills.*
—Canto lxxxiii

These examples are typical and varied enough to show
that the technique which began in a two-line "hokku-like
sentence" proved to be so adaptable to Pound that its use
marks his style throughout his work. It has had a special
importance in the *Cantos*, because their lack of formal
structure in the usual sense is baffling—any formal technique giving coherence is welcome. Equally important,
the "form of super-position" has been a technique which
has enabled him to write poems and passages of great
imagistic beauty. "Whistler and the Japanese" have been

more than a critical password for Pound. They, and especially "the Japanese," have admitted him to realms of technique that have given greater dimensions of beauty and significant form to his poetry.

iii. Haiku and the Image

In addition to the importance which it has had for his poetic practice, haiku has also entered into the formation of his literary theory, especially his theory of imagery. In *Poetry* for March, 1913, he stated his famous "Don'ts for those beginning to write verses." Part of the background for these proscriptions are the theories of T. E. Hulme, F. S. Flint, Remy de Gourmont, and Impressionistic practice, but it seems certain that Pound had Japanese poetry especially in mind when he was forming his theories at this time. Some of the "Don'ts" suggest this, and later writings confirm it.

"Use no superfluous word, no adjective which does not mean something.

"Don't use such an expression as 'dim lands of peace.' It dulls the image. It mixes an abstraction with the concrete. It comes from the writer's not realizing that the natural object is always the *adequate* symbol."

Concision, separation of imagery from abstract statement (as in the "form of super-position?"), and an emphasis upon natural images are what these paragraphs stress. These are also outstanding characteristics of Japanese poetry, and the very qualities which Professor Schwartz believed haiku brought to French poetry. A few years later, in *Pavannes and Divisions* (1918),

Pound writes similarly of natural imagery: "I believe that the proper and perfect symbol is the natural object, that if a man uses 'symbols' he must so use them that their symbolic function does not obtrude; so that *a* sense, and the poetic quality of the passage, is not lost to those who do not understand the symbol as such, to whom, for instance, a hawk is a hawk."

It might be supposed that this consistent advocacy of natural objects for symbols has no connection with Pound's interest in Japanese poetry, that, for example, his theories were derived from those French poets loosely grouped as Symbolists. But the article on "Vorticism" quoted in part earlier makes it clear that such a supposition does not hold. He begins by theorizing:

"The other sort of poetry [the imagistic] is as old as the lyric and as honorable, but, until recently, no one had named it. Ibycus and Liu Ch'e presented 'the Image.' Dante is a great poet by reason of this faculty and Milton is a windbag because of his lack of it. Imagisme is not symbolism. The symbolists dealt in 'association,' that is, in a sort of allusion, almost of allegory. They degraded a symbol to the status of a word. . . . The symbolists' symbols have a fixed value, like numbers in arithmetic. . . . The imagistes' images have a variable significance like the signs, *a*, *b*, and *x* in algebra. The point of *Imagisme* is that it does not use images as *ornaments.*"

He turns from theory to illustrations, and for illustrations to Japanese poetry: "The Japanese have had the same sense of exploration. They have understood the beauty of this sort of knowing. A Chinaman said long ago that if a man cannot say what he has to say in twelve lines he had better keep quiet. The Japanese have evolved the still shorter form of the *hokku*."

At this point he quotes the poem about the fallen blossoms which turn out to be a butterfly. He quotes another haiku, goes on to talk of "the one-image poem," and to tell how he made the "hokku-like sentence" which led him out of the impasse to which he had been brought by his experience in the Metro. *Lustra* (1916) was the first volume of poems published after this article. If we look at the short poems it contains for evidence of the poets and the literatures Pound mentions, we search almost in vain for Dante, for Ibycus, or for Liu Ch'e—apart from one poem. But since most of the short poems quoted earlier as illustrations of the super-pository technique appear in this volume, it seems just to say that Japanese poetry is basic to this, the formative period of Pound's theorizing and composition.

Given this postulate of the importance of Japan, it is relatively easy to relate Pound's well-known definition of the image to his other theoretical writings and his poetry. He defined an image as "an intellectual and emotional complex in an instant of time. . . . It is the presentation of such an image which gives that sudden sense of liberation; that sense of freedom from time and space limits; that sense of sudden growth, which we experience in the presence of the greatest works of art." Published in *Poetry* (March, 1913), this definition comes a year after the poetic expression of his experience in the Metro through a form borrowed from haiku. The emphasis is not so much upon the poetic function of the image here, as upon its effect on the apprehending sensibility: the "sudden growth." The only other discussion of the image on the basis of its subjective effect seems to be the story of his writing the poem on the Metro, where he spoke of the same "sudden emotion." In both articles he stresses the sudden and transcending revelation which the image brings to the poet and the reader. Pound's remarks have a real integrity when they are examined closely, and it may be said of him, as it can be said of few poets, that his theory and his practice support each other almost perfectly.

A somewhat different problem in regard to his literary theory is involved in the great schism of the Imagists, that moment when Pound went to Vorticism, and the others to Amy Lowell. The quarrel itself is a tedious and unenlightening bit of literary history, of which all the good that can be said is that nobody was stopped from writing poetry his own way and that Pound's genius as a critic and poet was never questioned. The real problem is whether or not he changed his esthetic theories at this time, as is often assumed. A little study should make it amply clear that he did not. In the article on "Vorticism" in the *Fortnightly*, from which so much has already been quoted, he makes it clear that "vortex" is a metaphor for "image"—a rush of feeling and meaning flows into the psychological or esthetic vortex created by an image. Furthermore, he says plainly: "Vorticism has been announced as including such and such painting and sculpture and 'Imagisme' in verse. I shall explain 'Imagisme' and then proceed to show its relation to certain modern paintings and sculpture." The new flag of

Vorticism was an excuse to join more capable fellow artists to fight the old cause of Imagism more effectively. Since the poetry shows no sudden change at this period which can be attributed to Wyndham Lewis or Gaudier-Brzeska, it is wrong to say that Vorticism represented more than a change of name and scene. The impression which many critics have given of Pound's thought as a kaleidoscopic helter-skelter chasing after this or that interesting discovery distorts the continuous and essentially integrated nature of his artistic theory and his poetry.

iv. From Image to "Ideogram"

Still another development in Pound's career began when Mrs. Ernest Fenollosa gave him her husband's manuscript notebooks in 1912. Some of the first fruits of this new field were the adaptations of Fenollosa's translations of nō plays, published in 1916. And by 1920, he had found an opportunity to publish in *Instigations* an important but disputed piece, taken from the Fenollosa manuscripts, which he called "An Essay on the Chinese Written Character."

A good part of the considerable disagreement over this essay has resulted from a tendency not unusual in cases of this kind to substitute personalities for issues. On the one hand, Pound has been ridiculed for going beyond his depth and for proceeding on false premises about the nature of "the Chinese written character" and, on the other, his opponents have been belabored as uninspired pedants who cannot see beyond their dictionaries. While the real problem is somewhat more complex than this, it can be resolved into a few clearly definable issues. What was Pound's conception of the Chinese written character? Is the conception correct? How does this idea fit in with his other literary theory? And what was the result of his theorizing for his writing? If the issues are raised and dealt with in this order, most of the confusion will disappear.

Pound's studies in Japanese and Chinese poetry in translation had prepared him for an interest in the written language of these two literatures. The partial change from his Japanese to his Chinese interests was all the easier since both written languages employ the Chinese characters, and since Fenollosa had learned his Chinese from Japanese scholars. There are two distinctly opposed schools of thought concerning the nature of the Chinese characters. One, the "old" school to which Fenollosa and therefore Pound adhered, believes that the written character is indeed ideogrammic, that it is a stylized picture or drawing of the object or concept which it represents and—this is what was fundamental for Pound and Fenollosa—that poets write with the primitive, pictorial meaning in mind. The second school of thought is the prevailing authoritative opinion today, and holds that while the character may perhaps have had ideogrammic origins in prehistoric times, these origins have been obscured in all but a few simple cases, and that in any case native writers do not have the pictorial significance in mind as they write. For many reasons, of which two may be stated, Pound and Fenollosa are wrong and the "pedants" are right. To begin with, anybody who has attained any fluency at all in reading and writing Chinese or Japanese can verify the fact that, while using the language, one has no more consciousness of the ideogrammic aspects of words than one has of Greek or Latin roots in using English. Second, if we consider the nature of language, we see that the Chinese characters are arbitrary symbols for words, that language consists, in another sense, of "dead" metaphors and that one of the jobs of the poet is continuously to refresh old idiom. The semantic problem of language, especially poetic language, would be unbearably complex if understanding the language involved apprehending every dead metaphor or written component to a character in its primitivistic freshness. Pound sees this and he does not see this. When Fenollosa writes, "The chief work of literary men in dealing with language, and of poets especially, lies in feeling back along ancient lines of advance," Pound appends a footnote: "I would submit in all humility that this applies in the rendering of ancient texts. The poet in dealing with his own time, must also see to it that language does not petrify on his hands. He must prepare for new advances along the lines of true metaphor, that is interpretive metaphor, or image, as diametrically opposed to untrue, or ornamental metaphor." He does not see that he is arguing against his own main point here, since the "ancient" poets faced the same problems as the moderns. We cannot travel back far enough in history to the point where each Chinese character was a magic picture of what it represented. He is more primitivistic than realistic in his hopes, and remarkably like Francis Bacon and Sir Thomas Browne, who thought that in the discovery of Chinese the Western world might have recovered the primitive, pre-Babelian language which was superior to the European tongues because the characters represented ideas as well as sounds.

While Pound's misunderstanding has given cause for some mirth to scholars who have, in addition, noted inconsistent romanization of characters or characters stood on their heads in printing, the real issue involved is why Pound should make such a mistake when it involves a contradiction in his own ideas. The most likely explanation is one which relates his conception of the written character to his other literary theories. He seems to have made his mistake, as Fenollosa had before him, because he was excited by the poetic potentialities of ideogrammic writing. To a poet who sought fresh images or metaphors in English, metaphors of things, colors, sounds, and concepts through the medium of the sounds represented by twenty-six letters, the possibility of discovering a world which had a given image (represented when spoken by a sound) made into an image once more and visually through an ideogram must have made Chinese seem like a brave new world indeed, that had such images in it. To use his own example of an image from a natural object, if "hawk" could mean such and such a bird to the phlegmatic reader, and yet have a highly connotative value in an Imagistic poem, what additional richness might it not have if it were not spelled *h-a-w-k*, but written as a "picture," 鵰 where the right component means "bird" and the left one means "family" or "clan"? (The ingenuities of deciding why "bird" plus "clan" equals "hawk" or explaining other characters is an innocent pastime found among new students of

Chinese and Japanese.) The reasons why Pound became enthusiastic over the supposed ideogrammic quality of the Chinese character are wholly understandable: he was merely projecting his theories about the image to another dimension. Moreover, it will be recalled that he defined an image as "an intellectual and emotional complex in an instant of time." This definition implies a certain tendency toward abstraction in his theory of imagery which is often overlooked. An image is for him not only an "emotional," that is sensuous, but also an "intellectual complex." In consequence, the abstract qualities of the Sino-Japanese characters—abstract insofar as they are only signs of the things which they represent—appealed to him along with the sensuous qualities inherent both in the objects which they may represent and in the pleasing formations of the stylized characters themselves. The logic of his mistake is the logic of a poetic mind come upon a wholly new kind of metaphor.

The most interesting illustration of his use of the Chinese character as a new kind of image is to be found in the *Pisan Cantos*, where he adapts the character to a technique he had devised earlier, that of the super-pository image. In Canto LXXVII, for example, we read that

> Things have ends (or scopes) and beginnings. To know what precedes 先 and what follows 後 will assist yr/ comprehension of process.

He uses the two characters which represent the concepts "precede" and "follow" as if they were super-pository images, which in a sense they are, since they embody the abstract concepts of preceding or following in visual terms similar to those which a well-chosen image would supply. A more beautiful, and more complex, example is furnished by a passage in Canto LXXIV.

> A lizard upheld me
> The wild birds wd not eat the white bread
> from Mt. Taishan to the sunset
> From Carara stone to the tower
> and this day the air was made open
> for Kuanon of all delights,
> Linus, Cletus, Clement
> whose prayers,
> the great scarab is bowed at the altar
> the green light gleams in his shell
> plowed in the sacred field and unwound the silk
> worms early
> in tensile
> in the light of light is *virtù*
> "sunt lumina" said Erigena Scotus
> as of Shun on Mt. Taishan
> and in the hall of the forebears
> as from the beginning of wonders
> the paraclete that was present in Yao, the precision
> in Yu the guider of waters.

There are two strands of metaphor in this passage, the lizard / scarab imagery and the imagery of light. The passage begins with a description of animals about the speaker, suggesting perhaps the Biblical legend of Elijah fed by ravens, and the lizard-bird image becomes a sacred scarab of jade glowing at the altar. The glowing, light-laden beetle is plowed under for good crops in the sacred field and is metamorphosed into the silk worms. So far the imagery suggests qualities of sacredness, propitious light, and wished-for change. The light metaphor is developed then from the "ideogram" used in super-pository fashion, 明 , which is made up of the radicals for sun and moon and means "to dawn" or "to open" (and to Pound, "reception and reflection of light; hence, the intelligence"). In this way, the idea of spiritual rebirth, or light as spiritual strength emerges. Scotus is credited (in full quotation a bit later) with saying, "all things that are are lights," as he might have said of Shun (or "Chun" in French transliteration, as it appears elsewhere), the principle or god of earth-governing. The spiritual light is designated as the paraclete, the Holy Spirit, which descends from heaven and which was therefore "present in Yao," the proper knowledge of the heavens, as we see in Canto LIII:

> YAO like the sun and rain
>   saw what star is at solstice
>   saw what star marks mid summer.

This light-spirit was also present in "Shun the compassionate," and therefore just, ruler, and in "Yu the guider of waters," or the spirit of cultivation. Yao, Shun, and Yu appear to be both ancient rulers who exemplified these virtues and also the divine manifestations of them. In any case, the *ming* character, 明 , the brightness of sun and moon and the spiritual dawn, is the superposed ideogram, as it may be called, which acts as a coherent for the diverse elements in the passage.

Another and simpler illustration of the way in which Pound regarded the "ideogram" as a poetic image can be seen in the prose of *Guide to Kulchur*, where he goes out of his way to use an "image" taken from Japanese history.

CIVILIZATION, to define same:

I

To define it ideogramicly we may start with the "Listening to Incense." This displays a high state of civilization. In the Imperial Court of Nippon the companions burnt incense, they burnt now one perfume, and now another, or a mixture of perfumes, and the accomplishment was both to recognize what had gone materially into the perfume and to write apposite poems . . . . It is a pastime neither for clods nor illiterates.

In this passage, Pound's development may be seen in reverse: the "ideogram" has become image, and the image has become Japanese technique and illustration. (There is a confusion in Pound's example, however, which was probably taken from Fenollosa's notes. Two homonymous verbs, *kiku*, represented by different characters, are involved. One means "listen," and the other "taste" or "smell.") For the price of one major error in the conception of Chinese written characters and a few incidental blunders, Pound was able to gain an extension of his earlier imagistic technique. The loss of face has had abundant recompense in poetic gain.

v. Nō Drama and "Unity of Image"

Among the notebooks which Mrs. Fenollosa turned over to Pound, there were many which dealt with nō, the classical, aristocratic, and essentially religious Japanese theatre. Since Pound has always regarded nō with the highest esteem, and since some of his "translations" are important for his own poetry, it is necessary to consider the influence which this form has had on his thought and writing.

The first notable aspect of his discovery of nō is the enthusiasm which it generated in him. It may be a mis-impression, but in all the excitement and brave sounds produced by the Imagists in their enthusiasm for haiku, one seems to hear a note of hesitancy or uncertainty. However beautiful these seventeen-syllabled poems seemed to them, with whatever skill they were written—and, it must be remembered, in a language which none of the Imagists understood—and however valuable they were for teaching Western poets how to reform their writing, the haiku remained an unknown, uncertain quantity. With the best will in the world, how could anybody confine himself to seventeen syllables in English and call himself a poet? But the nō justified the faith which Pound and other poets had had in Japan. Here was the same high degree of civilization which they saw in haiku, the same genius of technique, but in the generously sustained length of a dramatic form somewhat comparable to the classical drama of the Greeks. These are the undertones of Pound's enthusiasm; his explicit statement in a letter to Harriet Monroe will speak for itself: "Here is the Japanese play [*Nishikigi*] for April. It will give us some reason for existing. . . . I think that you will agree with me that this Japanese find is about the best piece of luck we've had since the starting of the magazine. I don't put the work under the general category of translation either. It could scarcely have come before now. The earlier attempts to do Japanese in English are dull and ludicrous . . . . You'll find W. B. Yeats [who sailed for America late in January, 1914] also very keen on it."

He states his opinions in more historical, if somewhat falsely historical, and critical terms in the three short paragraphs which constitute his introduction to the Fenollosa-Pound translations:

"The Noh is unquestionably one of the great arts of the world, and it is quite possibly one of the most recondite.

"In the eighth century of our era the dilettantes of the Japanese court established the tea cult and the play of 'listening to incense.'

"In the fourteenth century the priests and the court and the players all together produced a drama scarcely less subtle."

There can be no doubt of his enthusiasm, or of the way in which he soon infected Yeats with it. The question is rather about the quality of the translations and the function played by nō in his poetry.

The only large body of English translations of nō which are comparable with Pound's from a literary standpoint are those of Arthur Waley, who is unquestionably one of the world's great translators, on the basis alone of his

Tale of Genji (*Genji Monogatari*), a translation of Mur-
asaki Shikibu's early eleventh-century novel. Waley's
translations, published as *The Nō Plays of Japan*, are
executed with both scholarship and delicacy and are,
so to speak, the authoritative English texts. The Pound-
Fenollosa version is a poet's translation. Scholarly where
he can be, but unfamiliar with the historical, literary,
and linguistic contexts, Pound undertook an impossible
task in his translation. As often as not he has succeeded,
and where he has his translations are not infrequently
superior to Waley's in quality. But he often fails. He
botches the end of *Kinuta* so that it makes little sense and
unaccountably cuts *Sotoba Komachi* down to an insignif-
icant two pages, where Waley uses eleven. Some faults
must be ascribed to Fenollosa or to the imperfect state
of his notes, but there is no excuse for the introduction
to *Awoi no Uye* which muddles a fine translation. Also,
considering his great poetic powers, *Hagoromo* is a dis-
appointment, perhaps the greatest of all. He understood
the play perfectly, translated much of it superbly, and
yet the end of the play, one of the most beautiful passages
in nō, is put into a prose which bumps along heavily at
the end.

His real successes are *Suma Genji, Tsunemasa, Awoi
no Uye, Genjō, Kumasaka, Kagekiyo, Kakitsubata,* and
Nishikigi, in perhaps that ascending order. One can
quote meaningfully from only the more lyrical passages
in these plays, but such a passage as this speech of the
separated lover in *Nishikigi* gives some idea of the beauty
of the translations.

There's a cold feel in the autumn.
Night comes. . . .
CHORUS [speaking his words]
And storms; trees giving up their leaf,
Spotted with sudden showers.
Autumn! our feet are clogged
In the dew-drenched, entangled leaves.
The perpetual shadow is lonely,
The mountain shadow is lying alone.
The owl cries out from the ivies
That drag their weight on the pine.

Another lovely passage is worth quoting, both for its own beauty and for the relevance its imagery of light bears to the same imagery in the *Cantos*. These verses are from *Kakitsubata*, where the spirit of the Lady Kakitsubata (Iris) tells of her love for Ariwara no Narhira, a courtier of legendary attractiveness and one of Japan's greatest poets. Their love lasted only a brief time, and now the dead lady's spirit is torn between her longing for him, pride that he never forgot her, and her need for Buddhist salvation through renouncing all earthly attraction.

And here in the underworld
The autumn winds come blowing and blowing,
And the wild ducks cry: "Kari! . . . Kari!"
I who speak, an unsteady wraith,
A form impermanent, drifting after this fashion,
Am come to enlighten these people.
Whether they know me I know not.

A light that does not lead on to darkness . . .

The image set off in the last line here shows us that Pound was so taken by theories about the super-pository nature of haiku and the desirability of the technique that he could not resist the opportunity, even in such a translation as this, to separate the image of light in the last line from the more descriptive statements which precede.

At the first flush of enthusiasm, Pound felt that the adaptations which he had made were re-creations—and there is much indeed even in these fine passages which bears not only his personal style but a good deal that is different from the original. But by November, 1927, he had realized, possibly from reading Waley's translation, possibly from knowledge acquired elsewhere, that a goodly number of his translations were fragmentary and that he had not done as well as he might with these plays. On November 9th, he wrote to Glenn Hughes suggesting that he would like to revise his translations if he could get competent assistance and if he could expect enough of a sale to make the time spent worth his while. Both Japan and the West must count it a major poetic misfortune that this retranslation was never carried through. Had he redone the plays after seeing Yeats's dance plays and with a better understanding of nō, the work would probably be ranked among his finest.

His efforts to understand and to translate nō contributed an important element to his poetic theory, however, an element which was formulated about the time he joined the Vorticist movement. Once more the evidence is to be found in "Vorticism," the article in *The*

Fortnightly for September 1, 1914. It is plain from what he says here that he had been expounding his theories about the "one-image poem" and the "form of super-position" to those about him before he published the article—and, as the poetry of his acquaintances shows, his proselytizing had its effect. But some writers began to question him about this kind of poetry: "I am often asked whether there can be a long imagiste or vorticist poem. The Japanese, who evolved the hokku, evolved also the Noh plays. In the best 'Noh' the whole play may consist of one image. I mean it is gathered about one image. Its unity consists in one image, enforced by movement and music. I see nothing against a long vorticist poem."

He made this point about the structure of nō at least twice more in print, and most fully in his note at the end of the play, *Suma Genji*, where he writes that nō has "what we call Unity of Image. At least, the better plays are all built into the intensification of a single image: the red maple leaves and the snow flurry in Nishikigi, the pines in Takasago, the blue-grey waves and wave pattern in Suma Genji, the mantle of feathers in the play of that name, Hagoromo." This was published in 1916, two years after his article on Vorticism.

In the context of Pound's developing theory, these remarks are eloquent tributes to the importance of Japanese literature for his theory and his work. When we consider that haiku had shown him how to write concise, suggestive, imagistic poems and that nō taught him how longer poems might be organized, we have the right to call Japanese poetry one of the major determinants of his poetry and criticism. It would be foolish to vitiate this truth by overstatement, but from the evidence of his poetry and prose, it seems safe to say that at the least Japanese poetry was a justification for him, and at the most a primer for the technic of his poetry. The proper evaluation surely lies somewhere between.

One way in which nō assumed an importance for his poetic practice was as a source of materials. This mining in the nō can be tracked down in the many allusions to the plays which grace the Cantos, sometimes overtly, sometimes very subtly. On some occasions, as in Canto LXXIV, there is a direct reference to one of the plays, obviously *Suma Genji* in this passage.

> XAPITEΣ possibly in the soft air
> with the mast held by the left hand
> in this air as of Kuanon
> enigma forgetting the times and seasons
> but this air brought her here a la marina
> with the great shell borne on the seawaves
> nautilus biancastra
> By no means an orderly Dantescan rising
> But as the winds veer
> tira libeccio
> now Genji at Suma , tira libeccio
> as the winds veer and the raft is driven
> and the voices.

Several related stories are brought together here, beginning with the reference to Charity, or Christian love, which merges quickly with the image of Kannon (Chinese: Kuan Yin), the Buddhist goddess (or god) of mercy, a form of love. "Kuanon's" left hand clasps the mast, just as many statues show her holding a vessel or ornament in her left hand while her right hand is raised in blessing. Her Nirvana-reflecting, serene face is inscrutable to all time, even time which brought her over the sea. Here she merges with Venus, another form of love, shell-borne over the waves stormier than Dante's steady ascent to Paradise, storm-tossed waves like those which beat upon the shore when Prince Genji was exiled at Suma. We recall that Pound praised the image of "the blue-grey waves and the wave pattern" which unify both the play echoed here, *Suma Genji*, and this passage. The storm-driven sea seems finally to become the sea which dashed Odysseus's raft off the coast of Phaeacia. Pound has borrowed materials from diverse literatures, but the materials shape themselves into form, the form of the unifying image which he saw in nō.

In Canto LXXVII, the recollection of a nō play merges with the stark life of a military stockade.

> As Arcturus passes over my smoke-hole
>   the excess electric illumination
>   is now focussed
> on the bloke who stole a safe he cdn't open
>   (interlude entitled: periplum by camion)
> and Awio's *hennia*   plays hob in the tent flaps
>   k-lakk . . . . . thuuuuuu
>   making rain
>   uuuh.

The reference to *Awoi no Uye* is clear, although the transition from the Pisan military stockade to the nō is not. There does, however, seem to be some reconstruction possible. "The bloke" whom the speaker sees is imprisoned for a theft; time and events pass; since this passing is an interlude, and an interlude is a play, it has a title, "periplum by camion." The periplum is either a view of the landscape or a map with only the outlines marked and over which the modern Odysseus must travel. It is evidently a "periplum by camion," because the prisoner raced about the scene in a military vehicle, vainly trying to open the stolen safe. The intensely focussed light on his face makes it look like a spirit-mask, the hennia (i.e., *hannya*) of the jealous Lady Rokujō in *Awoi no Uye*, whose spirit comes to kill the stricken Awoi. There is a great commotion both on the stage and at the tent, and the onomatopoetic words describe both the flapping canvas in the pouring rain and the rosary beads clicking to the prayers recited by the Buddhist priest who exorcises Rokujō's spirit.

A passage in Canto LXXIX favorably compares the behavior of the principals in two nō plays with the behavior of the Greeks after the sack of Troy.

Greek rascality against Hagoromo
　Kumasaka vs / vulgarity
　　no sooner out of Troas
than the damn fools attacked Ismarus and the Cicones.

In *Hagoromo* a fisherman discovers the feather mantle of a *Tennin* ("Heaven-Dweller") and returns it to her when she tells him she needs it to fly back to heaven. The point of *Kumasaka*, as Pound has been fond of telling, is that the spirit of a brave warrior returns to earth for the purpose of telling a priest how skillfully he was *defeated* by a youth. These examples of courtly *gentilesse* are what he contrasts with Greek barbarity.

One thing which has already been hinted at must be added concerning these and other examples. It is a general structural principle of the *Cantos* that a large number of legends, stories, and examples from history are grouped about a few organizing archetypes as the passage which merges Kannon and Venus shows. If only the outlines (and not the names) are shown on the map or periplum, we may name a dominant mountain, for example, what we will—Fuji-yama, Vesuvius, or Taishan. This technique is used again and again in the *Cantos* until it becomes one of the most important structural devices; but unless it is clearly understood, such a passage as this—

> the lake flowing away from the side
> was still as is never in Sirmio
> with Fujiyama above it—

makes little geographical or poetic sense.

This method of unifying diverse materials through meaningful archetypes is another example of Pound's deriving a technique of form from Japanese literature, in this case "what we call Unity of Image," the technique which he felt the nō had to offer to make a long Vorticist poem possible. The range of such archetypal, unifying images in the *Cantos* is considerable. Some are from the common stock of poets, light for example; some are literary motifs, the literary voyage of the *Odyssey* or *Divine Comedy;* some are human activities given a metaphorical significance, merchandising; some are "local" images to which Pound attaches values of significance or beauty, the wave image of the passage alluding to *Suma Genji;* and some are images uniquely Poundian. Such an image as only Pound might have used is the "ideogram" made into an archetypal symbol of value, in which case it functions as any other image: again we see a technique developed from Japanese literature absorbing the written character. From the many possible examples of such unifying images, three may be chosen, both to illustrate the technique and to show how it often involves use of Japanese materials. These three are the heavenly earth-visitor, "the sacred influence of light" as Milton called the same kind of imagery, and the golden mean.

The unifying metaphor of the heavenly visitor to earth may well be called the Hagoromo image, since this play has meant so much to Pound's imagination. The passage which gives most explicit statement of the image and the other forms which it may take besides the "Heaven-Dweller" of *Hagoromo* is probably the one found in Canto LXXX.

"With us there is no deceit"
    said the moon nymph   immacolata
    Give back my cloak, *hagoromo.*
    had I the clouds of heaven
        as the nautile borne ashore
    in their holocaust
        as wisteria floating shoreward
with the sea gone the colour of copper
    and emerald dark in the offing

the young Dumas has tears thus far from the year's end
At Ephesus she had compassion on silversmiths
  revealing the paraclete
standing in the cusp
  of the moon et in Monte Gioiosa
   as the larks rise at Allegre
           Cytherea egoista.

This passage begins with a quotation followed by a para-
phrase from *Hagoromo*. With us immortals there is no
deceit, so give back my mantle of feathers and I will
dance the heavenly dance I promised you, the *Tennin*
says in effect to the Fisherman, and dances her way into
the heavens above Mt. Fuji. Pound assigns the words to
the "moon nymph," and although the *Tennin* is not
really quite that, he must have had Diana in mind, the
goddess of the moon who also visits earth and is caught
like the *Tennin* unawares while she is bathing and gazed
upon by the hapless Actæon who is mentioned just
after this quotation. The epithet attached to the *Tennin*,
immacolata, suggests the visit to Mary by the Holy
Spirit (if Pound has confused the Annunciation and the
Immaculate Conception). The "nautile borne ashore"
suggests Venus, as in a passage quoted earlier. Her affection for the silversmiths is transferred from her favorite island to Ephesus, with the Christian connotations
which are realized in the next line which mentions the
descent of the Comforter. The quotation ends by refer-
ring to Cytherean Venus once more.

The unifying image of light recurs again and again
in the *Cantos*. The passage quoted on page 132, for ex-

ample, shows the character for *ming*, 明 , used as a super-pository image in a passage which talks of Scotus' theory that "all things that are are lights." In the poem as a whole, this locally super-posed image of light is a unifying metaphor. The same image acts as a unifying element in the beautiful but complex fourth Canto. (The italicized English verses mark use of super-pository images.)

"Hither, hither, Actæon,"
Spotted stag of the wood;
Gold, gold, a sheaf of hair,
   Thick like a wheat swath,
Blaze, blaze in the sun,
   The dogs leap on Actæon.
Stumbling, stumbling along in the wood,
Muttering, muttering Ovid:
   "Pergusa . . . pool . . . pool . . . Gargaphia,
"Pool . . . pool of Salmacis."
   The empty armour shakes as the cygnet moves.

Thus the light rains, thus pours, *e lo soleils plovil*
The liquid and rushing crystal
   beneath the knees of the gods.
Ply over ply, thin glitter of water;
Brook film bearing white petals.
The pines at Takasago
   grow with the pines at Isé!
The water whirls up the bright pale sand in the
                              spring's mouth

"Behold the Tree of the Visages!"
Forked branch tips, flaming as if with lotus.

Ply over ply
The shallow eddying fluid
    beneath the knees of the gods.

Torches melt in the glare
    set flames of the corner cook-stall
Blue agate casing the sky (as at Gourdon that time)
    the sputter of resin,
Saffron sandal so petals the narrow foot: Hymenæus Io!
    Hymen, Io Hymenæe! Aurunculeia!
A scarlet flower is cast on the blanch-white stone.

The passage as a whole celebrates, one must say in
view of the tone, the involvement of the gods in meaningful, even sacramental, human passion. So Actæon's
death, devouring by his own dogs, is tragic, but Pound
chooses to emphasize the circumstances. Suffering today
is meaningless and ignoble (see Cantos xiv and xv),
while Actæon in another, happier age dies because he
has observed the naked Diana bathing, and his death in
a blaze of gold and light is an apotheosis. At such a
moment as this at the Salmatian pool, the light rains
down like crystalline water swirling about the knees
of the bathing Diana. This scene merges with Takasago,
the legend (and nō play, although neither Pound nor
Waley has translated it) of idyllic married love, and
the pines which symbolize the old couple's enduring love
merge into the pines of the great Shintō shrines at Ise.
The shrines seem to suggest the nimbus of gold flame
growing up and out of the lotus flower and behind the
Buddhist statue, of Kannon perhaps, standing before
it (although shrines are Shintō, and not Buddhist, sanc-

tuaries). The next verse paragraph ends with an echo of
Catullus' marriage hymn, another ecstatic experience
including a violation reminiscent of Actæon's—and
beautifully conveyed by the super-posed image of the
scarlet flower on the white stone—but a violation sancti-
fied by the gods in the light of the processional torches
and with the religious and marital overtones of Takasago.

There are many variants of the imagery of light. In
Canto xv, after the descent into the scatological modern
hell of xiv and xv, the voyager emerges like the thralls
of darkness from Plato's cave,

> blind with the sunlight,
> Swollen-eyed, rested
> lids sinking, darkness unconscious.

And the image is often iterated in passages which describe lanterns, often afloat, in beautiful passages like
the following two from Cantos xxvi and xxix.

> And at night they sang in gondolas
> And in the barche with lanthorns;
> The prows rose on silver
> taking light in the darkness.

> The sand that night like a seal's back
> Glossy beneath the lanthorns.

A final illustration shows how completely the imagery of
the heavenly visitor and light may be brought together,
very subtly and unpretentiously in such a passage as this
from Canto xxix.

> Eyes brown topaz,
> Brook water over brown sand,
> The white hounds on the slope,
> Glide of water, lights and the prore,
> Silver beaks out of the night,
> Stone, bough over bough,
> > lamps fluid in water,
> Pine by the black trunk of its shadow
> And on hill black trunks of the shadow
> The trees melted in air.

This passage of ideal beauty recollects the loveliness and light which once were in sharp contrast to the "things as they are" of the rest of the canto. Many now-familiar images are recalled: the brook water of Diana, the white hounds of Actæon, and the silver-prowed gondolas bearing lights. The pines recall Takasago and Ise, now covered with darkness where anciently all had been light, and all melts into the light-laden air, as even Mt. Fuji melts into the lambent haze (in Pound's translated version of *Hagoromo*, at any rate) as the *Tennin* with her feather mantle dances heavenward.

The unifying metaphor of the middle way or the golden mean of Confucius (not of Aristotle, whom Pound dislikes) is represented by the character, *chung*, 中, which means "middle," "center," "mean," etc. (and to Pound, "just process" and "pivot"). The first expression of this image—perhaps really "an intellectual complex" rather than an image in the usual literary sense—would appear to be a passage in Canto XIII, the first "Confucian" canto.

And he said
      "Anyone can run to excesses,
"It is easy to shoot past the mark,
"It is hard to stand firm in the middle."

We hear little more of this, although it is implicit in much of the poem, until one of John Adams' letters is quoted in Canto LXX. Again the "ideogram" appears in the local text as super-pository image but functions in the larger context of the poem as a unifying image.

Americans more rapidly disposed to corruption in
                          elections
      than I thought in '74
fraudulent use of words monarchy and republic

I am for balance. 中

This image is most common in the *Pisan Cantos* as two passages, from Cantos LXXVII and LXXXIV, show.

some sort whereto things tend to return
Chung

      in the middle
whether upright or horizontal.

John Adams, the Brothers Adams
    there is our norm of spirit

our

    whereto we pay our
              homage.

It is typical of the diverse and imagistically unified *Cantos* that the last of the Pisan series should end by paying homage to these American men of affairs, good governors, with a Chinese character expressing a Chinese (and universal) ethical ideal through techniques gained from Japanese poetry and drama, through an image at once super-pository and unifying. "There," to reapply Pound's remark, "there is our norm of spirit."

Many other Japanese elements are of course absorbed into the broad stream of the *Cantos*. Sadakichi Hartmann, the art historian who claimed so much for the influence of Japanese art on Western literature, is discussed briefly. "Miscio" (i.e., Michio) Itō, who danced for Yeats's plays and whose friendship Pound sought is one of the many lesser characters in the poem. There are many references to Japanese art; the large part of one canto concerns Japanese history; and frequent allusions to Japanese industry, famous places, religion, and so on decorate the poem. But the chief function of Japan in Pound's thought and writing has been the way in which Japanese art through Whistler colored his early work, and Japanese poetry and drama have given meaningful forms throughout the poetry of his mature period. The contribution of China to his imagination has been immense, but chiefly in the form of ideas and a concept of history; and insofar as his thought apart from literary theory is involved, his debt to China is great. To the extent that he is a poet dealing with problems of form, style, and imagery, he has contracted lasting debts to Japan. And while like the greatest of English translators from Oriental poetry, Arthur Waley, Pound has never been in the Orient, he has absorbed more of its spirit and reached a greater fundamental understanding of its rich cultures than many of us who have been in those realms of gold.

It is interesting, if on the whole somewhat fruitless, to speculate about the extent to which Pound's ideas about Japanese poetry have influenced T. S. Eliot. It is clear that Eliot knew about this side of Pound's studies, since he reviewed the Fenollosa-Pound translations from the nō for the *Egoist* (August, 1917) in an article entitled "The Noh and the Image," which shows how aware he was of Pound's developing theories of imagery and their Japanese derivation. On one occasion, he went with Pound to a performance of W. B. Yeats's *The Hawk's Well*, where Yeats was present and Itō danced the role of the hawk. But the basic question is whether or not his knowledge of Pound's theories and practice had any effect on his own. The last two lines of the "Preludes" and of "Cousin Nancy" have something of the effect of Pound's super-posed technique, but not enough to enable one to say outright that Eliot owes an indirect debt to haiku. The *Waste Land* is organized about certain repeated motifs in a technique somewhat akin to Pound's use of unifying imagery, and there are enough letters extant between the two poets to show that Pound had a large share in the technique of the poem. Eliot's techniques of using old materials are, however, as much like Dryden's in *MacFlecknoe* as Pound's, and it seems safest to conclude only that whatever of Pound's "Japanese" techniques Eliot found useful are so covered with traditional Western modes and forms that the Japanese element is all but completely submerged.

Japan has not had a uniform importance for Pound over the years. The period from 1912 to 1917 marked his first period of enthusiastic interest in "Whistler and the Japanese," haiku, and nō. About 1917 he became concerned with Chinese history and philosophy—especially that of Confucius—a concern which has lasted to the present. This shifting interest can be followed in his collected correspondence, which also shows a return of interest in Japanese literature in the 'Thirties and 'Forties. In a letter written just before the Second World War to Katsue Kitasono, a Japanese poet, he states that Japanese pronunciations for Sino-Japanese characters are preferable to the Chinese—because simpler in their lack of tones? one wonders—and in view of his early exclamations over the "ideogram," it is amazing to find him affirming the desirability of romanizations of Japanese literature. In recent years he has insisted upon the importance of nō as a dramatic form and the "need," to use his term, which our culture has for sound films of these plays. In a typical sentence from a letter, he says that "Noh contents are more interesting than Greek theatre apart from the Trachiniai." Other letters express the same opinion.

These are single interests. His broadest and most suggestive statement of his opinion of the importance of the cultural role of Japan in the modern world is his expression of hope in the letter to Katsue Kitasono that Japanese literature and culture will become the medium of Western understanding of the Orient. Pound is not the first writer to hope so much. Whitman had mused on the same possibility when he saw the Japanese envoys parade along Broadway, and Fenollosa's marriage of East and West was to take place in Japan. Amy Lowell and the lesser-known Sherard Vines have tried in their ways to dramatize Japan's role as a cultural intermediary. But what gives suggestive depth to Pound's broad statement is the role which he has played himself in attempting to bring the cultures of the Orient and Occident together in a gigantic lyric epic.

To the extent that he has been successful in writing a poem which brings together Oriental and Occidental cultures, in part through the medium of techniques taken from Japanese literature, Pound represents the vital center of this study. Because he made use of so much that others like Fenollosa had learned about Japan, and because he has played the role of teacher to an age, the other chapters in this study to a large extent either lead up to him or are shaped by his influence. And even when we come to examine the writing of the greatest poet of our age, William Butler Yeats, we shall discover unmistakable traces of Ezra Pound; for while all his great efforts have not been blessed with equal success, his work merits the epigraph chosen from his writing for this book:

What thou lovest well remains . . . is thy true heritage . . .

To have gathered from the air a live tradition
or from a fine old eye the unconquered flame
This is not vanity.
Here vanity is all in the not done,
all in the diffidence that faltered.

VI. THE ABSORPTION OF JAPAN INTO TWENTIETH-CENTURY POETRY

"I should say that the influence of haiku on the Imagists was much more considerable than almost anyone has suspected. It helped them make their poems short, concise, full of direct feeling for nature."—JOHN GOULD FLETCHER

By VIRTUE of the insights of the genius, the force and eloquence of his voice, and the accomplishment of his poetry, Ezra Pound has done more than anyone else to make Japan "a live tradition" in our literature. He has done most, but not all, and the history of the absorption of Japan into the poetry of the first half of this century is filled with the names of many poets who have some-times taught Pound, sometimes rethought his thoughts and borrowed his techniques, sometimes found voice for other interests in Japan, and sometimes expressed in verse a more intimate or detailed knowledge of Japan than Pound could lay claim to. As the influence of Japan has spread out, it has colored the work of more poets in more diverse ways than any except the most encyclopedic study could or need show. For our purposes, it is only necessary to suggest and illustrate the diversity of poets and poetic styles affected, and to study the poets in the groups to which they seem to belong by virtue of the kinds of interpretations of Japan they have made in their poetry. Pound's sometime associates, the Imagists, shared at least an acquaintance with him and Japanese poetry and seem to invite study as a group. There is also a large group of poets outside the Imagist camp who helped extend the range of poetry inspired in part by Japan, and diverse as they are, they may be usefully studied together for what they tell of changing responses to Japan. The third group is made up of those poets who have been to Japan and who—at this mid-century lull in English and American poetry—seem to have achieved a greater realism and ease in handling their shared experience of visiting Japan. All three groups illustrate the way in which the third period of interest in Japan has been absorbed into the mainstream of English poetry. More than anything else, the poetry of the first half of the twentieth century shows a consolidation of the discoveries of Japanese literature and art which so altered the poetic development and enthusiasms of Ezra Pound.

i. The Imagists

F. S. Flint played an important role in introducing Japanese poetry and French Symbolist poets to the Poets' Club, to whatever sections of the public would lend an ear, and to Ezra Pound. This role was of great historical and literary importance, greater probably than his own poetry, which is of relatively smaller significance; because where it does show flashes of success in adapting Japan, the brilliance is apt to be more a distant reflection of Pound than the creation of personal poetic style. The course of his use of Japanese materials and techniques

is, then, very like Pound's: he began with Oriental detail
in such a poem as "Chrysanthemums," and then turned
to Impressionistic techniques, as in "The Swan," a poem
which creates a vivid and coloristic picture—the same
picture, as a matter of fact, which appears on the cover
of the volume in which the poem appears, *Cadences*
(1915). The next step seems to have been imitation of
Pound's "form of super-position," a technique Flint
borrows for such poems as "The Beggar."

> Hark! the strange quality
> of his sorrowful music,
> wind from an empty belly
> wrought magically
> into the wind, —
>
> pattern of silver on bronze.

Somewhat later, he extended the super-pository technique to include aural and tactile images in such poems
as "Malady" and "The Star." And under the pressure
of Pound's imagistic methods and pictorial treatment of
natural scenes, much of the exoticism which adversely
affects his early poetry disappears. His poetic accomplishment is small, however, and his main contribution to our
poetry was the role he played in criticizing old techniques
and introducing new literatures. Although he has always
made very modest claims for himself, it seems clear
that he pointed out to fellow poets the Franco-Japanese
direction which made the first stirrings of the New
Poetry into Imagism; and he also seems to have been one
of the first to sense what Japanese poetry might do for
English poets at a time when Japan was still steadfastly

identified with Whistler and with the curios of the 'Eighties.

The only Imagist to hear Pound's declarations about the usefulness of Japanese poetry and not be materially affected appears to have been Hilda Doolittle ("H. D."), who has written of her acquaintance with Pound's ideas, but whose poetry bears out her belief that her style remained unaffected. Richard Aldington is another matter. His introduction to Japan was the usual one—the block print. As he recalls in a letter: "The early poem of mine called 'The River' was written in the B[ritish] M[useum] Print Room on a couple of Japanese colour prints. The landscape was certainly Hokusai's. The second one I don't remember, obviously a girl, perhaps an Outamaro, perhaps a Toyokuni." The second part of one of these poems—"The River"—illustrates once again that the early Imagists found the Japanese prints useful for pictorial and color-laden technique and exotic emotional response.

> O blue flower of the evening,
> You have touched my face
> With your leaves of silver.
>
> Love me, for I must depart.

Aldington seems to have been introduced to Japanese poetry by three sources. Many of the prints in the British Museum had poems or songs printed just below their upper borders; someone, perhaps Arthur Waley, had translated these poems. Aldington copied down these translations, and, he adds in his letter, "I kept them a long time." He must also have heard of Japanese poetry from

Flint and have read French translations. But it was Pound who interested him enough in haiku for him to carry a little notebook to the front lines, where, as we read in "Living Sepulchres,"

> One frosty night when the guns were still
> I leaned against the trench
> Making for myself *hokku*
> Of the moon and flowers and of the snow.

"The war poem 'Insouciance' has something of the *hokku* idea," he wrote, a something which turns out to be Pound's super-pository technique.

> In and out of the dreary trenches
> Trudging cheerily under the stars
> I make for myself little poems
> Delicate as a flock of doves.

> They fly away like white-winged doves.

From such statements and poems it seems clear that Pound had established haiku as short poems characterized by delicacy, natural imagery, and the super-pository technique.

Aldington was almost unique in being able to retain a refreshing sense of humor amidst all the solemn business of getting the "New Poetry" set in motion. In late 1914 or early 1915 he wrote a parody of "In a Station of the Metro" as section IX of "Penultimate Poetry" in the *Egoist* (January 15, 1915).

> The apparition   of these poems   in a crowd:
> White faces   in a black   dead faint.

He was obviously fully aware of Pound's insistence upon the importance of Japanese poetry, but could not suppress a snicker at the solemnity with which a new poetics was being promulgated on the basis of a two-line poem. Nonetheless, while one laughed at Pound, one also emulated him, and the super-repository technique is frequently used in the poems which Aldington wrote during these years—as, for example, in "R. V. and Another."

> You are delicate strangers
> In a gloomy town,
> Stared at and hated—
> Gold crocus blossoms in a drab lane.

The technique fades from his poetry in the early 'Twenties, and in the long run he seems to have benefited more from the clarity of imagery which haiku exemplified than from the super-repository technique.

It was plain to everybody concerned in the Imagist movement that Ezra Pound stood for one set of standards and Amy Lowell for another. What he represented was perfectionism of technique and knowledge of the Great Tradition—Occidental and Oriental—or at least those parts of it that he did not regard with distrust. She seems to have stood for energetic experimentation, for untrammeled freedom of the individual poet from the shackles of social and literary custom, and for poetry as a vigorous expression of beauty and emotion. If Pound made the New Poetry into a respected art, Amy Lowell made it popular—from the lecture stand as well as by her own unusual personality and the serious, if less-knowing, attempt she made to create a lasting poetry herself.

She was familiar with Japanese art and culture at a much earlier age than any other poet of the Imagist group. Her somewhat older brother Percivall had sent home books on Japan and Oriental *objets d'art* which fairly surrounded her with Japan. "All through my childhood," she wrote, these books and works of art "made Japan so vivid to my imagination that I cannot realize that I have never been there." This familiarity with Japanese art lay dormant, however, until she joined the Imagists in London, where she suddenly discovered that her childhood memories might be refreshed and made into poetry of the most advanced mode. An early fondness for Keats and a knowledge of the French painters led her to translate the pieces of Japanese art her brother had sent home into Grecian Urns in several poems of meditation and description. Such poems in *A Dome of Many-Coloured Glass* (1912) as "A Japanese Wood-Carving" and "A Coloured Print by Shokei" mingle a Keatsian afterglow with the bright colors of Impressionism and the Japanese prints. Her knowledge of Japanese art gave her another technique, the same kind of Japanese simile which French and American novelists had been finding so useful, but her use of this stylistic device is superior in its exactitude to perhaps any other writer. In *Sword Blades and Poppy Seeds* (1914), the poem "Sunshine through a Cobwebbed Window," for example, shows how carefully she has examined the prints of Hiroshige with their colored upper borders—"The layered branches horizontal stretched, like Japanese / Dark-banded prints." Other techniques or characteristics of Hiroshige's art appear in the description of rain in "Afternoon Rain in State Street"—

> Cross-hatchings of rain against grey walls,
> Slant lines of black rain—

or the metaphor of "one of those odd-shaped hills / You see in Hiroshige's prints" in "The Note-Book on the Gate-Legged Table," another Keatsian meditation—two poems from *Men, Women and Ghosts* (1916) and *East Wind* (1926).

The reader of *Pictures of the Floating World* (1919)—whose title is itself a translation of *uki-yo-e,* the genre of the block print—finds immediately that he is out of the realm of the simile and in the floating world of the block print itself. But this is also the world of Whistler, of "Whistler and the Japanese" as Pound said, and Impressionism has once more become the mode to convey an interest in the block print. Sometimes, as in " 'One of the Hundred Views of Fuji' by Hokusai," the debt to the block print is explicitly stated. Sometimes, as in "The Return," the borrowing is more subtle.

> Coming up from my boat
> In haste to lighten your anxiety,
> I saw, reflected in the circular metal mirror,
> The face and hands of a woman
> Arranging her hair.

Only a reader familiar with the block print would know that the composition of the picture she presents—a woman at her toilette with her features depicted only by their reflection in a mirror—is borrowed from an artist like

Eishi; and only Amy Lowell among the Imagists was capable of such a fillip of Orientalia as the metal Japanese mirror. At other times, she borrowed from Japan indirectly, through Whistler, as the subtitle of "The Back Bay Fens"—*Study in Orange and Silver*—indicates. But the poem which follows in this volume has a Whistlerian title also—"Free Fantasia on Japanese Themes"—and shows that she consciously attempted to combine Whistler's art and the print.

> I would sit in a covered boat,
> Rocking slowly to the narrow waves of a river,
> While above us, an arc of moving lanterns,
> Curved a bridge,
> And beyond the bridge,
> A hiss of gold
> Blooming out of blackness,
> Rockets exploded,
> And died in a soft dripping of coloured stars.

These verses must be compared with the identical subjects in Whistler's paintings of Battersea Bridge and Hiroshige's "Fireworks at Ryōgoku Bridge" for a proper understanding of the cross-fertilizing which has taken place between two cultures and three artistic media: all three present the same artistic composition. Ezra Pound was not the only one "accustomed to take pleasure in 'Whistler and the Japanese.'"

Pound did, however, provide her with a poetic technique that she probably would not have gained by herself—the "form of super-position." "Gargoyles," "Middle Age," and other poems from *Pictures of the Floating*

World and poems like "Afterglow" from *What's O'Clock* (1925) with its aural image set off in the last line show how she had learned Pound's lesson.

> Peonies
> The strange pink colour of Chinese porcelains;
> Wonderful—the glow of them.
> But, my Dear, it is the blue larkspur
> Which swings windily against my heart.
> Other Summers—
> And a cricket chirping in the grass.

Her purpose in utilizing Japan in such diverse fashions in her poetry is made clear from her somewhat naïvely philosophical Preface to *Pictures of the Floating World*.

"The march of peoples is always toward the West, wherefore, the earth being round, in time the West must be East again. A startling paradox, but one which accounts for the great interest and inspiration that both poets and painters are finding in Oriental art. . . .

"In the Japanese 'Lacquer Prints' [a section of this book], the *hokku* pattern has been more closely followed than has any corresponding Chinese form in the 'Chinoiseries'; but, even here, I have made no attempt to observe the syllabic rules which are an integral part of all Japanese poetry. I have endeavored only to keep the brevity and suggestion of the *hokku,* and to preserve it within its natural sphere. Some of the subjects are purely imaginary, some are taken from legends or historical events, others owe their inception to the vivid, realistic colour-prints of the Japanese masters."

Such an explicit statement tells us that, in addition

to the imitation of block prints and the Whistlerian Impressionism we have already discovered in the poems from this volume, we must see two new dimensions in her poetic intention. There is a vague impulse to unite East and West which was to concern her more deeply at a later point in her career; and there is an attempt to emulate the Japanese poetic forms.

Although haiku, or hokku, seems to have been foremost in her mind and even to have entered into her technique through Pound's device of the super-posed image, many of her poems show that she also knew the tanka, or waka, the thirty-one-syllabled Japanese lyric. These poems show it, both by her use of the subject matter of love which is alien to haiku but one of the chief concerns of tanka, and by her all but translating certain well-known tanka. "Temple Ceremony," with its subtitle "From the Japanese of Sojo Henjo," shows that she knew the most frequently translated of the Japanese anthologies of tanka, the *Hyaku Nin Isshū* ("One Poem from Each of a Hundred Poets"). Her poem may be compared with a somewhat more faithful rendering of the original.

> Blow softly,
> O Wind!
> And let no clouds cover the moon
> Which lights the posturing steps
> Of the most beautiful of dancers.

> *You heaven-born breezes, blow,*
> *And blowing close the paths*
> *Where the clouds pass to and fro,*

That these maidens' dancing forms
Will stop awhile their heavenward flight.

There are other poems in which she does not acknowledge her debt to Japanese poems. "From China" may
again be compared with a faithful translation of the
original, another poem in the *Hyaku Nin Isshū,* Abe
no Nakamaro's expression of loneliness while an envoy
in China.

I thought:—
The moon,
Shining upon the many steps of the palace before me,
Shines also upon the chequered rice-fields
Of my native land.
And my tears fell
Like white rice grains
At my feet.

> *Over the endless plains*
> *Of heaven and back I gaze,*
> *And ponder, Is this moon*
> *The one which rises over Kasuga,*
> *Above the slopes of Mt. Mikasa?*

These poems illustrate the degree to which she changed
or reshaped the Japanese poems which she used. A different time of day in "Temple Ceremony" or the very
un-Japanese comparison of tears to rice grains in "From
China" are cast in a free verse form and a characteristically
languishing tone, making these poems more like imitations of the translations she had read or free imitations

after her usual poetic style than true translations of the original.

Amy Lowell was undoubtedly right, however, in feeling that haiku was the most influential of all the forms of Japanese poetry and art in helping her form her poetic techniques. Her conception of haiku was determined in large measure by the block prints and tanka, but her acknowledged aim to "keep the brevity and suggestion of the *hokku,* and preserve it within its natural sphere" was on the whole successfully carried out. Her use of sharply defined images taken from nature made to express the tone and meaning of short poems characterized much of the work of the period of her association with the Imagists and for many years afterwards. And like tanka, haiku was often the source for specific poems. Slight changes in imagery or in situation do not disguise the degree to which she borrowed many of the short poems she had been reading in translation. "Nuance," for example, echoes Bashō's "First Snow" in its image of a flower bent under a very slight weight.

> Even the iris bends
> When a butterfly lights on it.

> *The first snowfall*
> *Is just enough to bend*
> *The jonquil leaves.*

"Autumn Haze" adapts the famous conceit in Moritake's "Fallen Blossom," the poem that Pound said was helpful to him in forming his technique of super-position.

Is it a dragon fly or maple leaf
That settles softly down upon the water?

To the barren branch
A flower returns; returning I see
It is a butterfly.

Haiku even proved useful for expressing such contemporaneous events as the armistice which followed
the First World War. Her image in "Peace"—of a butterfly contrasted with immensity, metal, and potentiality of
sound—is borrowed from Buson's haiku "On a Temple
Bell."

Perched upon the muzzle of a cannon
A yellow butterfly is slowly opening and shutting its wings.

A tiny butterfly is settled
Upon a massive temple-bell,
Asleep.

The pleasure of engaging in such a controversy as the
one which raged over free verse was not one which Amy
Lowell would have willingly denied herself. She never
seemed to question free verse either in theory or practice,
but she did experiment widely to find what varieties of
free forms were most effective in her writing. This
search, like the search of F. S. Flint, led her for a time
to experiment with haiku. She knew very well that Japanese poetry has rigid syllabic requirements which pre-
vent its being called "free"; and yet such an unusual
form was worth experimenting with anyway, especially
if one had already been using haiku for materials and

techniques. Her attempt to adapt the syllabic rules of Japanese poetry emerged in two poems in *What's O'Clock* (1925). In "Twenty-Four Hokku on a Modern Theme," the "modern theme" is unrequited love, and each haiku stanza of seventeen syllables presents a different aspect of the theme.

VI

This then is morning.
Have you no comfort for me,
Cold-coloured flowers?

The natural imagery suggests the Japanese origin of "Twenty-Four Hokku," but in "The Anniversary," the haiku form is used as a stanzaic unit in a narrative poem with no other connection with Japan. She dropped the attempt to naturalize Japanese prosody to English verse after these two poems, and wisely so. Syllabic rhythms adapted from a language with but slight accent to a poetry whose rhythms depend upon stress lose all their original qualities. And such a condensed form as haiku collapses when its traditional symbolic imagery is transferred to a culture and a language where these images have none of their religious and symbolic overtones. All in all, the experimentation in *Can Grande's Castle* (1918) with prose poetry or, as she called it, "cadenced prose," seems better advised.

While the technique of "cadenced prose" in this volume has nothing to do with Japan, one of the poems, "Guns as Keys: and the Great Gate Swings," is her epic of the meeting of East and West. She undertakes an assessment of the national characteristics of Japan and the United States as they were revealed at the historic moment of Perry's coercive opening of Japan. Her attempt to evaluate the significance of the meeting of East and West places "Guns as Keys" into the almost uniquely American tradition of such poems, a tradition which was started by Whitman in "A Broadway Pageant" and "Passage to India," developed further as a genre with a considerable intellectual apparatus and symbolism in Fenollosa's "East and West," and after Amy Lowell's attempt, taken into the greater fabric of Pound's *Cantos.* Her aim is made clear in the Preface:

"I wanted to place in juxtaposition the delicacy and artistic clarity of Japan and the artistic ignorance and gallant self-confidence of America. . . .

"I have tried to give a picture of two races at a moment when they were brought in contact for the first time. Which of them has gained most by this meeting, it would be difficult to say."

"Guns as Keys" is one of the most carefully conceived and ordered of her writings, but like Fenollosa's poem, it fails as literature. Drawing upon a surprisingly thorough knowledge of Japanese history and art, she alternates passages of her cadenced prose concerning America, Perry's preparations, sailing, and arrival with passages of free-verse poetic sketches of contemporaneous and contrasting scenes in Japan.

Her scheme of contrast between contemporaneous American and Japanese scenes produces a series of verbal pictures which are reminiscent both of Whistler and of her earlier attempts to make the block prints into poetry.

Although any of the sections of the poem would illustrate this in a general way, a passage from the first Japanese section makes her debt to Japan amply clear.

> At Mishima in the Province of Kai
> Three men are trying to measure a pine-tree
> By the length of their outstretched arms. . . .
> Beyond, Fuji,
> Majestic, inevitable,
> Wreathed over by wisps of cloud.

This "picture" is copied in all its details from the print, "Kō-shū no Mishima-goe," one of Hokusai's "Thirty-Six Views of Mt. Fuji." And another scene describing the procession of a feudal baron to or from his triennial visit to the shōgun in Tōkyō could have been copied from either "Hakone" or "Okayama" in Hiroshige's most famous series of prints, "The Fifty-Three Stations of the Tōkaidō."

> A Daimio's procession
> Winds between two green hills,
> A line of thin, sharp, shining, pointed spears
> Above red coats
> And yellow mushroom hats.

If any additional proof were needed to show the kinship which the Imagists felt with Whistler in their attempt to absorb Japan into their poetry, it could be found in the final section of the poem, "Postlude." Amy Lowell could not have stressed her debt at once to Japan and Whistler or her awareness of it more strongly than she does in choosing Whistler as her sole example of what the West had learned from Japan in fifty years of contact.

"Nocturne—Blue and Silver—Battersea Bridge.
"Nocturne—Grey and Silver—Chelsea Embankment.
"Variations in Violet and Green."

Pictures in a glass-roofed gallery, and all day long the throng of people is so great that one can scarcely see them. Debits—credits? Flux and flow through a wide gateway. Occident—Orient—after fifty years.

It is difficult to realize today how closely Japanese prints were associated with Whistler when any opportunity arose to use Japanese culture for English literary expression, but the conclusion of "Guns as Keys" shows, and Pound's insistence upon the necessity of knowing about "Whistler and the Japanese" shows, that it would be a mistake to regard Whistler apart from his Japanese interests when we are dealing with the idea of him held by the poets of this time. The contrast of vividly conceived pictures which are based, like Whistler's, on block print techniques or even specific block prints, distinguishes "Guns as Keys" from Fenollosa's "East and West." He too was interested in contrasting the racial characters of Orient and Occident, but he employed the didactic and ambiguously erotic language which marks the poem as such a typical product of the taste of the nineteenth century. Moreover, Whistler and the Japanese print, joined with a new knowledge of Japanese poetry and culture, have in this poem and the *Cantos* passed out of the realm of technique and into a form of thought. The very attempt in "Guns as Keys" or the *Cantos* to assess the cultural import of the meeting of East and West has become the idea of the confluence of cultures. For such American poets, the very techniques of imitation had to be rationalized in philosophical poems on the meaning of the contact of East and West.

John Gould Fletcher held himself shyly aloof from the Imagists until the schism, when he joined forces with the "Amygists." His standoffishness was not an isolation, however, and he was sufficiently touched by their interests to pursue a semi-independent study of French and Japanese poetry. Shortly before his death he recalled in letters his interests of those years. He remembered reading two English, one French, and two German translations of Japanese poetry and these at a time when he was deeply interested in the Japano-English poet, Yone Noguchi—a diet which gives some indication of the Imagists' appetite for Japanese poetry. Besides this intense study of Japanese poetry, he had a lifelong interest in Japanese art and philosophy. This interest in Japanese culture was manifested in his poetry after the typical pattern, first in exotic detail for Oriental atmosphere, and then in increasingly meaningful ways. The first poem to show what can be called a serious rather than exotic interest in Japan is "Irradiations VII" from *Irradiations—Sand and Spray* (1915).

> Flickering of incessant rain
> On flashing pavements:
> Sudden scurry of umbrellas:
> Bending, recurved blossoms of the storm.

The debt to Japan in this short poem is almost unbelievably great. The title suggests an Impressionistic picture, and the scene recalls many a block print; the poem ends with Pound's super-pository technique; and the situation is taken from Buson's haiku—

> *Through the spring rains*
> *An umbrella and raincoat hasten,*
> *Chatting together.*

Replying to a query about the possibility of Buson being the source of his poem, Fletcher replied, "I had most certainly read the Buson haiku you quote at the time I wrote my 'Irradiations.'"

His interest in Japan took a new direction when he discovered Fenollosa's works on Japanese art and its philosophical backgrounds. The Preface to *Goblins and Pagodas* (1916)—a Hearnian title—tells of his discovery of the Zen Buddhist "doctrine of the interdependence of man and inanimate nature" which he hoped to make use of in his poetry. He felt that if he could "link up" his personality with the essence of the objective world, he might "evoke a soul" out of inanimate nature and thereby produce a rich and new kind of poetry. Unfortunately, interesting as this attempt was, he was neither a Lafcadio Hearn nor an Ezra Pound; lacking the intuitive sympathy of the one and the genius of the other, his poems gained little more from this new philosophy than a sharper and more particularized use of imagery. This is a real gain, but the intellectual content of the poems in *Goblins and Pagodas* is much slighter than the Preface seems to promise. The new skill with imagery and the vain attempt at Buddhist transcendentalism are evident in many such passages as this one from "White Symphony":

> The pines groan, white-laden,
> The waves shiver, struck by the wind;
> Beyond from treeless horizons,
> Broken snow-peaks crawl to the sea.

However fresh these lines are, the attempt to "evoke a soul" from nature seems little different from the common metaphorical figure attributing animation to inanimate objects. Moreover, his debt to Japan seems more to Japanese art than philosophy, since such a passage as the following from "Green Symphony"—

> The trees are like a sea;
> Tossing . . .
> Darting their long green flickering fronds up at
>   the sky
> Spotted with white-blossom spray—

is probably inspired by Ogata Kōrin's screen-painting of "Waves at Matsushima," which W. B. Yeats wrote of having seen in London at this time, and which is now in the Boston Museum of Fine Arts.

With the publication of the poems in *Japanese Prints* (1918), Fletcher's chief interest in Japan had shifted from its art and philosophy to haiku, a fact which assumes some importance for the Japanese interests of the Imagist movement as a whole, since he wrote that these poems were composed from 1914 to 1916, "during the time I was most close to the Imagists." The long Preface to the volume gives a history of Japanese poetry from its origins through haiku, and although it is not free from errors of fact and interpretation, this little literary history is interesting for the application which he gives it to the contemporary poetic situation. He sees three meanings in haiku: "a statement of fact," "an emotion deduced from that," and "a sort of spiritual allegory." He seems to frown upon Pound when he says "Good hokkus cannot be written in English," but the chief relevance of haiku for English poetry is expressed in his exhortation, "Let us universalize our emotions as much as possible, let us become as impersonal as Shakespeare or Bashō was." He admires haiku for two other reasons, for its use of the elemental stuff of poetry—"universalized emotion derived from a natural fact"—and condensation— "the expression of the emotion in the fewest possible terms." Probably none of the Imagists ever came closer than this to describing the meaning of Japanese poetry for those of their poems which were not specifically Japanese in subject matter or technique.

The poetry which grows out of this theorizing is, on the whole, even more disappointing than the poems in *Goblins and Pagodas.* He often uses natural images or objects associated with Japanese poetry or prints, but usually in either a conventionally exotic way or in settings which make the images dissonant by both Japanese and Western standards. "The Young Daimyo" rings false in this way, probably because it pretends to be so much more Japanese than it is.

When he first came out to meet me,
He had just been girt with the two swords;

And I found he was far more interested in the glitter
of their hilts,
And did not even compare my kiss to a cherry blossom.

The detail of the two swords seems to promise a truly
Japanese situation, but kisses are not compared to cherry
blossoms in Japan, kissing in public is frowned upon, a
boy was given his swords at an age when he would find
even his mother's caresses tedious, and the last thought
of a samurai would be to leave the company of men
after receiving such an honor. It is a pleasure to be able,
after all, to discover other poems which are the happier
for not striving too hard to be Japanese. "Midsummer
Dusk" is such a poem and so Japanese in spirit that it
almost seems to be modeled upon a specific haiku.

> Swallows twittering at twilight:
> Waves of heat
> Churned to flames by the sun.

One poem does have a haiku as its source; "Evening
Bell from a Distant Temple" echoes Buson's "Temple
Bell."

> A bell in the fog
> Creeps out echoing faintly
> The pale broad flashes
> Of vibrating twilight,
> Faded gold.

> *How cool the reverberations*
> *As they out-circle in the evening*
> *From the temple bell.*

Like Aldington's poems after the First World War, Fletcher's later work shows a turning to narration and other, less Japanese, poetic preoccupations. Fletcher never ceased to be an Imagist, however, and he continued his interest in Japan throughout his lifetime. His essay, "The Orient and Contemporary Poetry," in Arthur B. Christy's *The Asian Legacy in American Life* (1945) tells in very general terms of the meaning which Chinese and Japanese culture have had for the Imagists and later poets. His Foreword to Kenneth Yasuda's translation of haiku, *A Pepper-Pod* (1947), shows that he still hoped that haiku might "lead poetry back to first principles," and he seems to echo Oscar Wilde when he adds a hope, with a glance at the more sophisticated poets who followed the Imagists, that haiku might also "lead some of the more intelligent moderns to cast off the burden of too-conscious intellectualism that they carry." But as in Wilde's case, we are left with an irony of an unkind fate: Fletcher's theorizing has proved to be more interesting than most of his poetry. His critical sense was sound, however, and shortly before his tragic death he could summarize the indebtedness of the whole Imagist movement to Japanese poetry: "I should say that the influence of haiku on the Imagists was much more considerable than almost anyone has suspected. It helped them make their poems short, concise, full of direct feeling for nature."

Fletcher's estimation of "the influence of haiku" and Amy Lowell's attempt to express the significance of Japan in the twentieth century suggest the desirability of an assessment of the accomplishment of the Imagists in the light of their preoccupations with Japan. The work of these writers and of Ezra Pound as well reveals a consistent pattern of developing interest that started with an artistic fascination with Japan which usually expressed itself in exotic detail and similes and which gradually grew into an interest in Japanese poetry and an attempt to develop meaningful techniques from it. It should be emphasized again that the characteristics which distinguish the Imagists and twentieth-century poets generally in their use of Japan are the awareness of Japanese poetry and the ability to express this knowledge in meaningful techniques—often in ways inextricably bound up with Whistlerian Impressionism and Japanese art. The Americans among the Imagists—Pound, Amy Lowell, and Fletcher—seem also to have needed, almost by the fact of their American heritage, to express their ideas about the significance of their discovery of Japanese culture. The American consciousness of the role of the United States in absorbing many cultures stimulated these writers to try, in their poetry and criticism, to unite East and West. The English Imagists remained content to borrow techniques, details, and images from their experience with Japanese art and poetry.

It has been fashionable for many years now to deride the Imagists—apart from Ezra Pound—but it seems wiser to use the advantages of retrospect for objective assessment. It is plain enough that these poets were rather longer on theorizing than they were on poetic gifts, but they deserve the benefit of historical perspective. Their great source of strength lay in the use they made of the pan-Impressionist heritage—chiefly French painting and poetry, Whistler, and Japanese art and poetry. This heritage enabled them to develop a modern tradition of clear, definite, imagistic poetry. But it was also their undoing. Their poetic abilities aside, these poets, and often Ezra Pound as well, seem to have concentrated so intently upon achieving clearly defined poems, especially poems made up of visual images or "pictures," that they failed to write their poems in moving language. The necessary revolution against the verbiage and vagueness of the worst sides of the late Victorian tradition went too far, and they often failed to be sufficiently verbal. A corollary of this extremism was their breakdown of conventional forms to escape the Swinburnian and Tennysonian intoxication with rhyme and rhythm; all too often, however, they ended in the sobriety of prose. Another aspect of their break with the nineteenth century also had baneful consequences, for while they seem justified in their rejection of late Victorian didacticism and moralizing, their amoral—because highly pictorial and imagistic—style often lacks that fiber of intellectual and moral toughness which gives English poetry its characteristic texture. Pound is of course the exception to most of these strictures, but he exemplifies what the Imagist tradition was at its essential best. The others went too far in the direction of rejecting the English and European literary tradition and ended by slaying themselves as well as the Victorian dragon—the attempts of Hilda Doolittle and Richard Aldington to apply their Imagistic techniques to their new interest in Cavalier and Metaphysical poetry have proved to be little more successful than the late poems of Amy Lowell and Fletcher. But the Imagists had cleared the way and handed on the tradition of their interests—Japanese and otherwise—to their contemporaries and successors. If Pound had created "a live tradition," his fellow Imagists had ended a dying one and had helped to make possible a variety of new poetic styles.

ii. The Contemporaries of the Imagists: Aiken, Stevens, and Others

The narrative inclinations of Conrad Aiken and his disagreements with the pronouncements of Amy Lowell kept him from identifying himself with the Imagist movement. But like the Imagists, he became acquainted with Japanese culture through the block prints, "which," as he says, "I once quite elaborately collected—and I still have some very fine ones. . . . There was also much talk [at Harvard about 1909] of Fenollosa and the Boston Collection." This American taste for the block prints amounted almost to a craze in the years just before the First World War and has left some traces in his poetry. Sometimes the result is only a casual reference, as in the first "Prelude":

the photograph, too . . .
The laundry bill, matches, an ash tray, Utamaro's
Pearl-fishers.

But occasionally, as in "The Divine Pilgrims," the block print is used to dramatize the climax of a narrative sequence.

What shall we talk of? Li Po? Hokusai?
You narrow your long dark eyes to fascinate me—

the speaker of the poem muses to himself, and then picks up a print of Hokusai and, while talking to the woman of it, imperceptibly leads her to accept him as a lover. This technique is not unlike the use made of block prints by the Impressionists and the Imagists in their shorter poems, but in other poems he goes farther. "Episode in Grey," "The Charnel Rose: A Symphony," and "Seven Twilights" reveal their Impressionistic origin in their titles and in their techniques. Their method and structure alike are largely pictorial—in terms of colors and visual perceptions rather than strict narrative.

Aiken's familarity with Japanese art and Impressionistic techniques soon took him, as they seem to have taken nearly everybody else—to Japanese poetry. It is an interesting commentary on this period that the enthusiasm for Japanese poetry among American college students should impel them to compose "Japanese" poems in the same way that the members of the Poets' Club were doing. He writes in the letter quoted earlier, "Of course [Japanese poetry] was all in the air—at Harvard [and everyone] around the Harvard Advocate was already aware of Hearn's hokku, and we all had shots at them. So when Fletcher and I dived into Japanese and Chinese poetry and art [in the years between 1915 and 1917] it was already old stuff for me." The debt to Hearn is expressed in a note to Part II of *The House of Dust* which states, "I am indebted to Lafcadio Hearn for the episode called 'The Screen Maiden' in Part II." The intermingling of talk about Hearn and haiku makes more sense than it at first seems to, because the section indebted to Hearn offers examples of Pound's super-pository technique which recur in Aiken's work of this period; here it describes the thoughts of a girl who dies on an operating table.

> Death was a dream. It could not change these eyes,
> Blow out their light, or turn this mouth to dust.
> She combed her hair and sang. She would live forever.
> Leaves flew past her window along a gust.

The final impression which Aiken's poetry leaves in the mind of the reader is that of a style which is mixed in its intentions to be both narrative and Impressionistic, story-telling and pictorial. It is a strange mixture, one which could be expected only from an age whose criterion of imagistic poetry impinged upon a poet like Aiken with narrative abilities that have found frequent expression in prose fiction as well as poetry.

Many writers besides the Imagists and their acquaintances show an abundant interest in Japan, but the weary reader soon finds himself in a jungle of mixed forms, meaninglessly imitated techniques, and exoticism which he would be readily willing to make into a desert and call peace. *Poetry, The Poetry Journal;* the host of now-forgotten little magazines—*The Wave, Seven Arts, The Chap Book*, etc.; such established magazines as *The Dial, The Athenaeum, The Fortnightly*; the newspapers; Braithwaite's annual *Anthology of Magazine Verse*; the *Others* volumes—everywhere, it seems, imitations of the Imagists' efforts to assimilate Japanese poetry and art abound.

Poetry alone carried the more-or-less imagistic early work of D. H. Lawrence, James Joyce, and William Carlos Williams—but also of Maxwell Bodenheim, Iris Barry, and other such worthies—in addition to the Imagists, Eliot, and W. B. Yeats. Only a few of these many poems related in one way or another to Japan are worth quoting, but a short one, "Marriage," by William Carlos Williams will do, both because it is highly representative and because it shows the attempt to emulate haiku in brevity and in the use of Pound's super-pository technique:

> So different, this man
> And this woman:
> A stream flowing in a field.

Dr. Williams, Joyce, and Lawrence later extended their literary interests over a broader field and are among the greater literary artists of our time, but the Japanese urge has bitten many would-be poets since the 'Twenties. It perpetrated such popular songs as the old one, "The Japanese Sandman," and since the war, such new ones as "Gomen Nasai" ("Please Forgive Me") and "Sayonara" ("Goodbye"). The same impulse excited, if that is the word, Tubman K. Hedrick to write platitudinous "hokku" for the *Chicago Daily News* after the First World War; an anonymous writer to contribute "A Tour of Duty in the Far East: Fifteen Hokku by an Ensign" to the *Atlantic* (June, 1953); and Maxwell Bodenheim to send such a piece as "Hokku Poems" to the daily *New York Times* (December 15, 1953)—all very eminent periodicals which ought to have known better. These are but a few of the ephemerae in the amber shadow of Pound's *Cantos*.

It requires a certain indulgence of the historical spirit to deal with the marvelous fact that readers a generation ago were excited by the writing of Yone Noguchi, the successor to Hearn as popularizer of Japan, and an acknowledged influence on John Gould Fletcher. He was praised, after all, by Richard Le Gallienne, Bliss Carman, Meredith, Richard Garnett, William Rossetti, Hardy, and others. But why? *Seen and Unseen* (1897) with its apt subtitle—"Monologues of a Homeless Snail"—echoes Emerson and Whitman more than the Japanese poets, and Noguchi kept echoing them in the unrhymed verse of *From the Eastern Sea* (1903), in the adaptations of Japanese poetic forms of *The Pilgrimage* (1912), and in the prose poetry of *The Summer Clouds; Prose Poems* (1906). There are at least two explanations for Noguchi's extraordinary popularity. To begin with, he was taken to be a real Japanese poet who just happened to write in English. How little he was the real article can be seen from his *Japanese Hokkus* (1920) where he sometimes tries to maintain the Japanese syllabic form and sometimes attempts merely to reproduce "the haiku spirit"— no mean thing when haiku has meant very different things to three centuries of poets. Furthermore, what this spirit meant to him is hard to say, since he translated, among other "hokkus," a few tanka by poets like Ki no Tomonori who died some seven centuries before the haiku form was evolved. But Noguchi seemed like the real thing to a generation who knew no Japanese. The second reason for his popularity is the ironic fact that he adopted the styles, often the worst styles, of contemporary poets in English. His "hokkus" are as exotic as any of theirs, his free verse is obviously inspired by Whitman, and his experiments with "prose poems" are almost indistinguishable from Amy Lowell's "cadenced prose" in technique. Here was Noguchi, doing his best to reflect current English modes of the more sentimental variety, and yet a Japanese: he assured the age that their own work was truly inspired by Japan. It is to his credit, however, that he protested, though in vain, in *Through the Torii* (1922), that suggestion was not the whole key to Japanese poetry. To his credit, because altogether too many poets were seduced out of sense by the false syllogism that Japanese poetry and art are suggestive, the poem x treats Japanese poetry or art, and therefore x must be suggestive and very modern. Noguchi's critical essays make more sense in retrospect than any of his poems.

There were a number of writers in these years who were either of Japanese descent like Noguchi or who had been to Japan and thereby were allowed reputations as poets in an age which seemed not to question anything Japanese. Jun Fujita is one of these who managed to scatter his "tankas," as he called them through the pages of *Poetry* and other magazines. He had a genuine sensitivity for imagery, but was no poet, and his scope is pretty well circumscribed by the little world of fallen leaves, grasses, and bare trees. These impulses from the autumnal woods, and others like them, teach us next to nothing, however, and it is amply clear that a poet must have a real talent in his own language before he can write moving poetry in response to Japan or any other stimulus.

One of the few poets for whom a Japanese "influence"

has ever been claimed is Adelaide Crapsey. Louis Unter-meyer seems to have started it in his *Modern American Poetry* (1920) when he said her cinquain-forms "doubt-less owe something to the Japanese hokku . . . she was an unconscious Imagist," a belief echoed by many. But her biographer, Mary Elizabeth Osborn, is no doubt right when she relates the cinquains to the tanka which Adelaide Crapsey read in her copy of *A Hundred Verses from Old Japan* (1909), William N. Porter's translation of the *Hyaku Nin Isshū* anthology. Tanka, or waka as the form is also called, is made up of five lines of five, seven, five, seven, and seven syllables. Adelaide Crapsey adopted the five-line scheme and reduced the syllables to two, four, six, eight, and two. The form may be illus-trated by "Anguish," which echoes Porter's translation of a poem by Mibu no Tadamine.

> Keep thou
> Thy tearless watch
> All night but when blue-dawn
> Breathes on the silver moon, then weep!
> Then weep!

> *I hate the cold unfriendly moon*
> *That shines at early morn*
> *And nothing seems so sad and gray*
> *When I am left forlorn*
> *At day's returning dawn.*

A couple of poems do seem to echo haiku, but the tone is the same tone of despair sounded in all her cinquains, and the form remains the same. "Trapped," for example, ought to be compared with Chamberlain's translation of Issa's "A Dew Drop World."

> Well and
> If day on day
> Follows, and weary year
> On year . . . and ever days and years . . .
> Well?

> *Granted this dewdrop world is but*
> *A dewdrop world—this granted, yet. . . .*

Even her poems in other forms were touched by Japan. The two quatrains, "Oh, Lady, Let Thy Sad Tears Fall" is obviously indebted to Ono no Komachi's most famous poem on the loss of her beauty, "Hana no iro wa" (Porter: "The blossom's tint . . . ").

If such a minor voice bore so heavy a Japanese accent, other more important ones have sometimes seemed to echo a Japanese tone or two. Robert Frost was in England long enough to learn about Pound's super-pository technique, as the last stanza of "A Boundless Moment" and other poems show:

> We stood a moment so in a strange world,
> Myself as one his own pretense deceives;
> And then I said the truth (and we moved on):
> A young beech clinging to its last year's leaves.

Similarly, in addition to allusions to Japan in his poetry, Archibald MacLeish shows his knowledge of Pound's interests in *Songs for Eve* (1954), where the first "Reply to Mr. Wordsworth" is strongly derivative.

The flower that on the pear-tree settles
Momentarily as though a butterfly—that petal,
Has it alighted on twigs black wet

From elsewhere? No, but blossoms from the bole.

These few lines echo Pound's "petals on a wet, black bough" and the haiku he quoted by Moritake to show what he meant by "the form of super-position" (see p. 114); and echo as well the last few lines about the chestnut tree in W. B. Yeats's "Among School Children" (see p. 247).

Interesting as these poems of Frost and MacLeish are, there is a more important debt to Japan in the poetry of Wallace Stevens, one of our major poets who has had an interest in Japan and China, an interest which he has transformed, like everything else, into the complex and subtle music of his "blue guitar." The extent of this transformation, the well-known difficulties of his poetry, and Stevens' lifelong chariness of saying anything about himself or his poetic interests make discussion of him a very exacting task. Professor Henry W. Wells has written about the importance of Japan for our poets that "The influence is vast. . . . It is all over Wallace Stevens' first book, *Harmonium*." And the poet himself was kind enough to answer a few questions. He wrote that while he knew about haiku, he could not ever remember writing with them in mind, and professed a greater interest in Japanese prints and other Oriental art. He concluded by saying that he possessed six or so books of Japanese and Chinese poetry, and disclaimed that his interests in Oriental poetry were cursory in nature. His poetry reveals that the effect of Japan upon his poetry lies somewhere between the disclaimer of an aloof poet seeking to be helpful and Mr. Wells's view that it is to be found throughout *Harmonium*.

It is necessary to begin by recalling that early in his career Stevens was associated with the "Others" group of poets (like Dr. Williams) who were for the most part aware of the Imagists but more interested in "objectivist" poetry. Stevens' "objects" were typically, however, the subjectively apprehended objects of French poetry, especially the poetry of the Symbolists. There is a curious and complex duality of Impressionist and Symbolist modes of cognition, a duality which seems to emphasize Impressionism more strongly in *Harmonium* (1931) and to shift to Symbolism and didacticism in the later volumes. The Impressionistic motive led him to the pictorial composition, the liberal use of color, and the insistence upon the beauty and reality of individual perception which we have seen in other poets touched by Impressionism. But he differs from these other poets in seeming to adapt these Impressionistic ideas directly from France, without benefit of "Whistler and the Japanese"; to this extent, any Japanese element in his Impressionism comes indirectly through the French absorption of Japan. His Symbolistic theory and practice led him to assign personal—or as Pound said of the Symbolists, arbitrary—ideas and values to the Impressionistic compositions, colors, and impressions. Impressionism gives his early poetry its rich, almost gay, texture; Symbolism makes his poetry increasingly intellectual, personal, and complex.

The best study of Stevens' poetry, Professor William

Van O'Connor's *The Shaping Spirit* (1950), helps clarify these general comments about his Impressionist and other motives. Professor O'Connor writes that Stevens' theory of the imagination leads him to believe "that color is not in the object itself (the black bark of a tree) but varies not only with the light but with the position of the beholder (the tree may appear purple, or gray, or bronze)." In later poems, an image of a tree or bird may become the metaphor of yet another, more conceptual image, of "the vulgar ocean" as in "Somnambulisma"—Imagism has been intellectualized, and Impressionism made Symbolist ratiocination. The impact of Japan on his poetry can be claimed with confidence only for the Impressionistic poems, where there is both an indirect debt to Japan through Impressionism and perhaps Imagism, and also overt or tacit echoes of Japan.

One would scarcely have a right to call Stevens' style Impressionistic unless his poetry reflected an interest in Oriental art and especially in Japanese prints. There are many references to porcelain in his poetry which seem to symbolize the superhuman stasis of art which Keats saw in the Grecian urn; to Chinese sages who seem to represent a timeless if somewhat disembodied human wisdom and a perception of eternal beauty and verities; and to Japanese prints, as in the third section of "Le Monocle de Mon Oncle."

> Is it for nothing, then, that old Chinese
> Sat tittivating by their mountain pools
> Or in the Yangtse studied out their beards?
> I shall not play the flat historic scale.

You know how Utamaro's beauties sought
The end of love in their all-speaking braids.
You know the mountainous coiffures of Bath.
Alas! Have all the barbers lived in vain
That not one curl in nature has survived?
Why, without pity on these studious ghosts,
Do you come dripping in your hair from sleep?

These verses are not in "the flat historic scale," since
he has chosen, in the manner of Pound, three different
ages and cultures to make his point. "Utamaro's beauties"
are the *bijin*—"beautiful persons" or courtesans—whose
beauty was frequently expressed in elaborate coiffures,
which is what Stevens means by the less accurate but
more specific term, "braids." The immediate point of
the speaker's address to the woman is that although the
Chinese sages cultivated their beards, and the Japanese
courtesans and ladies of society at Bath their piled-up
hair, all of this cultivation has not made one curl survive
in nature. In other words, for all the efforts of artists
(the barbers) to refine or beautify reality, it has remained
the same—a constant theme in Stevens' poetry. The image
of the woman who comes "dripping" in her hair from
sleep is most complex. Wetness is important secondarily
for its sexual appeal, as in Eliot's poems, but primarily
because wetting the hair straightens out whatever curl
has been put into it, and water must be taken as a symbol of reality which is inimical to art. The beards of the
Chinese are wet in the sense that they are reflected in
the Yangtse river. The associations of water with Bath
are obvious, but the associations of water with "Utamaro's

beauties" can only be called recondite. One of Utamaro's most famous pictures is a triptych of oyster-divers on a peninsula. The three women stand in different attitudes, and one is literally dripping as she wrings out her skirt. All have their long dark hair straightened by the water, unlike the usual women in his prints. So the woman, "wet" with sleep, represents a reality which is hostile to art, but which remains attractive to the speaker for the sensuousness of its appeal. The seemingly haphazard references are extraordinarily precise and are given point only by the crucial images taken from Japanese prints.

Apart from these subtle verses, the most Impressionistic and most nearly Japanese poems are those which give a series of several quasi-Impressionistic pictures, apprehensions, or impressions of one subject. The most important of these for our purposes are "Six Significant Landscapes" and "Thirteen Ways of Looking at a Blackbird" from *Harmonium* and "Study of Two Pears" and "Variations on a Summer Day" from *Parts of a World* (1942). The titles of these poems recall such series of Japanese prints as Hiroshige's "Eight Views of Ōmi," Hokusai's "Thirty-Six Views of Fuji," or Utamaro's "Seasons." These poems are also closest to the Imagist method and haiku technique, and are especially reminiscent of Amy Lowell's "Twenty-Four Hokku on a Modern Theme." The best example from among these poems of the highly pictorial method merged with haiku-like technique is "Thirteen Ways of Looking at a Blackbird." The blackbird is the constant, objective reality which means different things according to the mood and impression of the observer. Several of the sections of the poem are most extraordinarily like the Japanese in their method and in their use of natural imagery.

I

Among twenty snowy mountains,
The only moving thing
Was the eye of the blackbird.

III

The blackbird whirled in the autumn winds.
It was a small part of the pantomime.

IX

When the blackbird flew out of sight,
It marked the edge
Of one of many circles.

XII

The river is moving.
The blackbird must be flying.

XIII

It was snowing all afternoon.
It was snowing
And it was going to snow.
The blackbird sat
In the cedar-limbs.

The third and twelfth sections are haiku-like in spirit, because they assume the interrelatedness of all nature. The river, for example, is a Taoist symbol for motion; it moves, and the blackbird may therefore also be expected to be in flight. Only one of the thirteen sections—but also perhaps the basic image of the poem as whole, the blackbird in autumn—seems to echo a specfic haiku, and this the thirteenth with its darkening scene and the dark bird sitting in the tree. This poem recalls one of the best-known haiku, Bashō's "On a Withered Bough."

> *On a withered bough*
> *A crow has stopped to perch,*
> *And autumn darkens.*

The haiku-like elements in these stanzas are, then, their short, condensed quality, the poetic weight placed upon a few natural images, and the interrelatedness of the elements in a natural scene.

One other poem from *Harmonium*, "The Death of a Soldier," seems to echo a haiku by Bashō on the same subject.

> Life contracts and death is expected,
> As in a season of autumn.
> The soldier falls. . . .
>
> When the wind stops and, over the heavens,
> The clouds go, nevertheless,
> In their direction.
>
> *Only ordinary grasses,*
> *These that wave above the soldiers*
> *After their high martial dreams.*

The likelihood that Stevens may have had the haiku in

mind here is given some indirect strength by his using the technique Pound took from haiku, super-position, in a number of his poems. "O Florida, Venereal Soil" and "Metaphors of a Magnifico" from *Harmonium* show the technique.

> Donna, donna, dark . . .
> Conceal yourself or disclose
> Fewest things to the lover—
> A hand that bears a thick-leaved fruit,
> A pungent bloom against your shade.

*　　*　　*

> Of what was I thinking?
> So the meaning escapes.
>
> The first white wall of the village . . .
> The fruit trees. . . .

Other such poems are "Of the Surface of Things," "Jasmine's Beautiful Thoughts Underneath the Willow," "Theory," and "Tea." This evidence, along with the imagistic technique which accompanies the Impressionism of *Harmonium,* suggests the extent to which Japan entered into Stevens' poetry—somewhat as subject matter, somewhat as technique. The degree of assimilation and transformation which they have undergone is perhaps unique among the poets who have had an interest in Japan, and many years of study by many people will be necessary before anyone will be able to say with much confidence just what were the sources of Stevens' art.

Although there have been some contemporaries of

Stevens and the Imagists who have visited Japan and brought a new kind of realism to their treatment of it, there have also been those who went to Japan and brought back poetry not unlike the imagistic and Impressionistic verse of an Amy Lowell or a Fletcher. Two such poets are Arthur Davison Ficke and Witter Bynner, who visited Japan together, collaborated in their poetry, and became esteemed critics of the Japanese block prints. Ficke's early work in *The Happy Princess and Other Poems* (1907) is almost wholly exotic. Several poems in this volume purport to be translations from the Japanese, but how totally un-Japanese they are can be epitomized by his description of Japan in the epigraph from, he says, "The Poet Yoshi": "Isles round which the foam of dream lies pearled." "The Dreamers of Dzushi" is somewhat different, since it combines the myth of the sirens with the legend of Urashimatarō, the Japanese Rip Van Winkle, but it stretches on rather too long.

The question arises why Ficke bothered to write about Japan at all. Part of the answer is the urge to exoticize. But a more restrained poem, "In the House of the Potter," gives another partial answer. These four dramatic monologues by Japanese craftsmen picture Japan as an artistic nation with high standards of form—"One comes to think so much upon the Form," as one of the artisans says—and formal perfection was one of the creeds of the new poetic movements, in spite of their interest in free verse. Another reason for his treatment of Japan seems to have been simply an affection and admiration for the beauty of the country and its culture, especially its religion, which he treats in "At Ise," "Murmadzu," "Before the Buddha," and several other poems. And, like many a nineteenth-century writer, Ficke seems to have turned to the Orient in such a poem as "Before the Buddha" in order that he might safely question the beliefs of his own culture by posing them in terms of his experience in Japan. *Twelve Japanese Painters* (1913) contains fifteen poems based upon Japanese prints and *An April Elegy* (1913) contains a section of a similar nature, "Seven Japanese Paintings"—all poems which show a partial transition from exoticism to Impressionism in the strong resemblance they reveal to Wilde's "Impressions."

Like so many other Americans, Ficke wrote his most serious poem on Japan to express his hope for a mingling of cultures. His "Song of East and West" in *The Earth Passion . . . and Other Poems* (1908) recalls Fenollosa's "East and West," but its emphasis is more political, social, and religious. He envisions the time when the cultures will mingle:

> Lo! now the day of mingled life is come.
> The high cathedral chimes, the temple drum,
> The minster organ, the pagoda bells,
> Unto each other shall no more be dumb. . .
> [in a]single quest for a united world.

Ficke's friend Witter Bynner was even more of an Imagist in technique, although both of them ordinarily employed meter and rhyme. He too began with the cherry-petal exoticism of Ficke in such poems in *The Beloved Stranger* (1919) as "Wings" and "Cherry-Blossoms." But the technique becomes more firm, and "Touch"—so strikingly

like Adelaide Crapsey's cinquains—has some of the vividness of the five-line tanka.

> Some one was there . . .
>
> I put out my hand in the dark
> And felt
> The long fingers
> Of the wind.

"Mist" and "The Morn" continue the Imagistic and Japanese use of imagery in free verse forms, and some of
his other poems employ Pound's super-pository technique.
Bynner's ordinary method is, however, to employ regular
verse forms to express his experiences in Japan, and the
general effect is verse more like Ficke's than anyone else's.
A Canticle of Pan (1920) has several poems dealing with
such experiences as a pine tree seen "Through a Gateway
in Japan," a visit "In the House of Lafcadio Hearn," and
musings on a woman "In the Yoshiwara"—Tōkyō's old
licensed quarter. "In Kamakura" is a meditation something like Kipling's before the statue of the Great Buddha
there, and in "The Edge" from *Against the Cold* (1940),
we find him musing on death and dissolution in Nirvana,
considering with the seriousness of Ficke and Hearn
certain Buddhist metaphysical beliefs.

Proof that Ficke and Bynner were studying the Imagists
and their techniques is provided by their elaborate literary
hoax, *Spectra* (1916), "A Book of Poetic Experiments by
Anne Knish and Emmanuel Morgan." Ficke-Knish and
Bynner-Morgan enjoyed themselves by parodying the
the several styles of the Imagists, T. S. Eliot, and others.

Bynner's "Despair Comes" is a resonably happy parody of Pound's high tone and his technique of super-position.

> Despair comes when all comedy
>   Is tame
> And there is left no tragedy
>   In any name,
> When the round and wounded breathing
>   Of love upon the breast
> Is not so glad a sheathing
>   As an old brown vest.
>
> Asparagus is feathery and tall,
> And the hose lies rotting by the garden wall.

Neither of these writers is a fraction of the poet that Pound is, but in a curious and altogether pleasant way they seem to have recognized it, and while in their parodies they present Pound's theories and techniques with a snicker, their serious work can be said to adhere to the principles and example of the Imagists with more fidelity than not a few of the poets represented in Amy Lowell's Imagists' anthologies. Although they saw the humorous sides to the pretensions of Imagism, they illustrate how effective Pound and his associates were in promulgating a new poetic method, even among those writers who could boast what the Imagists could not, first-hand experience in Japan.

iii. Japan at First-Hand:
New Realism in the Work of Visiting Poets

Such writers as Ficke and Bynner seem to represent the end of one aspect of the Imagist movement—the aspect of excited interest in Japan and imitation of poetic techniques. The Imagists were essentially Japanese enthusiasts, and so were Ficke and Bynner. But their poetry often shows a directness of response to Japan and experience in Japan which suggests that Japan is, after all, something geographically, culturally, and humanly real. In spite of this incipient realism, however, they were still held in thrall by the exotic image and committed to poetic forms which made consistent realism impossible. The new development in the poetic treatment of Japan —as a matter-of-fact poetic subject little different from any other subject—had to come from poets uncommitted to the exotic, Imagist, or Impressionistic treatment of Japan. Edmund Blunden is the kindly dean of this group, and his poems, articles and essays, and reviews for *The Times Literary Supplement* have rendered great service in keeping alive an intelligent interest in Japan.

Japanese Garland (1928) is the record of an Englishman's response to experience in Japan, a response which is neither exotic nor involved in a desire to create new poetic modes. Like the rest of the writers to be treated in this chapter, he formed his style before going to Japan, and the result of his visit was new materials and a heightened sensibility rather than the discovery of a new world. Japan called some of his best writing from him, he acknowledges in "Far East," but could not change his allegiance.

> Uplands and groves that from the West
> Have the last word for me,
> Think not your image in my breast
> Was sullied when I sang my best
> Beside an Eastern Sea.

But the beauty of Japan was irresistible: however English his Muse, he often writes his "best" when the subject is Japan, as in poems like "Far East" which describes the beauty to be found "beside an Eastern Sea."

Both his "English" and "Japanese" poetry are happiest when responding to natural beauty upon, as it were, second consideration or reflection. He writes of the fishing-boats in Japan's truly lovely "Inland Sea,"

> Now like sea-lilies loom their luring sails,
> Or heaven's envoys walking fountained vales;
> And now, by one deflection dark,
> Like staring vultures of the night
> Each pirate blackness skulks, a murderous mark
> Begotten by a thing of light
> Like apprehension's baffling destiny,

as if their chiaroscuro patterns were really changing thoughts and moral perceptions. As his Japanese poems are sturdily Georgian, so his English poems written since leaving Japan retain some of the qualities of the country he visited. He has said in a letter, "I have written many [poems since leaving Japan] in which experience in Japan and acquaintance with Japanese art and poetry play a part though inconspicuously." His years in Japan confirmed and heightened his interest in external nature and more frequently led him to compose a scene which speaks for itself through its details without additional comment. His ten essays on Japan in *The Mind's Eye* (1934) give new evidence of the realistic treatment of Japan and the Japanese which characterizes his poetry. There is no supercilious condescension, and there is no unaccountable rapture. There is praise and blame, such enthusiasm and irritation as a reasonable person is likely to feel among any foreign people during a protracted visit. There is perhaps a suggestion, as in the poetry, that Japan is something special, but this is counterbalanced by the ever sure knowledge that England is home.

The reader who, like Blunden, has visited Japan may well feel that his own interests differ from the poet's, or disagree about an enthusiasm or a dislike, but he would disagree more on the principle that tastes differ than out of an objection to a distorted picture of Japan. For the most part, the poetry of William Plomer strikes one the same way. What was said about the realistic intent of his fiction in an earlier chapter, and his desire to assess and define the Japanese National Character in stories closely related to his personal experience, is true of his poetry as well. In *Visiting the Caves* (1936) "Captain Maru," for example, is a fictionalized treatment of the Captain Mori whose ship bore Plomer to Japan and who remained an acquaintance for several years. (Even the name "Maru" shows his tendency to generalize, because it is the suffix applied to the names of all Japanese ships, not a family name; hence "Maru" is a generic type of

Japanese ship's master, and by extension a representative Japanese.) The poem ends with an assessment of what Japan meant to Plomer in 1936.

Maru at home, in an old gown and clogs
Scrambling along the rocky shore,
Or Maru standing all night on the bridge
The third night running and the fog no less,
Or Maru as a good companion, sharing
The lives of younger men for a day or two . . .
Back on the [ship's] bridge, and in the afternoons
Singing some elegy of ancient wars,
A cultivator of his faculties
And calm—but not the calm of rarest mastery.
And now he has appeared to someone in a dream
Or rather a nightmare, menacing, a giant . . .
It is the challenge of his race, the short man scorned
Not satisfied with power, but mad for more.

It seems best to quote at length in this way from one poem rather than briefly from many, because the poem best represents Plomer's urge to define what the Japanese are like. Actually, as he writes elsewhere, the Marus are the type of active Japanese, but there is another type, the passive, gentle, and refined person—often a woman—which also can be found in his stories. While in "Captain Maru" the "nightmare" represents the growing fear of Japan in the 'Thirties, other volumes show a more sympathetic love for the country, as well as providing additional satirical and critical poems. These poems are among the twelve poems on Japan in *The Family Tree* (1929), among the satires of *The Dorking Thigh* (1946), and in the verses of *The Fivefold Screen* (1932). The realistic or comic intent of these poems is welcome, but Plomer's persistent desire to relate or assess his own experiences seems to lend itself more successfully to prose fiction or autobiography.

Another traveler to Japan, Laurence Binyon, has shown his interest in Japanese art upon several occasions. His *Little Poems from the Japanese* (1925) is chiefly a translation of poems which appear on woodblock prints or in the *Hyaku Nin Isshū*, the anthology known to Amy Lowell, Adelaide Crapsey, and to others new to Japanese poetry. In *The North Star and Other Poems* (1941), he has written additional poems which show a sensitivity to the natural beauty and religion of Japan, a responsiveness revealed in their titles, taken as they are from three famous visiting-places. "Matsushima" and "Miyajima" celebrate two of Japan's loveliest islands, and "Koya San" is a meditation on a visit to the mountain shrine of the founder of Buddhism in Japan. "Koya San" is the most interesting of these, because unlike the poems by Ficke and Bynner which concern the desirability—perhaps—of believing in Buddhism—if one could—or the hope that East will meet West one day, Binyon has his speaker feel a direct human bond with the pilgrim at the temple altar:

> in him I seemed to share
> Longings that still were patient to persist
> Through Time and Death from lips that once were red.
> In the one image all my kind stood there.

This is a remarkable instance of simple and basic humanity, without exoticism, to have appeared just before the Second World War, or perhaps at any period.

Sherard Vines is a somewhat lesser known poet than Binyon, but in his poetry realism achieves a complexity which is more typical of modern poetry. His conceits remind one of Cowley, his allusions of Eliot, and his imagistic use of detail of Pound, but whether his subjects are Japanese or neo-Metaphysical, Vines adapts them to his own unique style with a large amount of recondite detail. His first book, *The Pyramid* (1926), was published in London while he was in Japan, a fact which seems to account for the prefatory poems by Yone Noguchi and Edmund Blunden. The conceit in "Proposal for a Vase" is an example of his neo-Metaphysical technique: the vase turns out to be a fragile, porcelain-like world inhabited by "the youngest of courtesans and the most guarded," whom the speaker woos. The Japanese characteristics of the imagery in many of the poems is carried to the extreme of including a three-line, haiku-like poem in the already rich context of this poem.

> But my true bud of gilt and purple ebony
> Laughed back to her at once
> So flashingly as to discover
> Those childish teeth that shame
> The radiant paper of my poem:
> "A bell spoke in a temple yard,
> A pendant tinkled in the breeze,
> And a convolvulus bloom fell over."
> Then laughter shook her little breasts
> As young oranges are swayed in the typhoon.

Other similar poems are "Serenade," "The Willow," and "The Pawlonia" (a Japanese tree).

Vines's second book, *Triforium* (1928), was somewhat more indulgent to the igorance of his readers and provided them with a gloss for part of *The Pyramid* as well as some of its own poems. The poems are in the same style as those in the earlier volume, and many use Japanese materials or situations. One of these is "The Eastern Merchant's Invitation" to a friend after he has seen a vision of his death—he refuses to die without one last good time with his concubines. Another poem is "The Emblem," whose subtitle, *Specification for a Japanese Print*, would suggest exoticism, were it not that the subject it proposes is one of industrial and commercial bustle.

One of the most interesting pieces in the volume is one which might have been called "Meditation on a Poem by Bashō" but which is not called anything; instead of a title, Vines prefixed the Japanese poem—

> Atsuki hi wo
> Umi ni iretari
> Mogamigawa—

which may be translated—

> *Having thrust the sun,*
> *Flaming into the sea,*
> *The Mogami surges on.*

Vines makes the sun into the male principle and likens it to Adonis who is periodically slain to revive again reinvigorated, and the sea into the female principle which slays the sun in the sexual act—and so far we seem to have a kind of Japanese Wastelandish technique; but the Mogami is also the type of all such rivers as the Tagus, so there are traces of Pound's technique of the unifying image as well. The poem comes to a climax describing the act of union in which the sun dies and the Mogami is treated like a Japanese woman.

> River, river, loose your girdle . . .
> Turn back to the blue forest shadow
> From this too brilliant confusion of substance,
> Concept intolerable to the sense,
> The deathless carcase of the sun
> Washed hissing down to sea.

"Élan Mortel" is cut from the same neo-Metaphysical cloth and has the added interest of being perhaps unique among poems written by Englishmen since Kipling in its attempt to bring East and West together, although Vines's avowed purpose is to express "an attitude of heroic materialism" and a "defence of humanism." Part I employs a serpent symbolism to represent the religious aspects of life—according to the Hindu belief that the spine is a serpent and the seat of the soul, and of the emotional side of life—in accordance with the phallic serpent emblems to be found at some Japanese shrines. Part II employs the familiar metaphors representing the East as the feminine and the West as the masculine principle who join in physical-cultural union. "My sister East, / That lemon-tinted Venus" is also basically passive —"Postured to yield to the embrace / Of cool negation on both sides of death"—and so teaches a kind of heroic resignation to the Western, unreligious, materialistic man:

how "To greet as a recovered friend / The naught that crowns the end"—or death.

Vines has a genuine, if not too original or strong poetic voice which is worthy of wider acquaintance. His personal style is shaped in large measure by such greater moderns as Eliot, Yeats, and Pound, but with his knowledge of the East he was able to make something new and fresh out of a neo-Metaphysical style which sometimes seems only parroted by our lesser poets. Better than Fenollosa or Amy Lowell, and like Pound, he was able to discover imagistic symbols or metaphors and a poetic style.

The *Collected Poems* (1949) of William Empson give evidence of his periods of teaching in the Orient. Three poems are called "translations" of poems by a Miss Hatakeyama—"The Fool," "The Shadow," and "The Small Bird to the Big." He states in a note that his "part was only to polish up her own English version." No doubt this may be so, but if so, they have both been inspired by the same Muse, who is not named Simplicity. "Aubade," however, is wholly his own and describes with delightful irony what seems to be a first experience of a Japanese earthquake—like most visitors to Japan he finds the first shock amusing, the later ones grim business. In bed with a married Japanese woman, the speaker of the poem is handicapped as much by his lack of experience with earthquakes as with the language, and both heighten the complexities of their delicate situation.

> It seemed quite safe till she got up and dressed.
> The guarded tourist makes the guide the test.

Then I said The Garden? Laughing she said No.
Taxi for her and for me healthy rest.
It seemed the best thing to be up and go.

The language problem but you have to try.
Some solid ground for lying could she show?
The heart of standing is you cannot fly.

None of these deaths were her point at all.
The thing was that being woken he would bawl
And finding her in earshot he would know.
I tried saying Half an Hour to pay this call.
It seemed the best thing to be up and go.

The verbal ambiguities multiply as the lines are repeated, but the attempt to assess his experience leads him to feel that the loss—"to be up and go" "after . . . one kiss" —teaches him that action is worthwhile even when it thwarts one's purposes. The concern with death which is one object of the humor and seriousness of "Aubade" is treated as the chief subject but not in the same tone in "Ignorance of Death." Buddhist, Christian, and Communist points of view are compared, but he remains skeptical that anyone knows very much about the topic: "It is one that most people should be prepared to be blank on."

After leaving Japan, his next sight of the Japanese came under the peculiar circumstances of riding southward through Manchuria on a Japanese train in 1937, after the war with China had begun, and while en route to a teaching position in China. The experience is treated in "The Beautiful Train," where "I a twister love what I abhor."

He was happy, and surprised to be happy, among the Japanese who had invaded China. "China" is a poem about the two nations caught in the Sino-Japanese wars of the 'Thirties and too complex to quote in bits, but the central idea is the familiar one that the Chinese culture "hatched" the Japanese, and that therefore China has nothing to fear from any invading force—China had absorbed so many other ideologies. These ideas, held so fatuously by us, have since been disproved by the conquest of China by a new ideology, and a note says Empson has changed his mind about Chinese history along with the rest of us.

Pound was not the first poet to discover Japan in this century and Empson has not been the last to treat it in his poetry, but the change in the poetic approach to Japan seems to represent the changing poetic function of Japanese culture in this period. For Pound and the Imagists, Japan has been an exciting source of new forms and techniques; for Plomer and Empson, Japan has been just another source of experience to be assessed, and whatever is special about Japan can be treated in techniques which are wholly of Western origin. At least this seems to be the change, but it may also be that the distinction to be made is really one of the poet's nationality. An Empson is really little different from a Kipling in his attempts to fit his Japanese experiences into a world-view and literary forms which he possessed before he went to Japan. A Pound, on the other hand, has been more concerned with the American idea of a union of cultures which might be expressed in forms borrowed from Japan. Whether the distinction is to be made, then, in terms of nationality or of historical development remains in doubt. Vines may be the typical poet of the future in his response to Japan—Japan has meant for him new subject matter, an enlarged imaginative response to experience and, if not new forms, new images and metaphors. He seems at once English and American, a Pound and an Empson in his approach. But even in the poetry of Vines, the tendency toward realism is discernible. Japan no longer seems the exciting discovery it was a half-century ago: two world wars, improved transportation and communication, and a steadily growing familiarity with the country and its language have changed the temper of our response. Exoticism has all but died, lamented by no one, but with it the wonders of discovery seem to have perished as well. The new realism in the treatment of Japan is doubtless a good thing for our poets and for the Japanese too, but the tameness and diminution of heart which realism always seems to bring is surely a loss. The loss is perhaps the price of a poetic coming-of-age.

VII. KABUKI AND NŌ AS DRAMATIC
CRITERIA

"The most interesting link of the Japanese theater is, of course, its link with the sound film, which can and must learn its fundamentals from the Japanese."—S. M. EISENSTEIN, *Film Form*

IF THE EXCITEMENT of rich, new discovery is no longer possible for the poetic response to Japan, the various forms of the Japanese drama have, in recent years, afforded something of a recompense. Relatively unknown until recent times, kabuki and nō and even the Japanese film seem suddenly to have become a source of fertile inspiration for writers and producers. This has not always been so. In the past, the best plays using Japan as a subject achieved their quality either, like *Madame Butterfly*, by avoiding for the most part the stock stage conceptions of Japan, or, like *The Mikado*, by transcending them. But these triumphs were basically fortuitous, and Japan could not affect our drama in any significant way until it was used as Japanese poetry had been used—as a source for form and technique.

i. Early Interest in the Japanese Theatre

The first discussion of Japanese theatre in English, outside of the travel books mentioned in the second

chapter, appeared as early as October, 1876, when Basil
Hall Chamberlain published his translation of a nō play
with some introductory remarks in the *Cornhill Magazine*. Many articles appeared in the decades which followed, a few suggesting that the Japanese stage was
just emerging from barbarism, but most full of praise
for the spectacle, beauty, and skill of the Japanese theatre.
Besides the intrinsic interest which this newly discovered
stage had for the West, there was also the compulsion,
exemplified by Kipling, to verify the portraits of actors
in the block prints by comparison with the figures on
the stage. The new understanding had somehow to grow
out of seeing the drama in terms of the print, and the
change was slow.

Just how slowly the change occurred can be judged
by the most sensitive response to the visit of a kabuki
company to the Criterion Theatre in Piccadilly Circus
in 1901. Max Beerbohm reviewed the event for the (English) *Saturday Review* (June 22, 1901) in an unaccus-
tomed vein of public seriousness. The title is exotic—
"Almond Blossom in Piccadilly Circus"—but his serious
purpose is soon heard. He feels it appropriate that the
Japanese actors came "to the very centre of our vulgarity"
—Piccadilly. "For have not we," he asks, "in our greedy
occidental way, made a very great point of vulgarising
down to our own level the notion of Japan? The im-
portation of a few fans and umbrellas set us all agog. . . .
In the fulness of our national pride, we had believed that
the old Japan was no more. We had flattered ourselves
that the Japanese were now as vulgar and occidental as
we. And yet here, classic and unperturbed, untouched

by time or us, these players stand before us, as though incarnate from the conventions of Utamaro and Hokusai." The tone is rare for "Max" the satirist, and for an Englishman, now doing public penance for a period of misunderstanding of Japan. But even here, the climax comes with the invocation of the block-print artists, and the understanding of Japanese drama is limited by the *visual* criteria established by the Impressionist interpretation of Japan. The Japanese drama was not yet to be seen as drama.

ii. The Use of Kabuki by Western Dramatists and Critics

The proper appreciation of kabuki in England and America has begun only since the Second World War, and even now it cannot be said that this splendid and spectacular drama has made more than a beginning in affecting the techniques and productions of our plays. The obstacle in the path of understanding and use of kabuki has been the lack of translations and, more seriously, the fact that so few Westerners have seen kabuki performed.

The difficulties inherent in adapting kabuki seriously to our stage when so little has been known about it can be best understood by careful study of John Masefield's play, *The Faithful* (1915). The story is the familiar Japanese tale of the forty-seven samurai who, after years of persecution, avenged their master's unjust disgrace and death by assassinating his accuser, only to be ordered to death by ritual suicide for their act. This story became popular in England and America after the heroism displayed by the Japanese in the Russo-Japanese War had attracted general attention. E. V. Gatenby has written that he had a letter from Masefield telling him that he had used four kinds of sources for his play—a series of prints, Mitford's *Tales of Old Japan*, two translations of the *Chūshingura* (the kabuki version of the story), and information supplied him by Japanese students in London. The poet laureate has also said that the account of the Garter Mission to Japan first drew his attention to the Japanese story.

These sources make it amply clear that Masefield's use of Japan was very much the same as Shakespeare's use of Italy—for an image or atmosphere, and for plot. There can be no quarrel with this search for dramatic materials, but the point holds that kabuki is not being used as kabuki, but as story-matter. This is made clear by the Preface in *The Poems and Plays of John Masefield* (1918), where he writes, "I had known the story of The Ronin for many years, and had long hoped to make a play of it, *but could not see a dramatic form for it.*" The italicized phrase states the problem exactly. Without an intimate knowledge of the kabuki version of the story as theatre, how was he to use his materials as drama? His talk with Japanese students might have been of some help, but when he consulted the series of block prints, he could learn little more than the costumes which were worn. He finally found his dramatic form, of course, but it was from Granville-Barker's Shakespearean productions "with 'continuous performance' for a double platform stage."

The play is basically Japanese in subject, and neo-Elizabethan in form, with a few Japanese overtones. The Japanese atmosphere is given some substance by the quality of the several interspersed poems in the play. Masefield is obviously aware of the Japanese use of natural imagery to convey human feelings, and so the poem written by the lord of the samurai just before his death is very like many of the Imagists' "Japanese" poems.

> Sometimes, in wintry springs,
> Frost, on a midnight breath,
> Comes to the cherry flowers
> And blasts their prime;
> So I, with all my powers
> Unused on men or things,
> Go down the wind to death,
> And know no fruiting-time.

And the last poem of the play, the death-poem of the faithful samurai, is composed in the syllabic fives and sevens of Japanese poetry with which Amy Lowell had experimented.

> That long-dead heroes
> Manning the ramparts of God
> May hear us coming,
> Baring our hearts to the sword
> For him we loved so.

The Japanese element in *The Faithful* is of considerable proportion, as the plot, characterizations, and intermittent poems show, but in spite of the fact that the play is based to a large extent on two translations of the kabuki version, kabuki has had no influence as drama.

There are some stirrings today which seem to indicate a truly dramatic interest in kabuki, however. Many Americans and Englishmen have seen kabuki performed in the postwar years of military occupation, and the Adzuma company of quasi-Kabuki performers has successfully toured the United States and Europe upon two occasions. The new familiarity has bred a new interest. The American producer Joshua Logan has visited Japan, and the press reports his plans to use many aspects of kabuki in his own productions. Such a knowledgeable interest in the Japanese stage and the numerous studies of the Japanese drama by writers with a knowledge of Japanese may well hasten the day, if it is to come, when the Japanese popular stage will become the world of our players.

iii. Kabuki and the Film

It seems true that there is no literary medium as international in its adaptability as the motion picture. The conventions of the film can easily be separated from the literary element of dialogue which must perforce be conveyed through language, and what is theatrically effective in one country may be readily adapted to another. This unique characteristic of the film as a medium has made it possible for Japan to have a roundabout effect on our film industry by the great importance it had in developing the film theory of Sergei M. Eisenstein. Eisenstein was preceded by Vsevold Meyerhold in recognizing the potentialities of Japanese drama and culture for the film, but Eisenstein went further, was a greater theorist, and his influence has spread wider. He plays much the same role in introducing Japan to the film as the Impressionists played in bringing Japanese art into English literature.

Eisenstein studied Japanese at the University of Moscow after the First World War and progressed far enough in his study to be able to manage some three hundred of the Sino-Japanese characters. His knowledge of Japan did not become artistically meaningful, however, until he began to consider the theoretical basis of the film as an art form and to seek film techniques in various phases of Japanese culture. The meaning of Japan in the formation of his art is most fully expressed in two essays, "The Unexpected" and "The Cinematographic Principle and the Ideogram," which have been translated and republished by Jay Leyda in *Film Form* (1949). These essays are not only of great interest for such a comparative study as this, but also offer some of the most illuminating insights of any Western writer into the kabuki theatre as theatre.

Eisenstein begins by stressing the way in which the song-dance-drama (the literal translation of *ka-bu-ki*) function as a single "monistic ensemble": "Sound-movement-space-voice here *do not accompany* (nor even parallel) each other, but function *as elements of equal significance.*" This perception is based upon the performances of kabuki which he had seen when Ichikawa Sadanji and his company visited Russia in 1928. He had also observed that the kabuki actor addresses himself "to a grand *total* provocation of the human brain," easily "transferring" his appeal from one sense to another or from "one category of 'provocation' [of the senses] to another." To illustrate this, he describes a performance of kabuki he had witnessed where an actor played a warrior leaving a castle. The actor began by moving from the depths of the stage to the front; then the background screen with the castle gate in "natural dimensions (close-up) [was] folded away"; it was replaced with a second screen "with a tiny gate painted on it (long shot)"; a curtain was drawn to indicate that the actor passed out of sight of the castle; the actor came onto the stage-ramp extending among the audience; "this further removal [was] emphasized . . . by the samisen, that is, by sound!!" He discovers in this succession four removals in stage technique —spatial in the steps of the actor, artistic in the changing background, an intellectual removal suggested by the effacing curtain, and synesthetic through music. This is a lesson, Eisenstein declares, for the film, a "contrapuntal method of combining visual and aural images" which leads to a new artistic sense—"*the capacity for reducing visual and aural perceptions to a 'common denominator'* " —and "this," he adds, "is possessed by kabuki to perfection." For Eisenstein, kabuki offered a kind of Wagnerian synthesis of the arts which linked it with the film: the sound film "can and must learn its fundamentals from the Japanese."

Many of his suppositions in "The Cinematographic Principle and the Ideogram" are extraordinarily close to Ezra Pound's. He shares Pound's misconception of the written character as an ideogram and, like Pound, goes on to derive fruitful techniques from the misconception. The "ideogram" is for him a depictive-intellectual sign, strongly recalling Pound's definition of the image as "an intellectual and emotional complex." And he treats the written character as Pound treats the image, as a vehicle for condensation and direct presentation of meaning; it is the key to "a cinema seeking a maximum laconism for the visual representation of abstract concepts." The "ideographic" method is, moreover, like the one-image poem Pound postulated on the basis of nō, a coherent for many diverse materials. As he says of the marionette theatre from which kabuki grew, "The most important fact is that into the technique of acting itself the ideographic (montage) method has been wedged in the most interesting ways." With Pound and Eisenstein alike, the written character provides a means of giving intellectual and emotional coherence to the diverse elements of their art.

Kabuki taught Eisenstein many of the techniques, or supplied a theoretical basis for many of the techniques, which anyone who has seen his pictures will recall. He calls them the "cut," "disintegration," "slow-motion," and the "super-close-up." The "cut" is non-realistic type of "acting without transitions"—fear may change to hope by flashing from one actor's face to another's, rather than by picturing one face in change. The death agony of a character in *Yashaō* showed him how an actor might have various members of his body "act" non-realistically in sequence and suggested film-disintegration by "a breaking-up" into separate shots of different parts of the body of an actor. And the stylized kabuki acting of suicide in *Chūshingura* pictured for him a kind of disintegration in time—a kind of slow motion which was not naturalistic but which nonetheless would succeed in film. For the super-close-up, he turns to the Japanese prints with their "monstrous disproportion of a normally flowing event." He asks, "Haven't Japanese prints used *super-close-up* foregrounds and effectively disproportionate features in *super-close-up* faces?"

It is difficult in this day of color, wide screens, and "3-D," to recall the excitement which accompanied the invention of the sound film. Eisenstein was one of those who hoped to make it into the great art form of all time, and while this hope cannot be said to have been realized, his own films are indeed recognized as classics in their art. The importance of Japan to his theory can be seen in the fact that each of the techniques he discusses in these essays is either borrowed from Japanese drama or culture, or is analyzed and justified esthetically in Japanese terms. To the extent that Eisenstein has shaped the theory and practice of the film as an artistic medium, Japan has played an important role in the formation of the theory and technique of yet another artistic medium.

Kabuki has played a second, indirect role in shaping film practice in recent years. The Japanese historical films which startled Europe and the United States as *Rashōmon* won prize after prize in the early 'Fifties borrowed many of their techniques from kabuki. These influential films have of course had their effect largely as films, but the stylized acting, pageantry, and visual effect have been modeled to a considerable degree upon the native tradition of kabuki. The discovery of the Japanese film is still new, however, and the degree of its influence is still difficult to judge today. Moreover, the whole problem of cross-cultural fertilization is a tremendous problem in these days of easy communication. When one realizes that the film was developed as a medium in the United States; that Eisenstein borrowed many techniques and based many theories upon kabuki, upon a misconception of the written character, and upon other aspects of Japanese culture; that Japanese directors have studied Eisenstein, kabuki, and Western directors; and that Western directors have studied Eisenstein and the Japanese film—one can only conclude that Kipling's East and West have more than met: they have intermingled in the fruitful confusion of the film.

iv. The Importance of Nō for Western Drama and Criticism

Until recently, kabuki has had only Eisenstein for an expounder, or at least he was the only one to draw dramatic criteria from it. Nō has fared better, principally we may suppose, because it has found adequate translators and more enthusiastic advocates, because it is more literary, and because its techniques have seemed more adaptable to the Western stage. Nō has been most important for its effect upon Ezra Pound's theory and writing and in shaping the plays and poems of W. B. Yeats; but there are other writers, chiefly playwrights and critics, who have come under the influence of Pound and Yeats, and who have found nō useful in establishing dramatic criteria for the European and American stage.

Next to haiku, nō has excited the greatest interest of any of the Japanese literary forms—paradoxically perhaps, since it is probably the most complex of the many difficult Japanese genres. From Chamberlain's article in

1876 to the present day, a steady succession of articles and books concerning nō has appeared before the public. In part this appeal has been exotic, in part a taste for an "aristocratic" form which is perhaps snobbish, but in part the appeal has been the genuine one of a rich, poetic drama to a culture which believes its finest artistic accomplishment to be the poetic drama of Shakespeare.

In his *World Drama* (1949), Allardyce Nicoll has referred to one group of playwrights that sought the techniques of nō to help create a new poetic drama. Yeats stimulated both Gordon Bottomley and Laurence Binyon to try plays in the style of nō, "with the ultimate result that both Bottomley and Laurence Binyon began, about the year 1927, to experiment in the writing of Japanese-inspired plays for John Masefield's garden theatre."

The three volumes of Bottomley's plays which most clearly show the results of his interest in nō are *Scenes and Plays* (1929), *Lyric Plays* (1932), and *Choric Plays* (1939). Since these volumes represent the bulk of his mature dramatic writing, the Japanese element in his work is of great importance. In a Note to *Scenes and Plays*, he says that his reason for borrowing from nō is that "in the aristocratic Nō drama . . . poetry and the dance and music have achieved a novel balance of expression and delicacy of effect." He adds that W. B. Yeats "has been the first user of our tongue to seek in an acclimatisation of this foreign form an escape from the difficulties with which the alienation of the modern theatre has confronted the dramatic poet." The elements which he adapted from nō are largely those techniques of Yeats which he found most useful for himself: a stage stripped of all but essentials, stylized action, "the paramount importance of perfect costume," the "advantage of masks for certain parts," the "importance of separate dancing," "harmonious movement that issues from poetry and accompanies it," musical accompaniment, and the technique of beginning and ending a play with the folding and unfolding of a curtain. Yeats was obviously playing the same proselytizing role as Pound in his efforts to get contemporary writers to adopt the techniques he had discovered from Japanese literature. Bottomley did not employ all of Yeats's techniques in any single play, but he experimented with each of them at one time or another. The result of his work is a kind of symbolist melodrama which seems curiously dated today, but *Kirkonnel Lea* and *Fire at Callart* have many fine passages.

Bottomley's friend, Laurence Binyon, and Yeats's friend, Thomas Sturge Moore, were also induced to write plays modeled after nō. But there is little in Binyon's dramatic work which might not have come from sources other than Japan, and that little appears to come from Bottomley from Yeats from Fenollosa-Pound. As a result, the most important evidence of his response to Japan is to be found in the poetry discussed in the preceding chapter. T. Sturge Moore was closely associated with Yeats both in friendship and art—Moore designed covers for several of Yeats's books—so it was probably inevitable that he should try to emulate his friend's success in creating what each of them called his "Noh plays." Moore says almost as much in a note at the end of his introduction to *Medea*, his finest play, collected in *Tragic Mothers* (1920). "My friend Mr. W. B. Yeats asked me to try my hand," he says—and that was it. But Moore was no dramatist, and a remark by his biographer, Frederick L. Gwynn, about another play pretty well characterizes them all—"a wordy Noh play."

The plays of these English writers fail primarily because they lack dramatic and poetic quality. But Bottomley, Binyon, and Moore also seem to have sought out the techniques of nō for no real reason of dramatic or personal necessity, as Yeats had. They tried to establish a poetic drama for its own sake and dipped into nō merely because all other springs had run dry. The situation in the United States was somewhat similar. S. Foster Damon, Amy Lowell's biographer, tried his hand at "A Noh Drama in Japanese Syllabics," *Kiri no Meijiyama*, for the *Dial* in February, 1920. The "Japanese Syllabics" are the fives and sevens which Masefield had employed, and while the play has some interest in showing what might be done in the style of nō with a Japanese legend— apparently "Rokurokubi" from Hearn's *Kwaidan*—the result is more a curiosity of the study than a play for the stage.

Part of the attraction of Japanese poetry for the Imagists was the way in which it gave them fresh literary conventions and poetic criteria. Nō was made to serve much the same function in the criticism of an important critic of the 'Twenties, Stark Young. *The Flower in Drama* (1925) takes various things which had been said about the nō by Arthur Waley, Pound, and Yeats and tries to give them some coherent form by which to judge American drama and acting. The title is inspired by Waley's translation of parts of the then newly discovered *Kadenshō*

("Book of the Handing on of the Flower") by Seami
Motokiyo (1333-1384), the Sophocles of the nō. The term
"flower" (hana) may be translated into less metaphorical
language as "vital perfection of beauty," or more simply,
"sublimity." Young is particularly concerned to depreciate
realism in the theatre, especially the vogue of Naturalistic
acting, and uses Seami's doctrines in his essays "The
Flower," "The Prompt Book," and an open "Letter to
Duse" to advocate a liberated, more expressive style of
acting.

Young was most concerned with using the nō and its
critical theory to advocate a new style of acting and production, but there have been writers since him who have
tried in various ways, to varying degrees, and with varying success to adapt the techniques of nō to stage forms
which were already in existence. Paul Claudel, who was
in Japan with the French diplomatic service, used such
techniques in his marionette plays, and Berthold Brecht has
attempted in several plays—most notably his didactic
Lehrstücke, Der Jasager and *Der Neinsager*—to adapt
the stylized forms and philosophical content of nō to the
Expressionistic stage. The most successful American
playwright to use nō techniques has undoubtedly been
Thornton Wilder, whose *Our Town* is in part indebted
to nō for its bare stage technique and whose one-act
plays often have a stage-manager who speaks the thoughts
of the characters like the chorus in the nō. He has generously acknowledged his "deep interest" in nō, but
feels that the "major influence" upon the "bare stage"
technique was "the theatre of Elizabeth and Philip II
and III." However, he added in his letter, that "In my

next play I hope to borrow from Noh the device of the 'ideal spectator' which I read about in Paul Claudel's essay on the Noh." The reference is to the waki, or second character in nō, who usually sets the play in motion and who often assists the sh'te, or first character, in the development of the action toward a moment of "enlightenment" or revelation. Such a development of a nō technique as Wilder envisions seems best calculated to succeed. The efforts of so many other writers to adapt Japanese forms in an unquestioned entirety can lead only to confusion or a dramatic form which can have wide appeal only if the writer possesses unusual dramatic powers.

Another American writer, Paul Goodman, has written five plays modeled on the nō and published them together as *Stop-light, 5 dance poems* (1941) with "an essay on the Noh." He feels that nō is a "Drama of Awareness," and that while "the working out of will" characterizes Western drama, "the movement of noh is rather [toward] enlightenment." It is this movement toward enlightenment—of a Platonic, not Buddhist cast—the stylized dance, and rich poetic texture which he attempts to naturalize in his plays. The plays are interesting, both for the attempt and in themselves, but by adding the complexities of unfamiliar dramatic conventions to Surrealist drama, he has very nearly made the plays impossible to understand. They can be understood by being read, but the issues are not fully developed in dramatic terms.

The difficulty in generalizing about the effects of ka-

buki and nō upon our drama lies chiefly in the fact that
these dramatic forms have only recently come to be used
by writers of ability. Unlike the poetic response to Japan,
the mature dramatic response has only begun. But some
of the motivations behind those of our dramatists and
film directors who have made use of Japanese dramatic
media in one way or another can be understood. The
most significant motive has been the one which has all
along proved to be the most fruitful for our writers—
the urge to borrow technique and form—whether it is
from haiku or nō, and whether it is for film or poem.
But there has also been the perennial urge in all English playwrights to emulate Shakespeare and the Elizabethans. For the first half of this century as well as for the
eighteenth and nineteenth centuries, the most obvious
way to vie with the great Elizabethan and Jacobean
dramatists seemed competition in the realm of poetic
drama, and sometimes in such techniques as the platform
stage. Christopher Fry and T. S. Eliot are perhaps examples, where some of the writers treated in this chapter
are only symptoms, of this persistent motive. There has
also been a revolt from the Realistic and Naturalistic
literature of the twentieth century which has led some
critics and writers to seek new techniques of more imaginative expression—sometimes in native European symbolism, and sometimes in the Japanese nō. But the problem
of rising above the level of Naturalistic prose, plots,
themes, and conventions into an imaginative world of
poetic drama is an all but insoluble one for a playwright
who stands in the overpowering shadow of Shakespeare.
Only a writer of great poetic abilities can free himself

from the disastrous lure of imitating Shakespeare's style, and only a writer with great dramatic skill is able to fashion a new theatre out of the Elizabethan ruins. Drama is so restricted a vehicle of the poet's own thoughts that for a new poetic drama to emerge, writers must have a sensibility closely akin to that of their age, a vigorous poetic style, and a strong dramatic sense. Dryden and his age almost succeeded, and so did W. B. Yeats.

VIII. "AN ARISTOCRATIC FORM": JAPAN IN THE THOUGHT AND WRITING OF WILLIAM BUTLER YEATS

"In fact with the help of those ['Noh Plays'] . . . I have invented a form of drama, distinguished, indirect, and symbolic, and having no need of mob or press to pay its way— an aristocratic form."—W. B. YEATS on his Dance-Plays

THE "bitter furies of complexity" which haunt the poetry and thought of Ezra Pound and W. B. Yeats have often kept their detractors at a hostile distance. But they have also harried those of their admirers who seek to understand and to accept the ideas of these poets. But difficult to understand—and sometimes to accept—as their ideas are, few people today dispute the common judgment that Yeats is the greatest poet of his generation and that Pound was somehow instrumental in his accomplishment. Pound's role in effecting the much-prized change which took place in Yeats's style just before the First World War has been frequently discussed, and perhaps exaggerated, but there can be no doubt that he was instrumental in exciting Yeats to a lively interest in Japan. Once Yeats's imagination had been kindled by Pound, he began to study Japanese culture with interests often similar to Pound's, but often very different. For Yeats,

Japan was most important for its relationship to other elements in his thought, for its role in his poetic development, and for the way in which it shaped his writings.

i. The Place of Japan in Yeats's Thought and Development

There are many important subjects in Yeats's thought and development which have little or no relationship to Japan—his personality and experience, Anglo-Irish politics, his discovery of a mystical metaphysics, French poetry—and most of them are of greater significance than Japan in their effect upon his ideas. As with so many poets, Yeats found Japan more significant for the literary forms which it had to offer than for ideas which it presented to a writer who was not intimately acquainted with its culture. As a result, it seems most prudent to examine the course of his literary development with a hope of discovering those points at which Japan touched his thought and his practice, rather than to attempt a systematic review of his ideas.

The logic of Yeats's poetic development seems to be his involvement in the particular literary and artistic movement which was at each point in his career the most important movement of its time in leading to the modes and idiom of modern poetry. Pound's style took a new direction with his discovery of Impressionism but, although this movement cannot be entirely ruled out for Yeats, it seems more accurate to say that his development was parallel to the course which led from post-Impressionism to Imagism and the modern style. He fixes his debts clearly in his *Autobiography* (1938) when he writes of the Rhymers Club of the middle 'Nineties: "If Rossetti was a subconscious influence, and perhaps the most powerful of all, we looked consciously to Pater for our philosophy. Three or four years ago I re-read *Marius the Epicurean*, expecting to find that I cared for it no longer, but it still seemed to me . . . the only great prose in modern English, and yet I began to wonder if it, or the attitude of mind of which it was the noblest expression, had not caused the disaster of my friends." Pater and Rossetti made up that part of the advance-guard which expressed many of the ideas and attitudes of such Francophiles as Whistler and Wilde in the more traditional and conventional literary forms. Pater seems to have been partially distorted by such poets as Lionel Johnson and Francis Thompson into a cult of rare and romantic experience for its own sake. Rossetti had been a friend of Whistler and had been introduced to Japan by him, but his part in the Aesthetic movement seems to have been an advocacy of the Keatsian medievalism which was satirized by Gilbert along with the taste for "all one sees / That's Japanese." The Rhymers Club moved and wrote in a twilight world, then, whether the twilight of the Romantic and Victorian ages, the Celtic twilight, or the shadowed, decadent experiences only softly lit by the gem-like flame of Pater. But this twilight was in fact difficult to distinguish from the first gray light of the dawn of a new poetic era. The "disaster" of Yeats's friends—he has Johnson and Thompson chiefly in mind—was that, unlike him, they could not or would not sense what was truly new and vital and adapt their poetry to it.

The early poetry of Yeats was Aesthetic in an ambiguous sense—it seemed headed either for the preciosity of the *fin de siècle* or the emotionalism coupled with objectivity characteristic of Impressionism. But at this moment, a new influence entered his life:

"Gradually Arthur Symons came to replace in my intimate friendship, Lionel Johnson. . . .

"When with Johnson I had tuned myself to his mood, but Arthur Symons, more than any man I have ever known, could slip as it were into the mind of another, and my thoughts gained in richness and in clearness from his sympathy, nor shall I ever know how much my practice and my theory owe to the passages that he read me from Catullus and from Verlaine and Mallarmé."

He had made the slight but saving shift of allegiance from the increasingly sterile refinement of English Aestheticism to the stimulating ideas of the French poets. Since Symons reiterated Jules de Goncourt's idea that "the triumph of *Japonisme*" was one of the three most important literary and artistic movements of the second half of the nineteenth century, it is possible that he introduced Yeats to Japan. Yeats wrote in his introduction to *Certain Noble Plays of Japan* (1916) of his "memory of theatrical colour-prints" which he had seen some years before in the British Museum; and if he had been encouraged to look at them before the War, it must have been under Symons' urging. But this is very suppositious, and it seems more likely that the Impressionist admiration for the prints was assimilated by Symons to the extent that what had been Impressionism in Wilde became Symbolism for Yeats.

Yeats's thought during these years is not, however, left to mere supposition. In addition to his *Autobiography*, there is W. T. Horton's volume of etchings, *A Book of Images . . . Introduced by W. B. Yeats* (1898). His main concern in this introductory essay, which follows closely upon his developed friendship with Symons, is to define Symbolism. As one might expect of him, he distinguishes between allegory and symbol, heaping ridicule upon allegory and praising the great symbolists in art and literature. It is exceedingly interesting to examine the best known among his choice group of those who, as he says, "accepted all symbolisms." Keats, Blake, Rossetti (in his pictures), Beardsley, Whistler, Maeterlinck, and Verlaine are the most important and are named in that order. The progress from Keats to Verlaine in poetry and from Blake to Whistler in art not only represents his personal development from Romanticism to Victorianism to Impressionism-Symbolism, but also parallels the development of modern poetry by the Imagist group. Where he differs from, say, Pound in his development is in the greater attachment which he had, as an older and more conservative person, to the native nineteenth-century tradition, and in the fact which is relevant for this study, that until he met Pound he scarcely associated "Whistler and the Japanese."

His inclusion of Whistler among the choice Symbolist spirits makes it necessary to see what Whistler must have meant to him. Most of Horton's etchings are very little like the symbolic drawings of Blake or the art of

Rossetti; they are in fact as much in the style of Whistler as anyone else. "Loneliness" is strongly like a Japanese print in subject and design, and "Nocturne" employs the terminology which Whistler made famous. There are also Impressionistic elements in some of Yeats's own writings. In *Discoveries* (1907), for example, three "essays" in particular stand out. "A Banjo Player" and "The Looking Glass" are two vignettes which seem almost like Lafcadio Hearn's in their style, and "Concerning Saints and Sinners" describes his hallucinations after taking "the India hemp." His mind functions, not like a medium's as he had expected, but according to the best Impressionist psychology—giving reality a subjective coloring—and according to the Whistlerian terminology of color harmonies: "I opened my eyes and looked at some red ornament on the mantelpiece, and at once the room was full of harmonies of red, but when a blue China figure caught my eye the harmonies became blue upon the instant." His concept of Symbolism was clearly influenced by the tradition from which Symbolism grew, Impressionism, and to the extent that Japan was one of the determinants of Impressionism and especially of the Impressionism of Whistler's variety, Yeats obviously absorbed Japan scarcely without knowing it. But in 1911 he fell ill and took on as a secretary his new friend, Ezra Pound, who shared a house with him in Sussex and soon introduced him to Fenollosa's discoveries of Japan. Yeats's interests now took new directions, and Japan changed from a slight, implicit element in his thought to an important and explicitly acknowledged determinant of his writings.

ii. The Effect of Japan upon Yeats's Criticism and Poetry

Mrs. Fenollosa gave her husband's manuscripts to Pound in 1912, and he shared his find with Yeats by reading his "translations" and talking over their significance for English poetry. By 1914, Yeats was modelling his own plays upon the nō, and it does seem wholly accidental that this is the period when his mature style began to take shape. It is necessary to stress the fact that his imitations of nō began at this early a point in his career, both because the discussion which follows deals with the most important work inspired by Japan—the plays—last, and because it is so generally assumed that the plays are little more than an outgrowth or appanage to the poems of *The Tower* and *The Winding Stair*. This is not the case: seven of his thirteen "Noh plays," as he called them, were published by 1926, while *The Tower* appeared in 1928. Far from being a poetic afterthought or a diversion from his true line of development, the plays are integral with his finest writing and helped to develop many of the techniques in the poetry. It makes better sense to say that the plays brought a dramatic intensity to his poetry than that the dramatic qualities of his poems overflowed onto the stage.

After a period of studying nō with Pound, references to Japan and its culture begin to appear casually, naturally one might say, in his writing. But not all of his allusions are related to nō; most perhaps are not, so the question arises where this other information came from. No sure answer can be given, but one or both of two explanations must be true. Either Yeats had been reading more about Japan before he met Pound than one assumes, or else Pound stimulated him to read a great deal about Japan in the years of the First World War when they spent lengthy periods of time together. At any event, Yeats seems to have acquired certain kinds of knowledge about Japan that Pound never had and to have created in his mind certain images of Japan which were different from Pound's.

The first and most trivial image of Japan to enter his nondramatic poetry is the image of Japan, the far-far-away country. While this image has persisted even to the present day, Yeats was the first major poet since the eighteenth century to use it, as he does, in the four most vapid lines of "In Memory of Alfred Pollexfen."

> But where is laid the sailor John
> That so many lands had known,
> Quiet lands or unquiet seas
> Where the Indians trade or the Japanese?

He even fell prey to something like the exotic image at times—and as late in his career as the publication of *The Winding Stair* (1933). "In Memory of Eva Gore-Booth and Con Markiewicz" presents "Japanese" women as an ideal of beauty which Kipling would have understood.

> The light of evening, Lissadell,
> Great windows open to the south,
> Two girls in silk kimonos, both
> Beautiful, one a gazelle.
> But a raving autumn shears
> Blossom from the summer's wreath.

The two girls are of course the two women of the poem in their youth, but they are "dressed up" by the Japanese attire, made into lovely flowers or animals so that they can be shown more susceptible to mortality. The autumn wind is a symbol of just such a sad and destructive force in Japanese poetry, although it is impossible to say with any assurance that Yeats had it in mind as a Japanese metaphor, since it is common enough to all literatures.

The setting of this poem, the house with its "great windows," however, suggests one of Yeats's most persistent images of Japan as an aristocratic culture. This image occurs over and over again in his writing, beginning with his comments on the nō: it expresses his persistent idea that a true state of culture is possible only in an aristocratic society in which social forms are cultivated and the arts are supported by "the lords and ladies of Byzantium," the Japanese, or similarly ordered hierarchical societies. He gives expression to this idea by using Japan as the standard of comparison in the part of his autobiography which deals with the period of his life from 1887 to 1891: "I thought to create that sensuous, musical vocabulary, and not for myself only, but that I might leave it to later Irish poets, much as a medieval Japanese painter left his style as an inheritance to his family, and I was careful to use a traditional manner and matter."

Or again, writing with enthusiasm of aristocracy in *The Bounty of Sweden* (1925), he declares that "the politic Tudor kings and the masterful descendants of Gustavus Vasa were as able as the American presidents, and better educated, and the artistic genius of old Japan continually renewed itself through dynasties of painters. The descendants of Kanoka [the Kanō were hereditary painters for the shogunate] made all that was greatest in the art of their country from the ninth to the eleventh century." His dates and facts are confused, but he continues to speak of Japanese art, and races on to three other Japanese "proofs" of the desirability of an aristocratic culture before reining in.

In addition to these images of Japan, there are also certain Japanese "images"—as he called his metaphors and visions—which entered into the pantheon of his mythology or became metaphors to heighten passages in his writing. Buddha is an antitype of the Sphinx in "The Double Vision of Michael Robartes,"—which so strongly foreshadows "The Second Coming,"—and in the late poem, "The Statues." A Japanese legend about painted horses coming to life gives him a striking close in his *Autobiography* to a survey of Chaucer, the Elizabethans, Tolstoy, Symons, and racial mythologies and also explains the power of images to move the human spirit: "Perhaps even these images, once created and associated with rivers and mountains, might move of themselves and with some powerful, even turbulent life, like those painted horses that trampled the rice-fields of Japan."

Sometimes, as in these lines from "On Woman," another Japanese legend seems to explain an obscure passage—

> But when, if the tale's true,
> The pestle of the moon
> That pounds up all anew
> Brings me to birth again.

His theory of the phases of the moon is clearly involved here, but the image—"that pounds up all anew"—seems best explained by the popular Japanese legend of the rabbit in the moon who pounds glutinous rice with a pestle for the festive dishes of New Year's Day and other occasions. With these last examples, we have really moved from his images of Japan to Japanese images in his poetry, a change from a more or less self-conscious use of Japanese images to a use of them as an integral part of his thought and writing. This is an important distinction, but it does not hold precisely, since the aristocratic image of Japan continues throughout his writing.

The extent to which Japanese images and the image of Japan merge in his poetry can be understood by a close look at the "Dialogue of Self and Soul." Once Yeats's interest in Japan had been aroused, he sought out the Japanese who were visiting London—and they sought him, since his early poetry was popular in Japan. One of the most significant of these Japanese acquaintances for his poetry was one who came to his hotel while Yeats was in New York. He was Satō Junzō, who belonged to an ancient and aristocratic family and who gave Yeats the sword which figures in several of the late poems, including the "Dialogue of Self and Soul." (Yeats had a clause in his will stipulating that the sword be returned to Satō's son, an official in the League of Nations.) This "Dialogue" is one of many poems in which the two sides of human personality are in conflict. The Soul is the abstract side of man and is symbolized by the tower, the winding stair, "the Babylonian starlight," and other images. The Self is symbolized by the body, the heart, violence, sexual activity, and other images. These two sides are at odds in poem after poem, with Yeats shifting his allegiance to now one and now the other. In the "Dialogue," the Self has almost the whole say and the poem ends with what is perhaps its greatest triumph in his poetry.

> When such as I cast out remorse
> So great a sweetness flows into the breast
> We must laugh and we must sing,
> We are blest by everything,
> Everything we look upon is blest.

Why, one asks, should the Self triumph here, when in such a poem as "Sailing to Byzantium" the Soul wins out? In each instance, Yeats seems to have given the victory to that side of his personality which, in the context of the individual poem, is most creative and artistic. In "Sailing to Byzantium," the Soul (the old man) looks to a country where all of nature is abstracted into art. But in "A Dialogue" the Soul is passive and sterile, and the Body is associated with art, and not just with art, but with traditional, aristocratic art, which is the point of Yeats's using the symbol of Satō's sword. The Self declares that the sword and the brocade in which it is wrapped (itself a symbol of love and "Heart's purple") are "emblems of the day against the tower":

> The consecrated blade upon my knees
> Is Sato's ancient blade, still as it was,
> Still razor-keen, still like a looking-glass
> Unspotted by the centuries;
> That flowering, silken, old embroidery, torn

From some court-lady's dress and round
The wooden scabbard bound and wound,
Can, tattered, still protect, faded adorn.

The Self has a similar triumph in "Symbols," where
the same metaphors are employed.

A storm-beaten old watch-tower,
A blind hermit rings the hour.

All-destroying sword-blade still
Carried by the wandering fool.

Gold-sewn silk on the sword-blade,
Beauty and fool together laid.

The triumph of the Self-Fool over the Soul-Hermit is not
overt here, but it is implicit in the granting of two thirds
of the poem to its metaphors—Satō's sword with its brocade wrapping: art, love, and violent activity.

Yeats's study of the nō led him to create techniques
modeled on this "aristocratic form" and was the most important single element in the development of his new drama. Some of these techniques, an increased dramatic intensity reflected in poems of dialogue, and the important
metaphor of the dance were carried over into the nondramatic poems of his mature period. "A Dialogue of
Self and Soul" possesses this dramatic intensity and also
begins with the technique he devised from the nō of a
summons or a calling-up in a kind of prologue which sets
the scene and introduces the characters to the audience
gazing at the bare stage. The Soul begins,

I summon to the winding ancient stair;
Set all your mind upon the steep ascent,
Upon the broken, crumbling battlement . . .
Fix every wandering thought upon
That quarter where all thought is done.

This is the same technique employed in the opening summons to the audience in the musicians' first song in *At
the Hawk's Well*, the first of the plays modeled upon
the nō.

I call to the eye of the mind
A well choked up and dry
And boughs long stripped by the wind,
And I call to the mind's eye
Pallor of an ivory face,
Its lofty dissolute air,
A man climbing up to a place
The salt sea wind has swept bare.

The dramatic form of the poem as much as the imagery, then, has been formulated unobtrusively but nonetheless significantly from the Japan which Yeats created
in his thought and poetry.

The symbol of the dance or the dancer is one of the
most pervasive and most important of the symbols in
Yeats's poetry, and another symbol which he developed
from his experience with nō. One of his problems in getting his dance-plays performed (and which led him ultimately to substitute patterned movement for the dance)
was finding someone who could dance convincingly and
movingly. The problem was solved temporarily when he

met Itō Michio, temporarily because Itō left for America after dancing a number of times in Yeats's plays. There is a story, perhaps apocryphal, of Itō's days spent at the London Zoo, imitating and stylizing the movements of birds for the dance of *At the Hawk's Well*. He swirled and gyrated before a crowd which thought him either mad or some Eastern bird-worshipper, while Yeats stood apart, deeply and solemnly engrossed in Itō's practice. Whether true or fanciful, the story is symptomatic of his interest in the dance and of his admiration for Itō. This same respect for Itō is implicit in a poem published two years after *The Hawk's Well*, "Upon a Dying Lady" (1919).

> Because to-day is some religious festival
> They had a priest say Mass, and even the Japanese,
> Heel up and weight on toe, must face the wall
> —Pedant in passion, learned in old courtesies,
> Vehement and witty she had seemed.

"The Japanese" is of course Itō whose stance is the stance of a Japanese dancer; and the point of introducing him into the poem at this point is that *even* he, a man of great dignity and presence (he overawed Pound), and who represented aristocracy and statuesque nobility to Yeats, turned away in emotion from the rites about the dying woman.

The artistic and aristocratic associations which Itō carried for Yeats and the attractiveness of the dance as an image which conveyed these qualities made it almost inevitable that he should employ it in his later poetry. The image recurs frequently—in "Byzantium" for example, where the dance symbolizes the way in which human passion and violence are transmuted into art.

> And all complexities of fury leave,
> Dying into a dance,
> An agony of trance,
> An agony of flame that cannot singe a sleeve.

But the most stirring use of the symbol of the dance is that at the end of "Among School Children," an extraordinarily rich and complex poem full of many antinomies—age and youth, man and woman, nuns and mothers, Plato and Aristotle, body and soul, and so on—which the poem, almost uniquely among such poems, unites. The symbol of the dance is only the last and most climactic of several in the poem which show that for at least this occasion Yeats has brought the rich oppositions by which he saw the world into a unified vision.

> Labour is blossoming or dancing where
> The body is not bruised to pleasure soul,
> Nor beauty borne out of its own despair,
> Nor blear-eyed wisdom out of midnight oil.
> O chestnut-tree, great-rooted blossomer,
> Are you the leaf, the blossom or the bole?
> O body swayed to music, O brightening glance,
> How can we know the dancer from the dance?

The chestnut-tree is a metaphor for many things in the poem, but especially for the three stages of human maturity treated in the poem and for the political significance it seems to have had for Yeats—taking us back to "Labour is blossoming" and the talk of Maud Gonne earlier; Lady Gregory quotes his remark in her *Journals* (1946) that "Berkeley was the first to say the world is a vision; Burke was the first to say a nation is a tree. And those two sayings are a foundation of modern thought."

This metaphor soon gives way, however, to the metaphor of the ecstatic dance in which the body and the soul are indistinguishable. In the rhythmical sway and abstract pattern of the dance, the dancer's passion is not lost as in the holy fires of Byzantium; the face brightens and Body and Soul have become one. This metaphor is an apt symbol in itself, but it becomes even more understandable when we remember that in Yeats's dance-plays as well as in the nō, the climax often resolves the contrary forces of the play in a dance to music while the chorus chants its final song.

These images of Japan, Japanese images, and techniques which Yeats derived from nō have little indebtedness to Pound other than Pound's sharing his discovery of nō and other Japanese literary forms he found in the manuscripts given him by Mrs. Fenollosa. But there are also those poems which show that Yeats borrowed more than an enthusiasm for Japanese culture from Pound. Several poems show that he too had heard about the "form of super-position." The technique appears in its simplest, visual form with the image set off at the end of "Veronica's Napkin."

> The Heavenly Circuit; Berenice's Hair;
> Tent-pole of Eden; the tent's drapery;
> Symbolical glory of the earth and air!

The Father and His angelic hierarchy
That made the magnitude and glory there
Stood in the circuit of a needle's eye.

Some found a different pole, and where it stood
A pattern on a napkin dipped in blood.

He employs the same technique in "The Nineteenth Century and After," where the image is one of the most powerful images of nineteenth-century poetry—the sound of the receding sea from which man is isolated.

Though the great song return no more
There's keen delight in what we have:
The rattle of pebbles on the shore
Under the receding wave.

Wordsworth's "mighty waters," Tennyson's sea, and Arnold's Dover Beach at ebb-tide echo here in a half-ironic "keen delight" and the technique Pound adapted from haiku.

The most important poem to use this technique is undoubtedly "Byzantium," with its image of the tortured sea used in super-pository fashion at the end of the poem.

Astraddle on the dolphin's mire and blood,
Spirit after spirit! The smithies break the flood,
The golden smithies of the Emperor!
Marbles of the dancing floor
Break bitter furies of complexity,
Those images that yet
Fresh images beget,
That dolphin-torn, that gong-tormented sea.

The final, super-posed image grows naturally out of the passage as a whole, but it had an especially vivid sensuous appeal for Yeats. The gong suggests the "smithies" who "break the flood," and by extension Cuchulain fighting the waves in *On Baile's Strand*. But the image of dolphin and gong is also sharply visual in origin; it puts into words the seal of the Cuala Press. This seal, printed on the title pages of books edited by Yeats and printed by his sister, shows a bell suspended over a sea in which a dolphin is cavorting. There was every reason for Yeats to set off an image of such meaning to him to give a climax to his poem.

It was to be expected that when a poet of the stature of Yeats borrowed from Pound, the results would be as much his own as Pound's, and this is true as much of poetic materials as of the form of super-position. Often the degree to which he reshaped these materials almost disguises their source, as in a late poem, "Imitated from the Japanese."

> A most astonishing thing—
> Seventy years have I lived;
>
> (Hurrah for the flowers of spring,
> For Spring is here again.)
>
> Seventy years have I lived
> No ragged beggar-man,
> Seventy years have I lived,
> Seventy years man and boy,
> And never danced for joy.

The title and the tone tell us that the source for this ironic poem is not Gilbert's

The flowers that bloom in the spring, tra la,
Bring promise of merry sunshine.

The Japanese which this poem imitates is a portion of the
Fenollosa-Pound translation of *Kakitusbata*, a nō play.
A famous poem by Ariwara no Narihira is woven into
the texture of the play in the typical fashion of nō and
becomes part of a speech by the Lady Iris who both
bemoans the joy that went out of her life with Narihira
and exults in the pride of her attachment to him. A more
faithful translation of the original makes it clear that
Yeats adheres more closely to Pound's loose translation
than to the Japanese.

> The spring
> Is not the spring of the old days,
> My body
> Is not my body,
> But only a body grown old.
> Narihira, Narihira,
> My glory comes not again.

> *Is there no moon?*
> *Can it be this spring is not the same*
> *As that remembered spring,*
> *While this alone, my mortal body,*
> *Remains as ever without change?*

iii. The Nō and Yeats's Plays

"Imitated from the Japanese" was published among
Last Poems, a volume covering the period from 1936 to

1939, after Yeats had known of the nō for some twenty-five years. He had written an essay, "Swedenborg, Mediums and the Desolate Places," dated October 14, 1914, as a long postscript to Lady Gregory's *Visions and Beliefs* (1920)—an essay which tells how he came to learn about nō. "Last winter Mr. Ezra Pound was editing the late Professor Ernest Fenollosa's translations of the Noh Drama of Japan, and read me a great deal of what he was doing." He had heard about the nō by the winter of 1913-1914; by October his study of Japanese drama leads him to annotate and illustrate with Japanese references what he says on such a topic as the visions and beliefs of the Irish peasantry. By March, 1916, he was using nō as a model for a new kind of drama. Pound wrote in March to Kate Buss that she would do well to wait if she was planning an article on "the new Theatre," since "Yeats is making a new start on the foundation of these Noh dramas." After Pound had published his translations of nō in 1916, Yeats got his permission to republish four of the plays—*Nishikigi, Hagoromo, Kumasaka*, and *Kagekiyo*—as *Certain Noble Plays of Japan* (1916). Yeats added a long introduction to this volume with the purpose in mind of showing what the nō had to offer as a literary form and a cultural standard.

He asked Pound for the plays, he says, "because I think they will help me explain a certain possibility of the Irish dramatic movement." Nō, he argues, should be the model for one part of the Irish drama, and he discusses a play which he has written in the new form, *At the Hawk's Well*. It is to be an inexpensively produced drama which can be performed in a drawing-room; it is to be stylized, and "the music, the beauty of the form and voice will all come to a climax in the pantomimic dance." He states his debt to the nō in the next few pages.

"In fact with the help of those plays . . . I have invented a form of drama, distinguished, indirect and symbolic . . . an aristocratic form. . . .

"Therefore it is natural that I go to Asia for a stage-convention, for a chorus that has no part in the action and perhaps for those movements of the body copied from the [Japanese] marionette shows of the fourteenth century."

He justifies his decision on broad historical and cultural grounds as well as on the immediate needs of the Irish theatre.

"Let us press the popular arts on to a more complete realism, for that would be their honesty; and the commercial arts demoralize by their compromise . . . their idealism without sincerity or elegance, their pretense that ignorance can understand beauty. . . . Europe is very old and has seen many arts run through the circle and has learned the fruit of every flower and known what this fruit sends up, and it is now time to copy the East and live deliberately.

"The men who created this convention [of beginning a nō drama with a traveler asking his way] were more like ourselves than were the Greeks and Romans, more like us even than Shakespeare and Corneille. Their emotion was self-conscious and reminiscent, always associating itself with pictures and poems."

Yeats found that the nō fulfilled his ideal and dream of what the modern drama might be. He writes that Itō's dancing made *At the Hawk's Well* possible, and that when he saw the play danced by him in the natural light of day, only then "did I see him as the tragic image which has stirred my imagination." He was conscious that many people must have thought that he was eccentric or a mere imitator, and in his Note to the same play when it was published in *Four Plays for Dancers* (1921) he justified himself on the basis of dramatic necessity.

"I have found my first model—and in literature if we would not be parvenus we must have a model—in the 'Noh' stage of aristocratic Japan. . . . I do not think of my discovery as mere economy, for it has been a great gain to get rid of scenery, to substitute for a crude landscape painted upon a canvas three performers who, sitting before the wall or a patterned screen, describe landscape or event, and accompany movement with drum and gong, or deepen the emotions of the words with zither and flute."

Bottomley, Moore, and the others discussed in the last chapter who tried to imitate the nō did so out of a desire to create a poetic theatre for its own sake or in order to escape the modern world. Yeats's motivation was different. His comments show that he felt that no other form was as useful for him and that no other form could possibly express satisfactorily "the tragic image" which the modern world presented to his mind. The difference is one between fancy and necessity.

Moreover, Yeats always felt that he was creating a form which he might hand down to succeeding generations, and one which would re-create on the stage the glories of the Irish past and an aristocratic social order.

Synge, Lady Gregory, and O'Casey developed an Irish drama from the prose tradition of the modern English stage. Yeats helped and encouraged them but he aimed higher, as he thought, in his attempt to go against the current of his age, to create a poetic drama, and to bring tragic nobility once more to the hearts of men. Instead of a popular drama, he sought a "people's theatre," an aristocratic, national theatre which, like nō, would use the legends and stories that the simplest and humblest people know, but which would give them expression in all the beauty which art and intelligence can provide, instead of prostituting beauty and truth by vulgarizing them to the standards of taste and the notions of the ignorant. This stand for an aristocratic art brought criticism during the 'Thirties, when he was called an "obscurantist" and a "fascist." Such charges seem manifestly frivolous today, but they do show that Yeats overestimated the possibility of creating a dramatic form which would be as popular, to cultured people, as the nō once was in Japan. "As the nō once was"—even in Japan support of such a theatre has dwindled in the glare of the movies and television, and the stylized, dignified movements of the nō seem as unusual there in the whirl of modern life as Yeats's masked dancers do against the swinging legs of chorus girls in Radio City Music Hall or television's "spectaculars." It seems impossible to decide with assurance today whether or not his plays will ever obtain the audience he sought. It seems unlikely, perhaps, that modern society has room for such "an aristocratic form"; but nonetheless, there have been a few occasions when the plays were performed and they have met with a favorable response from the audience and the press. In the past few years, *Calvary* has been performed at Hamline University in St. Paul, Minnesota; *The Player Queen* at Harvard University; *A Full Moon in March* adapted to dance in Minneapolis; and an excellent production of several plays has been given by the Poet's Theatre of Cambridge, Massachusetts. No doubt there have been other productions in the United States and abroad, and only time and the ambition of our producers and players will tell whether or not the moving dramatic qualities of many of these plays warrant continued performance.

It is possible to speak with more confidence of the past —of Yeats's own purposes and the techniques which he took or adapted from the nō. Like the nō, the action of his plays is short, condensed, or "reduced," as Ronald Peacock says so well in his *Poet in the Theatre* (1946), "reduced to its simplest form, or at any rate to as simple a form as it can be brought to without our losing the sense of its place in the world. The characters that are involved in it are freed from everything that is not part of that action. . . . [The action] is an energy, an eddy of life purified from everything but itself." This reduction to essentials is one of the things which Pound felt was most important in Japanese literature, and it is significant that Yeats should wonder—apparently with complete independence from Pound—"I wonder am I fanciful in discovering in the plays themselves . . . a playing upon a single metaphor, as deliberate as the echoing rhythm of line in Chinese or Japanese painting."

Just as Pound was to do later in the *Cantos*, Yeats found it possible to adapt the "Unifying Image" which they saw in the nō to sustained poetic forms. The well of the hawk, the herne's egg, the words upon the windowpane, and the imagery of the cat's eyes and the moon are all unifying images which found their way into the titles, as well as dramatic embodiments of the actions and meanings of these plays. In other plays, the image may be of Christ holding His cross in *Calvary* or the sight of His wounded body in *The Resurrection*, or Cuchulain lying on his death bed in *The Only Jealousy of Emer*, but in all these plays written since *At the Hawk's Well* there are one or two images, either presented in the action, or represented symbolically on the stage, or wrought into the poetry or prose to give the plays a unity of form. The nō has furnished his plays with unity as well as technique.

Not all of the plays are successful—*The Death of Cuchulain* (1939) is an incredible mélange, and *Calvary* (1920) very imperfectly unites traditional Christian thought with Yeats's private philosophy. But the nō was useful to him for the dramatic form and techniques which it gave him, and it is possible to follow the development of this form throughout plays of representative types. *At the Hawk's Well* (1917) is the logical place to begin, since it was his first play to be modeled upon nō, and since it represents the conventions he borrowed in their least assimilated form.

The play opens with the musicians' "call to the eye of the mind" quoted earlier. They play on drum, gong, and zither and are a chorus like that in the nō—they do not take part in the action. As they sing, the chorus unfolds a cloth, a technique which Yeats thought he saw adumbrated in nō. Their closing the cloth marks the end of the play. The imagined well choked by leaves remains a unifying image throughout the play, represented merely by a square of blue cloth—a device probably a-dapted from *Awoi no Uye*, where the stricken Lady Awoi is represented by a single kimono or brocade cloth laid upon the stage. The well is the well of immortality which bubbles only rarely; Cuchulain and an old man wait for the water to rise and bring them eternal life and vigor, but Cuchulain is lured away, while the old man sleeps, when the hawk-woman (Itō) performs a provocative dance before him. This dance is, according to Yeats and the structure of nō, the climax of the play, and the effort of the men to drink the water ends in tragedy. The dance obviously represents the supernatural forces which always thwart man's quest for immortality and power. Yeats regards as heroic the effort to obtain these, although commonplace men in the chorus watch the dance, appalled:

> O God, protect me
> From a horrible deathless body
> Sliding through the veins of a sudden.

They seek an easier life "Among indolent shadows," and the play ends with the tragic lesson that "Wisdom must lead a bitter life." The verse is not sufficiently dramatic, the play lacks a real beginning, middle, and end, and the place of Cuchulain in the play is somewhat uncertain. But Yeats had made a start, and as such the play is a success.

One cannot, however, take exception to *The Only*

Jealousy of Emer (1919), a nearly flawless tragedy of great power. The increased dramatic power of the verse can be seen even in the expository "summons" of the chorus which opens the play while unfolding the cloth. The verse is taut, the images vivid, and the rhythms develop to a climax and fall away.

> I call before the eyes a roof
> With cross-beams darkened by smoke;
> A fisher's net hangs from a beam,
> A long oar lies against the wall.
> I call up a poor fisher's house;
> A man lies dead or swooning,
> That amorous man,
> That amorous, violent man, renowned Cuchulain,
> Queen Emer at his side.

Emer's tragic choice is to lose Cuchulain to the supernatural forces against which she struggles, or to win him back to life at the cost of renouncing his love forever. As in the *Hawk's Well*, the climactic dance is not by the central character—only Itō could dance properly and his English was not sufficient for dialogue—but by a supernatural being. In this play, however, the dance and the central figure are both part of the drama, since the masked, metallic dancer's ritualistic motions represent the force against which Emer struggles and are, so to speak, the counterpoint to the surgings of her own heart. At the end, she calls Cuchulain back, renouncing his love, and sees him revive and turn to the arms of his mistress who believes that her kiss has recalled him to life. Emer stands to one side as the chorus folds the cloth,

"A statue of solitude," suffering, but with too much nobility to complain. Yeats succeeded in making *Emer* one of the few plays of our time to show convincingly the nobility of human suffering.

Three of the plays deal with religious subjects—*Calvary* (1920), *The Resurrection* (1931), and *Purgatory* (1939). *The Resurrection* is one of Yeats's finest plays and representative of the group in its technique. The play, which was dedicated "to Junzo Sato" who gave Yeats the sword, owes much to the nō in its structural rhythm. It begins like the earlier plays with songs by the chorus during the unfolding and folding of the cloth at the beginning and end of the play, but Yeats's opening stage directions make it clear that he wrote the play so that it could be performed on a regular stage, and most of the play is written in prose. What remains, in addition, of the original nō form is the structural rhythm of the play. The climax occurs at the point where the supernatural being (Christ) reveals his true form and brings, as in nō, spiritual enlightenment. The two central characters are the abstract Greek, who holds that Christ is not a man but an Idea and the materialistic Hebrew, who argues that He is not God, but merely the best man who ever lived. The Hebrew is proved wrong when Christ climactically and miraculously appears in the locked room, and the Greek when he reaches into the torn side of what he thinks is only an "Idea" and clutches a beating heart. The well-known songs at the beginning and end of the play and the counterpoint to the main action of the raving Dionysians' shouting and coupling in the street add to the central revelation of the play to make it one of almost unbearable intensity.

The Player Queen (1922) is, like *The Cat and the Moon* (1926) and *The Herne's Egg* (1938), a comedy and the least like the nō in technique. It is episodic and slow to get under way, but enormously funny when once in motion. It was, however, originally planned as a tragedy and contains many of Yeats's most characteristic and most complex ideas. Its connection with the nō is slight in the sense that the techniques which Yeats had developed are not employed here. It is a curious sort of drama which almost defies characterization—and yet a wonderful success. It moves from the carefree, seemingly haphazard humor of *The Shoemaker's Holiday* toward the stylizing of Yeats's earlier plays. And this structure is like the nō in a more fundamental sense—it leads to a revelation and a change in the central character which is celebrated in a dance. The basic structure of nō is maintained, but overlaid with many alien elements.

The Dreaming of the Bones (1919) and *The Words upon the Window-Pane* (1934) employ the same structural motif, a motif taken from the nō play translated by Pound and reprinted by Yeats, *Nishikigi*. Yeats found *Nishikigi* especially appealing because it seemed to him so close to Irish ways of thought. He commented on the play in his introduction to *Certain Noble Plays of Japan*, remarking how much it reminded him of one of Lady Gregory's stories about a boy and girl of Aran who come after death to a priest for marriage. In *Nishikigi* the spirits of two lovers haunt the scenes of their life, seeking to be united by the sympathetic Buddhist priest. In *Dreaming*, the two lovers are Diarmuid and Dervorgilla who brought the Norman invaders into Ireland so that they might consummate their illicit love. These two spirits return to Ireland after seven centuries to seek forgiveness from a young Irish revolutionary who is fleeing the English— and who is the play's equivalent of the priest in *Nishikigi*. When he discovers who they are, he sees an analogy between them and those Irish who betrayed the country to the English in 1916, the time of the play, and he refuses to grant them the forgiveness which would unite them and free them from suffering. The conventions of the cloth-folding, of the songs that go with it, and of the musicians-chorus are employed here and help make the play one of the most beautifully stylized of Yeats's works. He also borrows from *Nishikigi*, and nō generally, the technique of having the central character speak impersonally of himself, as the girl's spirit does here, and also the convention of climactic revelation of identity, when the young revolutionary discovers who the pair are. This play has many virtues—its stylization; its skillful adaptation of subject, technique, and form from nō; and its dramatic intensity—but it is anticlimactic, and the motivations of the revolutionary are not clear. It is as though Shakespeare had muddled the conflict in Anthony and, just before the battle of Actium, sent him off from Cleopatra to raise grapes in Sicily with Octavia. But the play has a strong literary interest and it is a tribute to Yeats the dramatist that this play should stand alone among his dance plays as a drama better read than acted.

Words upon the Window-Pane is in prose, and in many other ways is not one of Yeats's "Noh plays." But it is clearly the product of the form of theatre he had developed from the nō. Like *Kumasaka*, one of the nō which he republished, it is a supernatural play on a historical subject—the appearance of Jonathan Swift, Vanessa, and Stella to a séance in a house where Stella had once stayed. The motif of the ghostly lovers brought together years after their death is the same *Nishikigi*-motif employed in *The Dreaming of the Bones*, but here there are two women who love Swift instead of the one in the earlier play —a triangle posing a problem of dramatic focus which Yeats solves brilliantly through the device of the séance where only one of the dead can speak at a time, first the impetuous Vanessa, and then Swift. Stella does not speak a word in the play, but her presence is implied throughout by Swift's address to her and by the "Unifying Image" of the words upon the window-pane taken from the poem which she wrote for Swift's fifty-fourth birthday. The group at the séance is a medley of ignorance and sensitivity and, as a group, are the equivalent of the priest in *Nishikigi* or the revolutionary in *The Dreaming of the Bones*; like these characters, they experience a revelation of the central, supernatural characters in the play. This play is one of Yeats's finest and, in spite of its completely English subject matter, shows how well he was able to refine and adapt to the modern stage the conventions of the form which he borrowed from the nō.

A Full Moon in March (1935) and *The King of the Great Clock Tower* (1935) are late plays which revert to Yeats's earlier form of "Noh play." Masks, poetry, a kind of chorus, revelation of character, and climactic dance all suggest *At the Hawk's Well*, but the violence of passion and action, the symbolism, and the concern with the artist's life as a superior type of experience mark these plays as characteristic products of Yeats's last period. The form of these plays must be understood against the background of his borrowings from nō, but their poetic qualities make them integral with the Crazy Jane poems and the Lear-like sanity in madness of *Last Poems*. But to say this is to say no more, really, than what is true of all of his plays. They belong with the poems written at the same time or a little later, and the poems must be seen with the plays for a full understanding of his poetic accomplishment. Many of the plays are as excellent and as moving as anything he ever wrote, and might well be studied with the attention that has been so rightly given to his poems.

These plays are not, however, only poems or stories; they are of course dramas which need performance for full appreciation. If they have not been given the full chance they deserve in the theatre, Yeats has nonetheless been justified in another way. His translation of Sophocles' most famous play was the hit of the season at the Canadian Shakespeare festival in the summer of 1954. *Oedipus the King* can certainly hold the boards in almost any production, but this production was clearly based upon Yeats's idea of what the play means and was based upon his ideal of the tragic modern drama as a stylized, ritualistic play. His own plays are obviously the product of a more eccentric genius than that of Sophocles, so that it would be foolish to believe that they will ever have the universal human significance of Greek or Shakespearean tragedy. But if these great dramatists, our ultimate Western standards of judgment, are to be rigorously set off against other playwrights of whatever period, who shall 'scape whipping? Like Dryden, Yeats was born into an age in which, for all of his protests, he was completely at home; but it was also an age in which social and cultural forces made an Elizabethan drama impossible. He chose to "copy the East and live deliberately," and to attempt to create a new form of drama out of a form that the West had scarcely known before. "This," to quote Pound,

> This is not vanity.
> Here error is all in the not done,
> all in the diffidence that faltered.

IX. THE SUMMING-UP

T͟HE TASK of bringing to a close such a study as this, of summing up a tradition which is still alive today, is comparable to the attempt to write a final biography of a man yet alive. Dr. Johnson's title for the last chapter of *Rasselas*—"The Conclusion, in Which Nothing is Concluded"—is by far the most appropriate here, and perhaps the attempt to sum up shows a want of judgment. But there are certain things which can be said in retrospect about the motivation for the persistent literary interest in Japan, and certain observations which may be made about the nature of the literature which this interest has inspired.

The persistency of the spell of Japan for our culture can be understood by looking about at the social and artistic life of the United States at mid-century. Many American families have flowers arranged in a Japanese style in vases which are Japanese or copied after the Japanese, in houses whose design is borrowed in part from Japanese architecture, and lit by Japanese lamps. When we look up from a recent book—say *Playbook* (1956)— that contains I. A. Richards' play, *A Leak in the Universe*, which seems modelled after the nō and which contains a Japanese Buddhist as its raisonneur—when we look up and see our wives and daughters wearing Japanese sandals or mitten-toed socks purchased at the drug store, we are apt to be teased out of thought and even out of patience as we try to decide what it all means in any sort of significant historical or cultural terms. These are difficult problems which one is happy to turn over to the cultural historian or to the anthropologist. And still the problem teases, because the impulse which leads our wives to hang a scroll with a Japanese landscape whose symbolism is all but lost on them and us is the same impulse which has urged our thinkers and writers to an abiding interest in Japan.

It is not easy to account for this consistent appeal of Japan and the Orient—whether over the four centuries or in the living room today. There are clearly some imponderable elements in the Western spirit which can be explained only by the postulate of an Oriental cultural attraction for the West. (No doubt there has also been a cultural tradition of suspicion and revulsion, but this unhappy story is not one which needs to be told here.) From 1550 to 1950, and for millennia before, the Orient has had an appeal which seems irresistible to the Western mind and transcendent of all but that strongest of ethnological deterrents to cultural intercourse, war.

The attraction has existed and continues, but it seems to defy explanation. Such a study as this deals only with part of its results, that part which concerns literature in English up to the middle of the twentieth century, but the particulars of this attraction can be explained in part. Throughout the middle ages and most of the Renaissance, men believed that the world had been deteriorating since the Fall of Man. With the secularizing of modern thought, this belief has gone the way of many traditional Christian beliefs, but in its wake an attitude of pessimism has grown about the possibility of achieving a great literature in modern times. The more firmly the age of science has been established, the more uncertain and unconfident of their own role and significance our writers have become. This literary pessimism has increased since the mid-nineteenth century, deepening into the feeling that each successive generation is further down the descending cycle of Western culture. Yeats, Pound and Eliot —three of our greatest poets—have been obsessed by the problem, by the attempt to make poetry out of its own void: Yeats's strange beast, its hour come round at last, slouches towards Parnassus as well as Bethlehem to be born. Perhaps only in our century could such a title as Spengler's *Der Untergang des Abendlandes* receive the emotional acceptance it has had. But the world is really not in such dire straits, and Eliot has turned to religion, Yeats to mysticism, and Pound to history to fashion out a hope sufficient at least to make man's end more of a tragedy than a whimper. The search for answers to this problem has also led writers to look to other cultures. Many have looked to Japan and the larger Orient—as artists have also looked to African and other "unspoiled" cultures—for fresh and revivifying forms with which to give new and living expression to the Western tradition. When Yeats wrote that the men who devised the nō drama were more like us than the Greeks or Shakespeare and Corneille, he was only stating the matter in more extreme fashion than most writers would allow; and yet it is true in a sense that our age has followed his urging to "copy the East and live deliberately."

However, neither the imponderables of cultural attraction nor the notion of "the decline of the West" explains why Japan rather than India or China should have been most influential in this period of four centuries of cultural relations with English literature. Both India and China are among the world's great seminal cultures; both nations have made extraordinary achievements in philosophy and art; and both have contributed much to the West. And yet, Japan, a relative newcomer in the family of Oriental cultures, has been most influential upon our literature. Insofar as it is not to be attributed to the accidents of history, this situation seems most explicable upon the grounds of the needs of Western artists in modern times. While some periods, like the middle ages, seem to desire new ideas and imaginative materials to fit into accepted forms of thought and expression, our modern literary artists have sought rather to find new forms with which to refresh the tradition and to treat the literary concerns of our times. Because our age has been an experimental and formalistic era in literature, the search for new forms of expression would seem to be the explanation of the modern interest in a Japan which our writers have found fertile in its literary forms.

The seemingly indestructible appeal of Japan as an ideal image—exoticism—may seem at first to belie this explanation. But exoticism is as much a search for what is ideal and what ought to be imitated as for what is merely different in nature. Exoticism seems, like primitivism, to take both chronological and cultural forms. There has been some chronological exoticizing of Japan—one may read a great deal about the wonderful days of "old Japan"

—but this impulse has born little fruit for our literature; or, to put it differently, this chronological exoticism of Japan has sought out Japan as material for a kind of sensibility which has produced very little literature of any merit. Cultural exoticism has exercised the stronger appeal by showing what Japan has had to offer our writers as a different and ancient but rich and continuous culture with a variety of usable literary and artistic forms. Moreover, Japan has been an exception among Oriental nations, at least until very recent times, because its high degree of civilization and its modernization along Western lines has increased the appeal of the country even to those who wished to flee the West and its burdens. Almost alone of the Asiatic cultures, Japan has played the important role of providing a meeting ground for East and West. It is difficult, after all, to exoticize or idealize the forms of Ubangi culture—or of the Indian and Chinese hinterlands—beyond a certain point, since few Westerners can really imagine themselves happy for a moment in such societies. But Japan, a civilization as highly refined as the West, is familiar and congenial in its modern conveniences, in addition to having the additional grace for a world-weary Westerner of new and idealized forms of behavior and art.

Some Westerners and some Japanese have felt that the cultural character or destiny of Japan has not been to create ideas or philosophies as China and India have created them, but to re-create through transmission and refinement what the older Oriental cultures have had to offer. This generalization seems to be truer than most and, along with the congenial Westernizing of the country, has had the effect of leading many of our writers to see in Japan the proper meeting-ground of East and West. This is probably the single persistent idea which Japan has contributed to our writers, although it has been so fertile in its provision of literary forms. This idea was first grasped by American writers, probably because Americans have been led by their experience to think of their own country in similar terms as the melting-pot, or heir, or meeting-ground of European traditions. Walt Whitman was obsessed by the idea of this manifest cultural destiny of the United States and was the first to interpret the Japanese as "the errand-bearers" of the Orient. Ernest Fenollosa next gave form to this idea by celebrating the meeting of "East and West" in poetry through the metaphor of a marriage—an extension of the ages-old images of the Feminine East and the Masculine West. Since Fenollosa, several poets have tried to give this idea expression in various forms—Amy Lowell in prose-poetry and Sherard Vines in neo-Metaphysical poetry, for example. Lafcadio Hearn sought to dissolve Western science and even his Impressionism into the fluid mysticism of Japanese Buddhism. And Ezra Pound is the most complex example of all. His *Cantos* attempt a synthesis of all that is important to him in Eastern as well as Western traditions, and he has expressed in his correspondence the idea that Japan is the ideal transmitter of Oriental culture. Moreover, in the very act of addressing himself to this synthesis, he has employed forms adapted from Japanese literature to help express the great international tradition. The idea of Japan—and America—the cultural intermediary, and the use of Japan as a source for literary forms, merge indistinguishably in his writing.

The search for imaginative forms in Japanese culture appears today to have taken place in three distinct cycles since St. Francis Xavier first raised the cross in Japan. The first and longest cycle lasted from that day in 1549 to the mid-nineteenth century. Japan was all but indistinguishable from China and India in this earliest period, or at least all three nations tended to be apprehended in the one image of Cathay throughout the Renaissance and Augustan periods. Increasingly, however, Japanese art and society were distinguished from the rest of the Orient, and the curiosity of Europe was aroused by this island kingdom which so unaccountably insisted upon isolating herself from the West. In this same period of three centuries, the East continued to function as an irritant to absolutist Western ideas of history and culture. Historians agree that the Orient was one of the major causes leading to that development of historical and cultural relativism which has made modern historiography and anthropology possible. This important change in Western thought was reflected in the literature of the first cycle of interest by the idealizing of Japanese society and government, by the literary device of the Oriental "Spy" or sage, and by the vogue for Oriental art which was expressed in many images in eighteenth-century writing. By the end of this first period or cycle, exoticism and imitation had given way to absorption of what was known, and most writers on Japan contented themselves by repeating what had been said before and thinking how interesting it would be if only Japan were to open its doors again.

The second cycle of interest began when Commodore Perry and an America bound for Manifest Destiny led the weakened Japanese feudal government and internationally minded native groups to open Japan to the Western powers. The result was a new period of exoticism and new images of Japan, but the early forms of thought by which Japan was interpreted in this period were largely determined—at first—by the ideas of Japan held by the seventeenth and eighteenth centuries and—increasingly—by beliefs and needs of the age which had little to do with Japan. Japan had become a special subject or reality for the mixed Victorian temper. This richly ambiguous attitude of mind is of course to be found in the mingled heterodoxy and orthodoxy, or mingled idealism and nihilism, of the major Victorian writers, who concerned themselves with subjects more important to their age than Japan; but the sensibility can also be seen in sharp focus in the writings of the Rudyard Kiplings and the Sir Edwin Arnolds who visited Japan. Empire, Propriety, and Progress—what we so limitedly define as the Victorian ethos—are found wanting or irrelevant in a culture which is different by equally civilized, and in some ways superior, standards to Victorian England. The attitude of these writers becomes one of adherence to both Empire and Japanese sovereignty, to Propriety and pleasurable deviation among women who might still be respected for their refinement, to Progress and a sense that Japan was well off without it, to Orthodoxy and an appreciation of the dignity and even in some ways the superiority of Buddhism. There were of course many visitors to Japan in the years before the turn of the century who liked almost all, and others who liked almost nothing, of what they saw; but the finest Victorian minds are ambivalent in their response.

Towards the end of this period in England, the interaction of old ideas about Japan and new European ideals helped to develop Impressionism. This broad movement with its many offshoots, for which pan-Impressionism is the most convenient label, was founded in great measure upon an interaction of the relativistic thought inspired to a large degree by contact with the Orient and the increasingly psychological approach to art. As the movement got under way, it soon found many of its forms and techniques, and much of its justification, in the Japanese color print.

Many of the attitudes and images of Japan created in the first two cycles of interest lived on, often in attenuated or corrupted form, into the third cycle which began about the turn of the century. This third period built upon the contributions of Impressionism and is chiefly distinguished from the other two by its discovery and use of Japanese literature. Ezra Pound no doubt expressed the debt of his generation to a Japan viewed through the lens of Impressionism most incisively when he declared that a knowledge of "Whistler and the Japanese" was necessary to anyone who claimed to be educated. In Japanese poetry and art, Pound and his contemporaries found pictorial techniques for poetry which were analogous to artistic composition; they found "images" or visual metaphors; and they discovered a restraint from obvious moralizing—an apparent Japanese belief in art for art's sake. These poets, and Pound chief among them, took from Japanese poetry and drama a precision of expression which they were seeking to establish in their own poetry; they saw a technique of imagery which conveyed meaning and tone without discursive statement; and on the example of haiku and nō they devised specific imagistic and structural techniques which have become widely current in our poetry.

The voluminous response of our prose fiction to Japan has been largely disappointing. A few competent writers have felt the appeal of Japan; but none of our major authors has agreed sufficiently with Hawthorne's belief —that Japan offered the least hackneyed subject in the world—to use Japan and its culture for little more than the stylistic device of comparison with the West. The most important contributions of Japan to the prose of Lafcadio Hearn came indirectly through Impressionism and directly in non-literary ways—through residence in Japan and from Japanese philosophy. Japanese fiction has not been well enough known to excite admiration and imitation by our writers, and the Japanese themselves have felt that they have had more to learn from Western novelists than to teach. Perhaps the day will come when English and American novelists will discover an importance in the Japanese fiction now being so well and so widely translated, but to the present time, Japan has been less important for our fiction than for our poetry and drama.

Indirectly, through the French author Julien Viaud— "Pierre Loti"—fiction inspired by Japan has provided a form of literature whose roots grow in the tainted soil of Imperialism. The theme of desertion has grown out of Viaud's *Madame Chrysanthème* into a host of stories and plays. Few of these versions of the theme have any more than historical importance, however, and the form is most interesting today for its culmination in Long and Belasco's play, and in Puccini's opera, *Madama Butterfly*.

English and American drama has contracted other and more important debts from Japan. The stock stage types of the "Jolly Jap," the unbelievably refined or intrepid Japanese, and the cruel Oriental have lived on in plays, motion pictures, and comic strips in spite of the more intelligent and more mature understanding of Japan which has been gained in recent decades. The perennial appeal of these ridiculous types has fortunately been overshadowed by more satisfactory and meaningful dramatic results from the study of Japanese theatre. Many critics and playwrights have discovered in nō valuable dramatic criteria which may be applied to Western dramatic forms and conventions, and techniques with which to revive the poetic drama or to judge Western acting and production. The importance of kabuki has consisted until very recent years in the basis which it provided Sergei M. Eisenstein for his creation of an esthetic of the film which has been widely influential upon world cinematic theory and practice. But a growing familiarity with kabuki since the Second World War seems to promise that, in time, it may prove to be valuable for the writing and production of drama in English. The appearance of Japanese movies has been so sudden and has met with such acclaim that it is difficult to judge what impact they may have on our film art. But the fact that they have become so widely familiar that parody of them on television programs can make sense to the wide audience of this newest medium seems to indicate that the Japanese film art may also enter into fruitful contact with our culture.

As this century has approached and passed its midpoint, there has been an increasing tendency to realism in the poetic and fictional treatment of Japan. The image of Japan seems less exciting to our writers and Japanese poetry no longer seems to offer forms to our best poets. This situation seems to be the result of the close of the third cycle of interest in Japan, although it may also be the result of a period of consolidation and quiescence in our poetry. It seems, in retrospect, that the most fruitful portion of the cycle of literary interest in Japan has come midway between early exoticism and late mature absorption of what Japan means to the age—the period, in short, of imitation and excited borrowing. This middle period has been more fruitful than the later period of more thorough understanding, it seems, because Japan has been much more important for the forms it has given our writers than for the ideas; and as all literary historians know, the excited discovery of forms in a foreign literature is more apt to be based upon half-understandings which illuminate because they tell the age what it seeks to know. But at the same time as the poetic response to Japan has become more realistic and tame, kabuki, the Japanese film, and perhaps the Japanese novel seem to be assuming greater importance. It is difficult to say whether the third cycle of interest in Japan is ending or whether it is simply taking new directions. Or, perhaps it is a mistake to continue to look for cycles of interest in Japan. Radically altered means of communication, the accumulation of knowledge about Japan, and the growing number of Westerners who know the language may be tending to produce an even-tempered, though ever-shifting, interest in Japan which makes cyclic analysis irrelevant.

The importance of Japan to English literature would comprise but a small chapter of our literary history had not two of the most important modern poets found answers to their poetic and critical needs in Japan. Ezra Pound, the poet of our critics and the critic of our poets, has probably done more than any other writer to make Japan a basis of poetic theory, a source of techniques, and a part of "the great tradition." And William Butler Yeats, who is usually called our finest modern poet, followed Pound independently to make Japan an important part of his poetry and the source of a new and richly complex form of poetic drama which he called his "Noh plays." While these two writers owe much to others and while they failed to gain a complete understanding of Japan, their transmutation of what they understood or even what they misapprehended constitutes the finest literary result of modern understanding of Japan, and also comprises an integral part of some of the most important literature of the twentieth century. There is no need to minimize the similar accomplishments of other writers, but because in the writings of Pound and Yeats a deep response to Japan is made into art by two of the finest talents of our age, their accomplishment is worthy of greater critical attention.

It is all too difficult to make a just evaluation of the importance of one literary tradition to another or of the importance of one source of inspiration in the total thought and work of a writer, and this is especially true when the outside tradition is as different as Japan. The importance of Japan has been great, but it must be seen in the light of history and not assumed to be a separate tradition in English literature. When the time is ripe, such novel and alien forms as haiku or nō—or the sonnet and the literary epic—can have an almost incalculable effect upon a literary tradition, but the historical moment must be suitable and prior to the discovery. It is obvious that no form of Japanese literature has played the part, or is ever likely to, that the literary epic has in the history of English literature; but it seems fair to conclude—from the acknowledgments of the writers and the evidence of their works—that Japan has played a major role in developing certain attitudes, certain images, and certain forms. While this role seems greater than anyone had thought, it would be both historically inaccurate and a gross distortion of the conservative nature of literary and cultural traditions to say that Japan has fundamentally altered the essential character of our literature.

What has happened, it seems, is that our tradition has been refreshed, redirected, and enriched by the absorption of Japanese culture and the experience of Western contact with Japan. Japan has been a real part of our culture since the Jesuits advertised it to Europe. But reality may be real in many ways, and different aspects of reality may assume different degrees of importance in different ages. Japan was, in this sense, no less real to the eighteenth century than Homer and Virgil—but it was vastly less important. Succeeding generations have had different conceptions of the nature and importance of Japan and have found differing literary forms to express what these conceptions signify. Each age must make its assessment of Japan—or of Rome—and decide what it means. Each successive age is apt to feel that its understanding is better or more "real" in an absolute sense than that of its predecessors, and it may truly be said that there has been, on the whole, an increasing understanding of Japan; but this is more the concern of the cultural historian or the anthropologist than the literary historian and critic. For literature, it is not so much the fact of the use of certain materials as the form, the meaning, and the beauty which have been wrought from them. Japan has been fortunate in this respect to have attracted the interest of many of the best writers in English. These poets, novelists, artists, and critics may be said, in Pound's words, to have gathered a live tradition from the international air and made it live again in literature of enduring quality; they have also reflected many of the absorbing interests of the passing times in the mirror of changing literary conceptions of Japan.

BIBLIOGRAPHICAL ESSAY AND
NOTES TO THE CHAPTERS

ALTHOUGH the lack of a formal bibliographical apparatus will not trouble most readers, there may be those who wish to check sources or further investigate aspects of this study. Such readers may obtain the doctoral dissertation from which this book has grown, "The Japanese Influence upon English and American Literature, 1850-1950," either by inter-library loan from the University of Minnesota, or on microfilm from University Microfilms, Ann Arbor, Michigan. The dissertation contains longer and more frequent illustrations and discussion of many lesser writers who seem out of place in a book of this length for a more general audience; and it is fully documented with footnotes, appendices, and bibliography. Some material has been added here, especially to Chapters I, VI, VII, and IX, but the chief changes have been those of complete reorganization and rewriting from first to last.

There are two other reasons for avoiding an ungainly apparatus—the stylistic aim to tell an unencumbered story and the fact that the literature produced by our writers constitutes the largest and most important body of source material for this study. There are very few cases where one decent edition of their writings is not as good as another.

Instead of a formal bibliography, then, I have added

four sections of notes intended to aid the understanding or satisfy the curiosity of interested readers. The first section describes the four Japanese literary forms referred to in this book and suggests certain readily available works on these forms. The second section lists some books, chiefly translations and anthologies, which have been of historical importance in shaping our writers' conceptions and misconceptions of Japanese literature. The third section notes those comparative studies which have preceded this book and which are not mentioned in the fourth and longest section, the Notes to the Chapters. This section of source notes is divided under the chapter titles and subdivided into, first, a paragraph discussing sources of general use to the chapter, and second, citation of the books referred to in each of the subdivisions of the chapters. Some books which seem useful although they are not named in the text are silently added, and some works referred to in the text have been omitted. There are two kinds of omissions: of those works, like Pope's *Rape of the Lock*, which are readily available, and of such works as those referred to without quotation or without relevance to the comparative aspects of this study—such works as St. Augustine's *City of God*. The method of citation in the Notes to the Chapters is by authors in the sequence in which they appear in the text; and by author, title, place, publisher, and date.

1. Japanese Literary Forms

The four Japanese literary forms most often referred to in this study are tanka, haiku, nō, and kabuki.

TANKA is also called "waka" and "uta" by Japanese as well as Western writers. It is a thirty-one syllabled lyric form written in five verses of five, seven, five, seven, and seven syllables. Tanka originated in some prehistoric period, may be called the "classical" Japanese poetic form, and has continued to the present day, most often treating nature, love, or occasional subjects. HAIKU is a form of seventeen syllables—with verses of five, seven, and five syllables—and is alternatively called "hokku" and "haikai." Each haiku must state or imply one of the five "seasons" (including New Year's Month), a fact which suggests the high degree to which the form is devoted to natural subjects and natural images. Haiku employs these natural images as more or less conventional symbols derived from the typically eclectic Japanese heritage of Taoism, Buddhism, and Shintō animism. The form was defined in the sixteenth century and remains popular to this day. NŌ is a relatively short dramatic form with certain qualities taken from the Japanese religions. Its use of ritualistic, symbolic dance seems to owe much to various Shintō rituals; its thought, subjects, and form are derived from Zen and other sects of Buddhism. Nō was perfected in the fourteenth century, and its repertory of plays with religious, historical, and literary subjects has remained all but unchanged from feudal times. It employs masks and rich costumes, a chorus which takes no part in the action, and a small, rhythmic orchestra; it is a highly poetic and stylized dramatic form presented on a bare, elevated stage open to the audience on three sides. KABUKI is even more synthetic than nō, but is made of many of the same elements—stylized acting and dance, rich costumes, musical accompaniment, and acting restricted to male performers. But kabuki is performéd on a larger stage, uses scenery, is secular and spectacular where nō is religious and restrained, and retains its popularity while nō continues as a precious artistic heritage in the possession of the tradition-minded literati. Kabuki are often very long—they may take up to three or four days of acting—and the preponderance of dance or drama varies widely from play to play. The subjects also vary, but plays on historical or domestic themes have had the most enduring popularity. Kabuki arose during the seventeenth century, borrowing many features, including plots and techniques, from the nō and the bunraku or puppet theatre. The most striking features of the kabuki stage are its acting ramp extending at an angle through the audience from middle stage right to an entry door at audience left and the revolving stage which the Japanese were the first to invent.

One of the most readable books on these forms—apart from the tanka—is Donald Keene's fine handbook, *Japanese Literature* (London: John Murray, 1953; republished in the U. S. by the Grove Press). For the tanka, there is Arthur Waley's excellent introduction, *Japanese Poetry*; *The 'Uta'* (Oxford: Clarendon Press, 1919); and Earl Miner, "The Technique of Japanese Poetry," *Hudson Review*, VIII (Autumn, 1955). A more particularized and historical discussion of tanka and haiku with excellent documentation may be found in Richard N. McKinnon, "Tanka and Haiku: Some Aspects of Classical Japanese Poetry," *Indiana Conference on Oriental-Western*

Literary Relations (Chapel Hill: Univ. of No. Carolina Press, 1955). Many of the translations of Japanese poetry have helpful introductions. See, for example, the books by Miyamori Asatarō: *Masterpieces of Japanese Poetry, Ancient and Modern,* 2 vols. (Tōkyō: Maruzen, 1936) and *An Anthology of Haiku Ancient and Modern* (Tōkyō: Maruzen, 1930; 1932); Kenneth Yasuda, *A Pepper-Pod* (New York: Knopf, 1947); and R. H. Blyth, *Haiku,* 4 vols. (Tōkyō: Hokuseidō, 1949-52).

There is not yet a satisfactory book on all forms of the Japanese drama. Donald Keene's *Japanese Literature,* cited earlier, has a brief chapter. Otherwise, Frank Alanson Lombard, *An Outline History of the Japanese Drama* (London: Allen and Unwin, 1928) and Arthur Lindsay Sadler, *Japanese Plays . . .* (Sidney: Angus and Robertson, 1934) are somewhat dated and over-detailed, but often preferable to Faubion Bowers, *Japanese Theatre* (New York: Hermitage House, 1952), a readable but loose and often inaccurate book. There are, however, excellent studies available of nō and kabuki alone. For the nō, it is enough to have understood Arthur Waley's excellent book, *The Nō Plays of Japan* (London: Allen and Unwin, 1921; New York: Grove Press, 1950); but there is also Zemmaro Toki, *Japanese Nō Plays* (Tōkyō: Japan Tourist Library, New Series, no. 16, 1954). Kabuki has been receiving increasing attention. Adolphe Clarence Scott, *The Kabuki Theatre of Japan* (London: Allen and Unwin, 1955) is a fine recent study, and the introductions to two translations give excellent background and history: Donald Keene, *The Battles of Coxinga* (London: Taylor's Foreign Press, 1951) and Donald H. Shively, *The Love Suicide at Amijima* (Cambridge, Mass.: Harvard Univ. Press, 1951).

The best introduction to Japanese literature can probably be obtained, however, by reading the two anthologies compiled and edited by Donald Keene, with translations by various hands: *Anthology of Japanese Literature* (New York: Grove Press, 1955) and *Modern Japanese Literature* (New York: Grove Press, 1956), and by supplementing them with Arthur Waley's book on the nō mentioned above.

2. Translations and Other Works of Historical Importance

While such writers as Lafcadio Hearn, Yone Noguchi, and others mentioned in the text and the Notes to the Chapters have been most influential in shaping our writers' conceptions and misconceptions of Japan and Japanese literature, the works which follow have also had significant effect in creating images of the Japanese literary forms. W. G. Aston, *A History of Japanese Literature* (London: Heinemann, 1899). Basil Hall Chamberlain: "Japanese Miniature Odes," *Cornhill Magazine*, xxxvi (July, 1877); "A Lyric Drama from the Japanese," *Cornhill Magazine*, xxxiv (October, 1876); *The Classical Poetry of the Japanese* (London: Trübner and Co., 1880); and *Japanese Poetry* (London: J. Murray, 1911). Ernest Fenollosa and Ezra Pound, *"Noh" or Accomplishment* (London: Macmillan, 1916). Ernest Fenollosa: *Epochs of Chinese and Japanese Art,* 2 vols. (New York: F. A. Stokes, 1911) and *The Masters of Ukiyoe . . .* (New

York: Knickerbocker Press, 1896). Algernon Bertram Freeman-Mitford, 1st Baron Redesdale, *Tales of Old Japan* (London: Macmillan, 1871). Yoshisaburo Okakura, *The Japanese Spirit* (New York: J. Pott, 1905). William N. Porter, *A Hundred Verses from Old Japan* (Oxford: Clarendon Press, 1909). Michel Revon, *Anthologie de la littérature japonaise* (Paris: C. Delagrave, 1910).

3. Earlier Comparative Studies

There are a number of comparative studies of widely varying significance and differing relevance to the subject of this book. Besides those mentioned in the Notes to the Chapters, there are those which may be mentioned with some annotation for readers interested in developing specific aspects of Japanese-Western comparative studies. Irving Babbitt, "Romanticism and the Orient," *Bookman*, LXXIV (1931), is highly doctrinaire in the lines of the New Humanism, but stimulating. Charles S. Braden, "The Novelist Discovers the Orient," *Far Eastern Quarterly*, VII (February, 1948), has a number of interesting figures but is very limited in statistical criteria. Arthur Christy's compilation of essays, *The Asian Legacy in American Life* (New York: John Day, 1945), is important, but only partially relevant to Japan. Paul Claudel, *L'Oiseau noir dans le Soleil levant* (Paris: Libraire Gallimard, 1927), is a sensitive account of Japanese culture and experience in the Orient. Johannes Hoops, "Orientalische Stoffe in der englischen Literatur," *Deutsche Rundschau*, XI (August, 1926), perhaps deserves mention. F. S. C. Northrop, *The Meeting of East and West* (New

York: Macmillan, 1946), is a provocative but highly abstract study of little immediate relevance to literature. William Leonard Schwartz, perhaps the first scholar to explore the complex intercultural relations between Japanese art and poetry and our literature, published the first detailed study of the effect of Japan and China on one of our writers—"A Study of Amy Lowell's Far Eastern Verse," *Modern Language Notes,* XLIII (3 March 1928). H. L. Seaver, "The Asian Lyric and English Literature" in *Essays in Honor of Barrett Wendell* (Cambridge, Mass.: Harvard Univ. Press, 1926), covered some new ground. Royall Snow published two short impressionistic articles of some historical importance: "Marriage with the East," *New Republic,* XXVII (29 June 1921) and "Poetry in Borrowed Plumage," *New Republic,* XXV (9 February 1921). Mark Van Doren's article, "The Progress of Poetry in England," *The Nation,* CXII (22 June 1921), is somewhat more searching and is also of historical importance. Walter C. Young, "Some Oriental Influences on Western Culture," *Bulletin, Institute of Pacific Relations* (New York, 1929), is of little relevance to literature. By far the most important sources for this book, however, are those noted in the section which follows.

4. Notes to the Chapters

CHAPTER I: "THE MEETING OF EAST AND WEST"

A large portion of the factual information in this chapter has been borrowed from three excellent books: Sir George B. Sansom, *The Western World and Japan* (New York: Knopf, 1950); William W. Appleton, *A Cycle of Cathay* (New

York: Columbia Univ. Press, 1951); and Beverly Sprague Allen, *Tides in English Taste (1619-1800),* 2 vols. (Cambridge, Mass.: Harvard Univ. Press, 1937). The role of the Orient in developing Western relativistic thought has been a commonplace among historians for some years. Arthur Walworth's *Black Ships Off Japan* (New York: Knopf, 1946) is a lively account of the opening of Japan.

Sources cited. (i) The "noble Spanish traveler" was Don Rodrigo de Vivero y Velasco, quoted from an anonymous article on his journals, "Travels in Japan," *Asiatic Journal,* New Series, II (July, 1830). The Jesuit's praise of the Japanese is quoted from Sansom, *op.cit.,* p. 174. Sir William Temple, *Essay upon the Ancient and Modern Learning* (London, 1690). Oliver Goldsmith's Lien Chi Altangi is the "Chinese" letter writer in *The Citizen of the World.* Tobias Smollett, *The History and Adventures of an Atom* (London: Hutchinson, 1905). John Stalker, *Treatise on Japanning* (London: John Stalker, 1688). Ernst Cassirer, *An Essay on Man* (New York: Doubleday, 1953). Oliver Goldsmith, *Citizen of the World,* Letter VIII. Anon., *The Manners and Customs of the Japanese* . . . (London: J. Murray, 1841).

(ii) Herman Melville, *Moby-Dick,* ch. CXI. Bayard Taylor, *A Visit to India, China and Japan* . . . (New York: G. P. Putnam, 1855). Nathaniel Hawthorne, *The English Notebooks of Nathaniel Hawthorne,* ed. Randall Stewart (New York: M. L. A., 1941). Henry Wadsworth Longfellow, *Kéramos and Other Poems* (Boston: Houghton, Osgood and Co., 1878). Walt Whitman, *"Salut au Monde!"* "Facing West from California's Shores," "A Broadway Pageant," and *Passage to India,* are readily available in Modern Library ed., but "A Broadway Pageant" was originally published in different form and under the title, "The Errand-Bearers," in the New York *Times, IX,* no. 2736 (27 June 1860). Ernest Fenollosa, *East and West . . . and Other Poems* (New York and Boston: T. Y. Crowell, 1893).

CHAPTER II: "NEW IMAGES AND
STEREOTPYES OF JAPAN"

A pioneering, if almost wholly factual, article by E. V.
Gatenby, "The Influence of Japan on English Language and
Literature," *Transactions and Proceedings of the Japan
Society* (London), xxxiv (1936-37), was helpful in discovering some of the English writers who responded to Japan.
The splendid unpublished doctoral dissertation of John Ash-
mead, Jr.—"The Idea of Japan 1853-1895. Japan as Described
by Americans and Other Travellers from the West" (Harvard University, 1951)—ranges farther than its title sug-
gests and contains a valuable bibliography; my quotations are
from the Summary of the dissertation. Charles Lee Purdy's
Gilbert and Sullivan: Masters of Mirth and Melody (New
York: Jules Messner, 1946) has useful biographical details.
The discussion of the relations between John Luther Long,
David Belasco, and Giacomo Puccini owes most of its facts
to two books: William Winter, *The Life of David Belasco,*
2 vols. (New York: Moffat, Yard and Co., 1918) and Arthur
Hobson Quinn, *A History of American Drama from the
Civil War to the Present Day,* 2 vols. (New York: Harper,
1927). And it is a pleasure to acknowledge a letter from
Professor Quinn. Much of the most illuminating information
for this and subsequent chapters comes from boring through
the popular, theatrical, and literary magazines of the period.
  Sources cited. (i) Charles MacFarlane, *Japan: An Account
. . .* (Hartford: Silas Andrus and Son, 1856). W. Burges,
"The International Exhibition," *Gentleman's Magazine,*
July, 1862. Sir Edwin Arnold: *The Light of Asia* (London:
Trübner, 1870); *Japonica* (New York: Scribners, 1891); *Seas
and Lands* (New York: Longmans, Green, 1891); and *The
Tenth Muse and Other Poems* (London and New York:
Longmans, Green, 1895). Rudyard Kipling's travel letters
on his first visit to Japan were published in the two vols.,
From Sea to Sea, xiii and xiv, of *The Works of Rudyard
Kipling,* 23 vols. (New York: Scribners, 1925), and his ar-

ticles describing his second trip in *Letters of Travel*, xiv of the *Works;* his story, "Griffiths the Safe Man," is in *Abaft the Funnel* (New York: B. W. Dodge, 1909); "The Undertaker's Horse" is in *Works*, x, Part One, and "The Rhyme of the Three Sealers" in *Works*, x, Part Two; and "Buddha at Kamakura" is in *Works, xxiii*. W. E. Henley, "Ballade of a Toyokuni Colour Print," *The Works of W. E. Henley*, 7 vols. (London: David Nutt, 1908), ii. Margaret Veley, "A Japanese Fan," *Cornhill Magazine, xxxiv* (September, 1876). Alfred Noyes's poems, "A Triple Ballad of Old Japan," "Haunted in Old Japan," "A Japanese Love Song," and "The Two Painters" are in *The Collected Poems of Alfred Noyes*, 2 vols. (New York: Frederick A. Stokes, 1913); his short story, "The Log of the Evening Star," is in *Walking Shadows* (New York: Frederick A. Stokes, 1918); "Nippon" is in *The New Morning* (New York: Frederick A. Stokes, 1918); there are many similar poems in these volumes and in *The Lord of Misrule and Other Poems* (New York: Frederick A. Stokes, 1915).

(ii) Ruth Benedict, *The Chrysanthemum and the Sword* (Boston: Houghton Mifflin, 1946). Wallace Irwin, *Mr. Togo, Maid of All Work* (New York: Duffield, 1913). Stephen Crane, *The Work of Stephen Crane*, 12 vols. (New York: Knopf, 1925-26), x. Jack London, *Martin Eden* (New York: Macmillan, 1927). Frank Norris, *The Octopus* (New York: Doubleday, Page, 1901). Henry B. Fuller: *The Cliff-Dwellers* (New York: Harper, 1893) and *With the Procession* (New York: Harper, 1895). Theodore Dreiser, *The Titan* (New York: Boni and Liveright, 1914). William Dean Howells, *The Rise of Silas Lapham* (Boston and New York: Houghton Mifflin, 1884). Henry James, *The Golden Bowl*, 2 vols. (New York: Scribners, Grosset and Dunlap, 1922). Edith Wharton, *The Age of Innocence* (New York: Grosset and Dunlap, 1920). Robert Louis Stevenson, "Yoshida Tora-Jiro," *Works of Robert Louis Stevenson*, 22 vols. (New York: Scribners, 1895-98), xiv. Louis Marie Julien Viaud ("Pierre Loti"), *Madame Chrysanthème* (Paris: Calmann Lévy, 1888).

Anon., "In the Shadow of the Daibutsu," *The Chapbook,* 7 January 1897. Winifred Eaton Babcock, *A Japanese Nightingale* (New York: Harper, 1901). James Michener, *Sayonara* (New York: Random House, 1954). William Plomer's stories are reprinted from earlier volumes in *Four Countries* (London: J. Cape, 1949); his novel, *Sado,* has been printed twice (London: Chatto and Windus, 1931; 1951); and *Double Lives* (London: J. Cape, 1943) is his autobiography; see also the notes to chapter VI.

(iii) W. S. Gilbert, *Patience* and *The Mikado, Plays and Poems of W. S. Gilbert* (New York: Random House, 1932). Anon., reviewer of "The Japs," *Theatre,* 1 Oct. 1885. Sir Edwin Arnold, *Adzuma; or the Japanese Wife* (London and New York: Scribners, 1893). *Madame Butterfly* first appeared as a novel by John Luther Long (New York: Century Co., 1897; 1903), and then as a play written with David Belasco: *Six Plays by David Belasco* (Boston: Little, Brown, 1928), in which *The Darling of the Gods* may also be found.

(iv) Lafcadio Hearn: *Exotics and Retrospects* (Boston: Little, Brown, 1898); *Gleanings in Buddha Fields* (Boston and New York: Houghton Mifflin, 1897); *Glimpses of Unfamiliar Japan,* 2 vols. (Boston and New York: Houghton Mifflin, 1894); *In Ghostly Japan* (Boston: Little, Brown, 1899); *Japan: An Attempt at Interpretation* (New York and London: Macmillan, 1904); *A Japanese Miscellany* (Boston: Little, Brown, 1901); *Karma* (New York: Boni and Liveright, 1918); *Kokoro* (Boston and New York: Houghton Mifflin, 1896); *Kotto* (New York and London: Macmillan, 1902); *Out of the East* (Boston and New York: Houghton Mifflin, 1895); *The Romance of the Milky Way* . . . (Boston and New York: Houghton Mifflin, 1905); and *Shadowings* (Boston: Little, Brown, 1900); see also the notes to the next chapter. Percivall Lowell, *The Soul of the Far East* (Boston and New York: Houghton Mifflin, 1888).

CHAPTER III:
"FROM *JAPONISME* TO IMPRESSIONISM"

Much of the historical information in this chapter has been taken from the first real comparative work on Japan— William Leonard Schwartz, *The Imaginative Interpretation of the Far East in Modern French Literature, 1800-1925* (Paris: H. Champion, 1927); "The Priority of the Goncourts' Discovery of Japanese Art," *Publications of the Modern Language Association (PMLA)*, XLII (1927); and his helpful correspondence. Quotations from painters and other valuable information have been taken from Jean Leymarie, *Impressionism* (Skira ed., no date or place), trans. James Emmons. Sadakichi Hartmann's *History of American Art,* 2 vols. (London: Hutchinson, 1903) and "The Influence of Japanese Art on Western Civilization" in *Japanese Art* (London: G. P. Putnam, 1904) must be used with care, but they are invaluable documents from the period around the turn of the century. Holbrook Jackson, *The Eighteen Nineties* (New York: Knopf, 1922), is perhaps the best introduction to the period. The two most useful studies of Wilde for this book have been a fine unpublished doctoral dissertation by Esther Kaufman, "The Use of Oriental Material by James Thomson, Oscar Wilde, and Rudyard Kipling" (Cornell University, 1947) and Edouard Roditi's *Oscar Wilde* (Norfolk, Conn.: New Directions, 1947). Paul Elmer More's essay, "Lafcadio Hearn," in *Shelburne Essays,* second series (New York and London: G. P. Putnam, 1905), is by all odds the best study of the relation between Hearn's thought and style; but George M. Gould's *Concerning Lafcadio Hearn* (Philadelphia: G. W. Jacobs, 1908) is also useful; and there is an excellent unpublished doctoral dissertation by Robert Felix Morrison, "The Growth of the Mind and Art of Lafcadio Hearn" (University of Wisconsin, 1941).

Sources cited.

(i)   See the preceding.

(ii) Arthur Symons, *Dramatis Personae* (Indianapolis: Bobbs-Merrill, 1923).

(iii) See opening paragraph.

(iv) Sadakichi Hartmann is quoted from *A History of American Art,* 2 vols. (London: Hutchinson, 1903), II.

(v) Algernon Charles Swinburne, *The Complete Works* . . . , 20 vols. (London: W. Heinemann, 1925): "Étude Réaliste," v; "A Flower-Piece by Fantin," v; and "Before the Mirror," I. James A. M. Whistler, *Mr. Whistler's Ten O'-Clock* (Portland, Maine: T. Mosher, 1925). Swinburne's reply to Whistler's "Ten O'Clock"—'Mr. Whistler's Lecture on Art 'Et Tu Brute' Freeing a Lost Friend"—appeared in *The Fortnightly Review,* June, 1888; and his "To James McNeill Whistler" in *Complete Works,* VI. Oscar Wilde, *The Complete Writings . . . ,* 10 vols. (New York: Pearson, 1909): "Impression du Matin," "Impression—Le Reveillon," "Les Silhouettes," and "Le Jardin" are from IX; "The Decay of Lying" is from IV; and "The English Renaissance" from VI.

(vi) In addition to Hearn's works cited in the note to ch. II, there are *Leaves from the Diary of an Impressionist* (Boston and New York: Houghton Mifflin, 1911) and *Chita: A Memory of Lost Island* (New York: Harper, 1889). John Gould Fletcher's remark is taken from a letter to me. Hearn's "Nirvana, A Study in Synthetic Buddhism" is in *Gleanings from Buddha Fields* and "First Impressions" from *Karma*—both cited in the preceding chapter.

CHAPTER IV: "TRANSITION TO THE NEW POETRY"

Frank Stewart Flint's "History of Imagism" in *The Egoist,* II (1 May 1915) is indispensable for this and the next two chapters, and other studies useful here are cited in the first paragraph of both those chapters.

Sources cited.

T. E. Hulme's miscellaneous prose writings have been edited: *Speculations* (New York: Harcourt, Brace, 1924; 2nd ed. 1936); "Notes on Language and Style," Criterion, July, 1925; and *Further Speculations* (Minneapolis: Univ. of Minnesota Press, 1955); his poems were published at the end of Ezra Pound's *Ripostes* (London: S. Swift, 1912) and in the 2nd ed. of *Speculations*. Edward Storer's poem, "Illusion," is borrowed from S. Foster Damon, *Amy Lowell* (Boston and New York: Houghton Mifflin, 1935), p. 200; Storer's *I've Quite Forgotten Lucy* (London: D. Rider, n.d.) contains the other verses quoted.

CHAPTER V: "EZRA POUND"

Pound's own critical prose is the most valuable commentary on his Japanese interests. The articles on "Edward Wadsworth, Vorticist" in *The Egoist* for 1 June 1914 and on "Vorticism" in *The Fortnightly Review,* cii (1 September 1914) are fundamental, but all of his criticism must be studied. A good portion of his correspondence has been edited by D. D. Paige, *The Letters of Ezra Pound, 1907-1941* (New York: Harcourt, Brace, 1950), and Mr. Pound has been kind enough to reply to my letters of inquiry. The Fenollosa-Pound translations of nō plays are most readily available in Hugh Kenner, *The Translations of Ezra Pound* (Norfolk, Conn.: New Directions, 1953). Pound has provoked a wide and various critical literature, from which the more interesting and valuable essays have been collected in Peter Russell's anthology, *An Examination of Ezra Pound* (Norfolk, Conn.: New Directions, 1950); the chapters by T. S. Eliot ("Ezra Pound"), Wyndham Lewis ("Ezra Pound"), and Hugh Gordon Proteus ("Ezra Pound and His Chinese Character") have been used and Lewis quoted in the epigraph. Many of the letters and much of the published material in chs. iv and vi are also of value for study of Pound.

Sources cited.

(i) T. S. Eliot, *The Selected Poems of Ezra Pound* (London: Faber and Faber, 1928; 1948). Pound's poetry apart from the *Cantos* can be found arranged in the order of earlier volumes in *Personae: The Collected Poems of Ezra Pound* (Norfolk, Conn.: New Directions, n.d.), and the *Cantos,* up to the most recently published volume, in *The Cantos* (Norfolk, Conn.: New Directions, 1948).

(ii) Donald Keene, *Japanese Literature* (London: John Murray, 1953). H. A. Giles, *A History of Chinese Literature* (London: D. Appleton, 1901).

(iii) Ezra Pound, "A Few Don'ts for an Imagiste," *Poetry,* I (March, 1913); *Pavannes and Divisions* (New York: Knopf, 1918).

(iv) Ernest Fenollosa and Ezra Pound, "An Essay on the Chinese Written Character," *Instigations* (New York: Boni and Liveright, 1920). Ezra Pound, *Guide to Kulchur* (Norfolk, Conn.: New Directions, n.d.).

(v) T. S. Eliot, "The Noh and the Image," *Egoist,* IV, (August, 1917).

CHAPTER VI: "THE ABSORPTION OF JAPAN INTO TWENTIETH-CENTURY POETRY"

Much of the most valuable information used in this chapter came in letters which it is a pleasure to acknowledge: from the late John Gould Fletcher and Wallace Stevens; from Conrad Aiken, Mrs. Hilda Doolittle Aldington, and Richard Aldington; and from Edmund Blunden, who first directed my attention to the poetry of Henley, Plomer, and Vines. Two useful books for this and the preceding two chapters are Glenn Hughes, *Imagism and the Imagists* (Stanford: Stanford Univ. Press, 1931) and Stanley K. Coffman, *imagism* (Norman, Okla.: Univ. of Oklahoma Press, 1951). Professors Hughes and Henry W. Wells have sent letters of assistance to this study. S. Foster Damon's distinguished biography, *Amy Lowell* (Boston and New York: Houghton Mifflin, 1935), is of much wider relevance than the title suggests.
Sources cited.

(i) F. S. Flint, *Cadences* (London: Poetry Bookshop,

1915). Richard Aldington: *Collected Poems* (New York: Covici, Friede, 1928) and "Penultimate Poetry," *Egoist*, 15 Jan. 1915. Amy Lowell: *Ballads for Sale* (Boston and New York: Houghton Mifflin, 1927): *Can Grande's Castle* (New York: Macmillan, 1918); *A Dome of Many-Coloured Glass* (Boston and New York: Houghton Mifflin, 1912); *East Wind* (Boston and New York: Houghton Mifflin, 1926); *Men, Women and Ghosts* (New York: Macmillan, 1916); *Pictures of the Floating World* (New York: Macmillan, 1919); *Sword Blades and Poppy Seed* (New York: Macmillan, 1912); and *What's O'-Clock* (Boston and New York: Houghton Mifflin, 1925). John Gould Fletcher: *Goblins and Pagodas* (Boston and New York: Houghton Mifflin, 1916); *Irradiations—Sand and Spray* (Boston and New York: Houghton Mifflin, 1915); and *Japanese Prints* (Boston: Four Seas Co., 1918); see also Fletcher's Foreword to Kenneth Yasuda, *A Pepper-Pod* (New York: Knopf, 1947) and "The Orient and Contemporary Poetry" in Arthur B. Christy, *The Asian Legacy in American Life* (New York: John Day, 1945).

(ii) Conrad Aiken, *Collected Poems* (New York: Oxford University Press, 1953). Yone Noguchi: *From the Eastern Sea* (London: Unicorn Press, 1903); *Japanese Hokkus* (Boston: Four Seas Co., 1920); *The Pilgrimage* (New York, London, and Tōkyō: M. Kennerly, 1912); *Seen and Unseen* (New York: 2nd ed., Orientalia, 1920); *The Summer Clouds*: *Prose Poems* (Tōkyō: Shunyodō, 1906); and *Through the Torii* (Boston: Four Seas Co., 1922). Adelaide Crapsey, *Verse* (n. p.: Manas Press, 1915); and see Mary Elizabeth Osborn, *Adelaide Crapsey* (Boston: B. Humphries, 1933). Robert Frost, *Collected Poems* (New York: Henry Holt, 1930). Archibald MacLeish, *Songs for Eve* (Boston: Houghton Mifflin, 1954). Wallace Stevens: *Harmonium* (New York: Knopf, 1923; 2nd ed. 1931) and *Parts of a World* (New York: Knopf, 1942); see also William Van O'Connor, *The Shaping Spirit* . . . (Chicago: Regnery, 1950). Arthur Davison Ficke: *An April Elegy* (New York and London: M. Kennerly, 1917); *The Earth Passion . . . and Other Poems* (Cranleigh: Samurai Press, 1908); *From the Isles* (London: Samurai Press, 1907); *The Happy Princess and Other Poems* (Boston: Small, Maynard, 1907); and *Twelve Japanese Painters* (Chicago: Alderbrink Press, 1913). Witter Bynner: *Against the Cold* (New York: Knopf, 1940); *The Beloved Stranger* (New York: Knopf, 1919): and *A Canticle of Pan* (New York Knopf, 1920). "Anne Knish" (Arthur Davison Ficke) and "Emmanuel Morgan" (Witter Bynner), *Spectra* (New York: M. Kennerly, 1916).

(iii) Edmund Blunden: *Japanese Garland* (n. p.: Beaumont Press, 1928); *The Mind's Eye* (London: Jonathan Cape, 1934); and *Poems, 1914-1930* (London: Cobden-Sanderson, 1930). William Plomer: *The Dorking Thigh* (London: J. Cape, 1946); *Double Lives* (London: Jonathan Cape, 1943); *The Family Tree* (London: Hogarth Press, 1929); *The Five-fold Screen* (London: L. and V. Woolf, 1932); *Selected Poems* (London: Hogarth Press, 1940); and *Visiting the Caves* (London and Toronto: Jonathan Cape, 1936); see also the Notes to ch. II. Laurence Binyon: *Little Poems from the Japanese* (Leeds: Swan Press, 1925) and *The North Star and Other Poems* (London: no pub., 1941). Sherard Vines: *The Pyramid* (London: Cobden-Sanderson, 1926) and *Triforium* (London: Cobden-Sanderson, 1928). William Empson, *Collected Poems* (New York: Harcourt, Brace, 1949).

CHAPTER VII: "KABUKI AND NŌ AS DRAMATIC CRITERIA"

Most of the information in this chapter comes from theatrical journals or books, but John Masefield and Thornton Wilder have kindly replied to my letters of inquiry with very helpful information. And Allardyce Nicoll's *World Drama* . . . (London: G. Hurrap, 1949) has been of some overall use.

Sources cited.

(i) [Basil Hall Chamberlain], "A Lyric Drama from the Japanese," *Cornhill Magazine*, Oct., 1876. Max Beerbohm, "Almond Blossom in Piccadilly Circus," *Saturday Review* (London), xci (22 June 1901).

(ii)   John Masefield, *The Poems and Plays of John Masefield*, 2 vols. (New York: Macmillan, 1918); see also E. V. Gatenby in Notes 3, "Earlier Comparative Studies."

(iii)   Sergei M. Eisenstein: *Film Form* (New York: Harcourt, Brace, 1949) and *The Film Sense* (New York: Harcourt, Brace, 1942).

(iv)   Allardyce Nicoll, *World Drama,* cited above. Gordon Bottomley: *Choric Plays* (London: Constable, 1939); *Lyric Plays* (London: Constable, 1932); and *Scenes and Plays* (London: Constable, 1929). Thomas Sturge Moore, *Tragic Mothers* (London: Grant Richards, 1920); see also Frederick L. Gwynn, *Sturge Moore and the Life of Art* (Lawrence, Kansas: Univ. of Kansas Press, 1951). S. Foster Damon, "Kiri no Meijiyama . . . ," *The Dial,* lxviii (Feb., 1920). Stark Young, *The Flower in Drama* (New York: Scribners, 1925). Berthold Brecht: *"He Who Says Yes and He Who Says No," Accent,* Autumn, 1946—translations of *Der Jasager* and *Der Neinsager, Gesammelte Werke,* 2 vols. (London: Malik-Verlag, 1938). Thornton Wilder, *Our Town* (New York: Coward McCann, 1938). Paul Goodman, *Stop-Light, 5 dance poems* (Harrington Park, N. J.: 5 x 8 Press, 1941).

CHAPTER VIII: "W. B. YEATS"

It is a pleasure to acknowledge a letter from Mrs. W. B. Yeats concerning Japanese books in her husband's library. *The Autobiography of W. B. Yeats* (New York: Macmillan, 1938) and *The Letters of W. B. Yeats,* ed. Allan Wade (London: R. Hart-Davis, 1954) are of such importance that they must be cited here among the general sources. The information in Joseph Hone's biography, *W. B. Yeats, 1865-1939* (London: Macmillan, 1942), and in T. R. Henn's excellent study, *The Lonely Tower* (London: Methuen, 1950), has also been useful. Ronald Peacock's chapter on Yeats in *The Poet in the Theatre* (London: Routledge, 1946) is probably the most illuminating study of the plays; but Eric Bentley's article, "Yeats as Playwright," in the *Kenyon Review*, x (Spring, 1948) and reprinted in the anthology by Joseph Hall and Martin Steinmann, *The Permanence of Yeats* (New York: Macmillan, 1950), is also of value for the way in which it sets Yeats's plays in the context of modern efforts to re-establish a poetic drama.

Sources cited.

(i) William Butler Yeats: *The Collected Plays of W. B. Yeats* (New York: Macmillan, 1953); *The Collected Poems of W. B. Yeats* (New York: Macmillan, 1952); *Discoveries* . . . (Dundrum: Dan Emer Press, 1907); *Four Plays for Dancers* (New York: Macmillan, 1921); *Plays and Controversies* (London: Macmillan, 1923); and *Wheels and Butterflies* (New York: Macmillan, 1935); see also Yeats's introduction to a selection from the Fenollosa-Pound translation of nō plays, *Certain Noble Plays of Japan* (Dundrum: Cuala Press, 1916) and W. T. Horton, *A Book of Images . . . Introduced by W. B. Yeats* (London: Unicorn Press, 1898).

(ii) See opening paragraph and i above.

(iii) Lady Augusta Gregory, *Visions and Beliefs* . . . , 2nd series (New York and London: Putnam, 1920).

CHAPTER IX: "THE SUMMING UP"

The generalizations in this chapter owe a good deal of their firmness to their confirmation by the distinguished Japanese philosopher and publicist, Hasegawa Nyozekan; I wish to acknowledge my gratitude for the time he gave me for conversations in the midst of his world-wide trip in the summer of 1956.

Source cited.

I. A. Richards, *A Leak in the Universe, Playbook* (Norfolk, Conn.: New Directions, 1956).

INDEX

[This is primarily an index of topics, names, and genres. Only a few titles are indexed, and only the most general subjects are entered under "Japan." Japanese names are entered in the order most familiar to the West—e.g., Bashō, Matsuo; but Okakura Yoshisaburō.]

Doolittle, Hilda, 108, 159, 181
drama, better able than fiction to use Japan, 52; debt to Japan, 276-77; display in "Japanese" plays, 58; lasting popularity of pseudo-Japanese plays, 57; mania for pseudo-Japanese plays, 55; problems in "Japanese" plays, 58; realistic attempts in "Japanese" plays, 58; stage images of Japan (1936-53), 60-61; use of Japan for subject matter, 52-62
Dreiser, Theodore, uses Japanese details, 44
Dryden, John, 26, 52, 153, 231, 265
Duret, Théodore, calls Japanese first Impressionists, 69

East, *see* Orient; Japan
East India Company, motives in trade, 4
Eisenstein, Sergei M., 214, 276; concept of kabuki, 220-21; concept of Sino-Japanese characters, 221-22; takes film theory from kabuki, 276; use of kabuki in film techniques, 219-24
Eishi, Hosoda, 164
Elijah, 132
Eliot, T. S., 23, 84-85, 109, 185; possibility of Japanese influence on, 153
Éluard, Paul, 75
Emerson, Ralph Waldo, 186; uses Indian Buddhism, 17-18
Empson, William, poetic response to Japan, 210-13
England, images of Japan, 1600-1850, 8-12

Augustan: interest in Japan, 272; literary images of Orient, 11; nature of interest in Orient, 15
Renaissance: images of Japan, 5-9; images of Orient, 9-10; nature of interest in Orient, 15, 272
Victorian: response to Japan, 25-40; complex temper of and Kipling, 37-38; effect of Japan on, 273-74; fad for *japoneries*, 53; great poets of do not write on Japan, 29-30; image of Japan, 66; temper of, 25-26; wane of interest in Japan, 97-98
exoticism, 213, 272; compared to primitivism, 29, 269; defined, 29; nature of appeal of, 269-70

Far East, *see* Orient; Japan
Farr, Florence, 100
Fenollosa, Ernest, 41-42, 43, 127, 128, 134, 155, 171, 173, 210, 237, 271; response to Japan, 22-23; Buddhist thought in poetry, 23; anticipates Imagists, 23; anticipates Pound, 23; develops Whitman's ideas, 22-23; honored by Japan, 23; interprets Japan symbolically, 22-23; on poetic diction, 129; popularizes Japan, 23-24; Pound on the career of, 23
Fenollosa, Mrs. Ernest, 127, 135, 238, 248
Ficke, Arthur Davison, 200, 202; response to Japan, 198-99; parodies current styles,

200; reasons for using Japan, 198-99

fiction, response of to Japan, 40-52, 275; difficulty in adapting Japan to, 43-44; French, effect of Japan on, 72-73; Japanese details in, 43-46; low quality of "Japanese" novels, 40-41, 46, 275; motives in writing on Japan, 51-52; postwar on Japan, 49; reasons for small Japanese effect on, 46, 275

film, modern Western, debt to Japan, 223-24. *See also* Japanese films; Eisenstein, Sergei M.

Fitzgerald, Edward, influence of in Orientalism, 18

Flaubert, Gustave, 88

Fletcher, John Gould, 91, 108, 156, 180, 181, 186, 198; response to Japan, 174-79; concept of haiku, 177; debt to haiku, 176-77; on Japanese influence upon Imagists, 156, 179; pseudo-Japanese poems, 177-78; uses Zen Buddhism, 175-76

Flint, Frank Stewart, 97, 104, 105, 108, 123, 169; response to Japan, 157-58; introduces Japanese poetry, 157-58; on Japanese interests of New Poetry, 100-01

Ford, Ford Madox, 108

Fort, Paul, 75

France, interest in Japanese art, 67-71; interest in Japanese poetry, 75-76; Japanese art and theories of fiction, 72-73; literary use of Japan, 71-74; use of Japanese similes in fiction, 71-72; vogue for haiku, 75-76

Franciscans, flout Japanese proscriptive laws, 6; spoil Jesuit efforts in China, 8

Frost, Robert, 190; uses Japanese technique of Pound, 189

Fry, Christopher, 230

Fujita, Jun, 187

Fuller, Henry B., uses Japanese details, 44

Garnett, Richard, 186

Gatenby, E. V., 217

Gaugin, Paul, 69

Gautier, Judith, 68-69, 71

Gautier, Théophile, 68-69, 71

Gay, John, uses chinaware as metaphor, 11

Gilbert, William Schwenck, 33, 42, 214, 234, 250-51; inspiration for *Mikado*, 55-56; Japanese words in *Mikado*, 56-57; *Mikado* as satire of England, 10; satirizes Aestheticism in *Patience*, 29, 54-55; stock Japanese types in *Mikado*, 56

Giles, H. A., 117, 119

Goethe, Johann Wolfgang von, 25; influential Orientalism of, 18

Goldsmith, Oliver, 13; uses Oriental "spy," 10

Goncourt, Edmonde de, 69

Goncourt, Edmonde and Jules de, use of Japan in writings, 71-74

Goncourt, Jules de, 69, 235

Gonne, Maud, 247

Goodman, Paul, models plays on nō, 229

Gourmont, Remy de, 123

Grant, Ulysses S., 41

183, 191-92, 194, 220, 233, 235, 236-37, 271, 275; relation to Japan, 66-96, 88, 274-75; adapted to French and English poetry, 74; affinities with Naturalism, 72-74; and Pound, 110-12; development of, 67; effect on New Poetry, 103; in Hearn's thought and writing, 87-96; many-sided nature of, 79; Orient and, 14; Japan appeals to painters, 69-71; uses Japanese art to justify theories, 69-71
India, nature of appeal to West, 269-70
International Exhibition (London), starts exoticism, 29; 53, 97. *See also* Japanese Court
Irwin, Wallace, comic Japanese in fiction of, 43
Issa, Kobayashi, imitated, 189
Itō, Michio, 152, 153, 253-54, 259; dances Yeats's plays, 246

Jackson, Holbrook, on 1890's, 83-84
James, Henry, uses Japanese imagery, 45
Japan, appeal to West, 266-68; as meeting-ground of East and West, 270-72; closing of, 6; conclusions about importance for Western literature, 278-80; cultural role of, 270-71, cycles of interest in, 43, 97-98, 272-75, 278-79; dual image of, 42-43; in fiction, 40-52; popular image of, 61, 62; reaction to *Mikado*, 57;

reasons for appeal to West, 267-72; recent realism in response to, 277-78; small effect on Western fiction, 46, 275; travel literature on, 41-43; used in French literature, 71-74
Japanese, stage images of, 52-53
Japanese art, and medievalism, 28-29; French interest in, 67-71; 19th-century enthusiasm for, 43
Japanese Court at International Exhibition, excites England, 28
Japanese film, effect of on West, 276-77; recent interest in, 214
Japanese Mission (1860), 97; effect on America, 19-22; *New York Times* on, 21; results in plays, 21; Whitman's response to, 19-21
Japanese poetry, French interest in, 75-76
Japanese theatre, Ch. VII; early interest in, 214-16
Japonisme, French fad of, 68-69
Jesuits, 12, 279; admiration of Japan, 6-7; compare Japan with West, 7; missionaries to Japan and China, 5-8; panegyrics on Orient, 9-10. *See also* St. Francis Xavier
Johnson, Lionel, 234
Johnson, Dr. Samuel, 266
"jolly Jap, the," source and nature of, 53
Joyce, James, 185

kabuki, description of form, 283-84; influence of, Ch. VII, passim

extends imagistic practice,
127-34; super-pository technique from haiku, 114-22;
support of Vorticism, 126-27;
translates nō from Fenollosa's
notes, 136-39; use of haiku
in poetry, 112-23; use of
Japan for materials, 152-53;
use of Sino-Japanese characters in poetry, 131-33, 150-
51; uses non-pictorial "ideo-
gram," 134; variety of interests, 108
primitivism, compared to exoticism, 29
Proust, Marcel, 72
Puccini, Giacomo, 42, 48, 59
Pythagoras, fabled travels to
India, 8

Raleigh, Sir Walter, conventional history of, 12
realism, in modern response to
Japan, 202-13, 277-78
Regnier, Henri de, 69
relativistic thought, Orient and
the growth of, 7-8, 12-14,
272
Renan, A., 69
Renard, Jules, 68
Revon, Marcel, 75
Richards, I. A., 266
Rodgers, Richard, writes *South
Pacific*, 60
Romanticism, Orient and, 14
Rossetti, Dante Gabriel, 234,
236, 237
Rossetti, William, 186
Ruskin, John, 78
Russo-Japanese war, effect on
Western attitudes, 39

Sadanji, Ishikawa, 220

St. Augustine, equivalent for in
Confucius, 10; source for
Christian historiography, 12
St. Francis Xavier, 5-6, 272.
See also Jesuits
Satō Junzō, 242, 243, 244, 260
Schwartz, William Leonard,
studies French interest in
Japan, 72-73, 76, 123
Scotus, Duns, 133
Seami Motokiyo, 228
Shakespeare, William, 52, 230,
231, 262, 268
Sino-Japanese written characters, 127-34, 221-22; Renaissance enthusiasm for, 9
Smollet, Tobias, uses Japan to
satirize England, 10
Snider, Vern, 60
Sophocles, 264-65
Solomon, Walter, 107
Spencer, Herbert, advises Japan,
39; influences Hearn, 92, 93
Spengler, Oswald, 268
Spenser, Edmund, 7
Stalker, John, enthusiasm for
Japan, 3, 11-12, 15
Stevens, Wallace, 198; response
to Japan, 190-97; mingles Impressionism and Symbolism,
191-92; use of block prints,
192-95; use of haiku, 195-97
Stevenson, Robert Louis, uses
Japanese subject, 46
Storer, Edward, 100; mingles
Japanese and other elements
in verse, 105-06
Stowe, Harriet Beecher, popularity of *Uncle Tom's Cabin*,
59
Sullivan, Sir Arthur S., *see*
Gilbert, William Schwenck